# SEX, SIN AND GRACE

Women's Experience and the Theologies of Reinhold Niebuhr and Paul Tillich

Judith Plaskow

UNIVERSITY
PRESS OF
AMERICA

BT
704
.P56

91279

Library of Congress Catalog Card Number: **79-5434**

To Valerie
and
To my father

# TABLE OF CONTENTS

# PREFACE

This book is essentially my 1975 Yale dissertation. When I began it seven years ago, I was most excited by the opportunity it provided me to reflect at length on the nature of women's experience. In the years since I finished the thesis, women's experience has remained my chief interest. Indeed, I have focused more and more on exploring the implications of women's experience, and moved further away from traditional theology. Nevertheless, I find it disappointing that other women more involved than I in the struggle with traditional religion have not taken up Valerie Saiving's cudgel and attempted to write systematic theology from a feminist perspective. It seems that so much reformist energy has been channeled into more immediate tasks -- the fight for ordination, liturgical reform, reinterpretation of Scripture -- that there has not been time for consideration of this fundamental and difficult issue. If the appearance of this thesis in print helps stimulate discussion of the nature and possibility of a feminist systematic theology, it will have served its purpose. I only hope that the next few years will witness the development of several such theologies so that the conversation Saiving began so long ago can come to fruition.

There are always other people involved in bringing a thesis to completion. Julian Hartt agreed to be my advisor even when he knew he would be leaving Yale for the University of Virginia. He provided support and encouragement when others tried to persuade me to choose a less controversial topic, and he gave me substantive help and criticism once my work was underway. Hans Frei read sections of the first draft and made many helpful suggestions for revision. Gordon Kaufman lent a helping hand at one crucial point when I had thought myself into a corner.

My husband Robert Goldenberg served as technical advisor for the final draft: he ironed out many an infelicitous phrase. Those that remain were not submitted to him for first aid. My sister Harriet Plaskow, despite her contempt for all things theological, gritted her teeth and typed the manuscript twice. She is living proof that "sisterhood is powerful."

At many points in this work, I acknowledge the help of Carol Christ. The footnotes mentioning her can only begin to suggest the enormous intellectual and moral comradeship (sistership?) she provided. Without her,

vii

this book would never have been written. That is easy
to say, of course, and is said often. But any woman
who has survived a male-dominated institution like Yale
only through the support of other women -- and any
woman who has failed to survive because she lacked that
support -- will know it is simply and literally the
truth.

# INTRODUCTION

In 1960, Valerie Saiving published an article entitled "The Human Situation: A Feminine View."[1] Speaking as a woman, she criticized the accounts of the human situation, particularly the interpretations of sin and love, found in the theologies of Reinhold Niebuhr and Anders Nygren. She wrote:

> It is my contention that there are significant differences between masculine and feminine experience and that feminine experience reveals in a more emphatic fashion certain aspects of the human situation which are present but less obvious in the experience of men. Contemporary theological doctrines of love have, I believe, been constructed primarily upon the basis of masculine experience and thus view the human situation from the male standpoint. Consequently, these doctrines do not provide an adequate interpretation of the situation of women -- nor, for that matter, of men....(2)

She argued that the concepts of sin and love in Niebuhr and Nygren are mutually dependent in such a way that their understanding of love is "normative and redemptive" only if it grows out of a correct interpretation of the profoundest needs of sinful humanity. In fact, however, the two theologians' representations of human sin as self-assertion, self-centeredness, and pride speak out of and to the experience of only half the human race.

> ...The temptations of woman as woman are not the same as the temptations of man as man, and the specifically feminine forms of sin...have a quality which can never be encompassed by such terms as "pride" and "will to power." They are better suggested by such terms as triviality, distractibility, and diffuseness; lack of an organizing center or focus, dependence on others for one's self-definition; tolerance at the expense of standards of excellence... In short, underdevelopment or negation of the self. (3)

Niebuhr and Nygren, in other words, are guilty of identifying their important but limited --male-- perspectives with universal truth. In pointing this out, Saiving called into question a whole line of recent theological development.

1

Since 1960, and particularly in the last few years, theological criticism from a "feminine" perspective has become increasingly frequent and wide-ranging. The whole history of Christian thought and doctrine has been subjected to feminist scrutiny. Numerous articles have appeared analyzing traditional attitudes towards and images of women, and much constructive work has been written from the perspective of women's experience.[4] In all this material, the inadequacy of understanding sin solely as pride has become almost a commonplace. "Women's sin," it is implied again and again, is not self-centeredness but what have historically been considered the Christian virtues. Self-sacrifice, obedience, etc., while perhaps necessary counterweights to the behavioral excesses of a stereotypically male culture, have been preached to and taken to heart by women, for whom they are already a way of life.[5] Practiced in excess, they undermine the self's relationship to itself and ultimately to God.

Criticism of the traditional equation of sin and pride certainly bears repetition, but most of the articles which have appeared since Saiving's have been limited in two ways. They have not gone much beyond her statement of the problem, and they have tended to assume rather than argue a particular view of female as opposed to male experience. This latter failing is especially unfortunate because Saiving's own distinction between masculine and feminine character was not flexible enough to serve as a consistent basis for theological criticism. Although she approached her subject by asking how men and women have experienced themselves rather than whether there are innate differences between them, she tended to see differences in experience as rooted quite solidly in biology. This raised questions as to how "underdevelopment or negation of the self," being inherent, can at the same time be considered sinful and why and how theology should seek to discourage what is inherent in the feminine character. To call for theological change on the basis of women's experience seems to require a view of women's experience which, while not necessarily denying all innate differences between men and women, focuses more clearly on the cultural factors shaping feminine personality and draws attention to the limits of current definitions of femininity.

It is the purpose of this book to develop such a view of women's experience in order to carry forward the analysis begun by Valerie Saiving. A definition of women's experience as the interrelation between cultural

2

expectations and their internalization will be used to examine in some detail the extent to which and the ways in which Reinhold Niebuhr and Paul Tillich take account of women's experience in formulating their doctrines of sin and grace.  I will argue that in the work of the two theologians, certain aspects of human experience are highlighted and developed while others are regarded as secondary or ignored.  Certain experiences are seen as having been judged and transformed by the work of God in Jesus Christ; others are **reinforced** by the Christian message or not illuminated by it at all.  I will then argue that the experiences which are developed, judged, and transformed are more likely to be associated with men in our society, while experiences regarded as secondary or reinforced are more likely to be those of women.  The effect of this tendency, which is not incidental but springs from the very definitions of sin and grace, is to identify human with male experience.  This identification not only impoverishes theology but leads it to support prevailing definitions of femininity.

Just as the structure of my argument depends to some extent on Saiving's paper, so its content will begin with her work and then develop it in a number of directions.  Thus I will accept and amplify her definition of "women's sin" as the failure to take responsibility for self-actualization, but I will also be concerned in a secondary way with the idea that women are closer to nature than men and the way in which this stereotype functions in women's lives.  Both these aspects of women's experience will provide the basis for the theological sections of **this work.  They will** examine whether Niebuhr and Tillich adequately account for the sin of self-abnegation or the experience of grace as the possibility of self-realization, and will ask how the two theologians understand the human relationship to nature.

While the thrust of these questions is mainly critical, the motivation behind them is constructive. I hope that the critical study of Niebuhr and Tillich will provide clues, negative if not positive, as to how theology might more fully reflect women's experience. This constructive concern will emerge from underground only in the last chapter, and even there it will lead to discussion of considerations underlying the formulation of a constructive position rather than the statement of a constructive position itself. On the other hand, this concern will be at work throughout this book, stimulating the many suggested revisions of the thought of Niebuhr and Tillich and influencing to some extent

3

the selection of issues and materials dealt with.

Though the goals of this study could be achieved through examination of the work of any number of recent theologians, there are several reasons for focusing on Niebuhr and Tillich. Perhaps most obvious is their prominence and influence. Because they have affected and continue to affect so many other twentieth century writers, their neglect of women's experience is more significant than that of lesser figures. Beyond this, the fact that both thinkers acknowledge the importance of human experience to theology, and in some sense begin with it, means that they are open to direct criticism from the perspective of a particular area of experience. In this respect they differ from Barth who, while certainly equally prominent and by no means immune to analysis from the perspective of women's experience, would have to be criticized in at least two stages.6 Lastly, the similarities and differences between Niebuhr and Tillich are interesting and revealing. The fact that Tillich deals with many of the experiences Niebuhr disregards and yet in certain respects is even less relevant to women's experience raises issues which are important from a constructive perspective and which will be discussed in the final chapter of this work.

Similar reasons might be adduced for focusing on the doctrines of sin and grace. It would seem that with reference to content, the question of the limits of a theology (from the perspective of women's experience) can be examined from two different sides. One can analyze the God-language of the theologian, the types of images (s)he employs and the experiences they reflect and elicit; or one can discuss the theologian's anthropology, his or her view of human beings as creatures, sinners, recipients of grace, etc. These two procedures are not strictly separable. The anthropological approach, however, because it deals explicitly with human experience, is more directly accessible to criticism from the perspective of women's experience. It is therefore the approach taken here. The doctrines of sin and grace in particular are chosen because they not only speak to and from human experience, but are theologically central as well. Evaluation of them is thus significant and, from a constructive viewpoint, most interesting.

The structure of this work, then, will be quite straightforward. I will develop a definition of women's experience in the first chapter. In chapters two and three I will present and evaluate in its light the doctrines of sin and grace of Reinhold Niebuhr and Paul

4

Tillich. In the final chapter, I will summarize the findings of the study and conclude by suggesting some ways in which future attempts to include women's experience in constructive theology will have to move beyond the thought of Niebuhr and Tillich.

While the purpose of this work has now been stated, its boundaries can be more clearly defined through some comments concerning what it is not intended to argue or accomplish. It will not be concerned, first of all, with either the two theologians' attitudes towards or their relationships with women. The connections between their personal lives and their thought might be the subject of an important book, but a book very different from this one. For my purposes, the fact that Niebuhr chided the church for failing to come up to the standards of secular society in granting equal rights to women[7] might increase the irony of his failure to speak to the situation of women, but it does not change it. The publication of Hannah Tillich's From Time to Time[8] may lead to all sorts of speculation concerning the relation between Tillich's work and experience, but does not affect the strengths and weaknesses of his theology proper. This study will deal only with theology in a very narrow sense, with the extent to which Niebuhr's and Tillich's doctrines of sin and grace do or do not reflect women's experience.

Second, I do not want to argue that the perspective of all male theologians is necessarily limited by their maleness. There are some male theologians who speak from a broader range of human experiences than others. Tillich's thought includes aspects of experience which Niebuhr's does not; Niebuhr's theology often provides the categories necessary for developing aspects of experience he himself neglects. While there is an obvious sense in which women can speak for women's experience in ways which men cannot, it does not follow that no one can transcend his or her perspective. If it did follow, this book would be pointless. It calls attention to theologians' disregard of women's experience because it assumes that in making our presuppositions self-conscious, we are to some extent able to alter them -- and certainly to avoid absolutizing them.

Third, I do not wish to argue that the experiences I describe as "women's experiences" are only women's experiences. The point is, as Valerie Saiving puts it, that "feminine experience reveals in a more emphatic fashion certain aspects of the human situation which are present but less obvious in the experience of men."[9]

By focusing on women's experience, we call attention to aspects of the human situation which might otherwise escape our notice. This point has a reverse side. I also do not wish to argue that the experiences on which Niebuhr and Tillich concentrate are not important human experiences or that they are not shared by women. I am attacking the universality of their claims. The two men do not define sin and grace for all people in all times or even for their generation. Rather, they deal with experiences which are more likely to be those of men in this society and do not deal with experiences which are more likely to be those of women.

Fourth, any argument with theological anthropology implicit in the criticisms of Niebuhr and Tillich will remain implicit. I will not be concerned with the limits of and warrants for theological anthropology in general but with the inclusion of women's experience in theological anthropology. However, were the plea for the incorporation of women's experience as women's experience to be generalized, it would be a plea for theological particularity. If I do not want to argue that "women's experience" is only women's experience, I also do not want to argue that because "women's experience" is also human experience, it can be appropriated by looking at experience in an "objective" or neutral way. I do not believe this is possible--if only because "human experience and "male" experience have so long been identified.

Fifth, and most important, I am also not arguing for the universality of my own definition of women's experience. "Women's experience" is a very broad category including a great variety of human experiences. My view of "women's experience" is one view of modern, white, western, middle-class "women's experience." I maintain, though, that it is a significant view and that it leads to results which are theologically interesting. Furthermore, it is more appropriate in this context than many other equally valid views of women's experience which might be proposed, because the two theologians it is used to evaluate are modern, white, western, middle-class men. Be that as it may, however, the phrase "women's experience" may be understood as having quotation marks around it wherever it appears.

Since the problems I deal with in Niebuhr's and Tillich's doctrines of sin and grace are basic to their work, aspects of them have been noted and described from perspectives other than that of women's experience. John Raines, for example, has criticized Niebuhr's concentration on the sin of pride from a Marxist viewpoint, while

6

Wayne Proudfoot has discussed Tillich's monism in a thesis on conceptions of God and ideas of the self.[10] The perspective of women's experience, however, yields insights unique to itself and brings together a variety of theological issues which would otherwise be seen only from separate standpoints. Focus on this perspective also raises to consciousness a general connection between our experiences as women and as men and what we say as theologians--a connection which has its own implications for theology. And at a time when the women's movement has made us aware of the centuries-old rigidity of our sexual stereotypes and the role of religion in perpetuating them, this is a connection which needs to be clearly and explicitly stated.

# CHAPTER ONE

## WOMEN'S EXPERIENCE

What I call "women's situation" or "women's experience" has two interrelated aspects: what has been said
about women, mostly by men, and the ways in which women
have experienced themselves. "What has been said about
women" is a large number of things, indeed. We need
only recall the astonishment of Virginia Woolf on
opening the British Museum's catalogue to "women" to
gain an idea of the number of volumes written on the
subject.

> Have you any notion how many books are written
> about women in the course of one year? Have you
> any notion how many are written by men? Are
> you aware that you are perhaps the most discussed
> animal in the universe?...Sex and its nature
> might well attract doctors and biologists; but
> what was surprising and difficult of explanation
> was the fact that sex--women, that is to say--
> also attracts agreeable essayists, light-
> fingered novelists, young men who have taken
> the M.A. degree; men who have taken no degree;
> men who have no apparent qualifications save
> that they are not women. Some of these books
> were, on the face of it, frivolous and facetious;
> but many, on the other hand, were serious and
> prophetic, moral and hortatory. (1)

Women have been endlessly pondered and pronounced upon;
the "riddle," the "puzzle," the "problem" of femininity
has been considered and reconsidered anew by every
generation. The limitations and potentialities of women
have been defined and confined; their "sphere" and the
correct and normal course of their development has been
prescribed.

On first consideration, it would seem that innumer-
able male pronouncements and philosophizings about women
can hardly be considered part of women's experience.
They come from outside, after all, not from women themselves. And even the best pronouncements seldom reflect
the richness and complexity of experience. But external
and limited as the source of these definitions may be,
the definitions enter the lives of women in many ways.
The "wisdom" all these male pronouncements express
arises out of and is reabsorbed into a general social
mythology concerning women which is part of the cultural
air we breathe.2 Not only is there no direction in

9

which women can turn without bumping into others' expectations of them, but also in the course of their education and growth, women internalize these expectations. There has been no women's experience in isolation or abstraction from them. Having no vantage point from which to question cultural assumptions concerning them, women have known themselves and the world only in lived relation to male definitions of women and male definitions of women's possibilities. These definitions have thus come to form a part of women's experience.

But while there has been no women's experience apart from these "outside" definitions, women's experience and the definitions are not simply the same. The relation between them has most certainly been a living and complex one. Each woman has had to compromise with and adjust to her culture's understanding of her role, or has had to struggle within or against it. Most often, women have accepted and lived within the limits of society's definitions of them, their compromises have for the most part been invisible, certainly unrecorded ones. On the other hand, there have been times when the experiences of women have contradicted these definitions, and in this way judged them and shown forth their restrictiveness. This is most obviously true of history's "great women," the Elizabeths, the Joans, and also her "firsts"--the first woman doctor, the first woman lawyer, and those who followed--all of whom did with excellence things of which women were judged incapable. But such judgements are also found in women's writing from and about themselves--in diaries, novels, political tracts. Charlotte Bronte's Jane Eyre, for example, pauses in the telling of her story to apologize for her feelings of confinement in the manor where she taught, for her "[longing] for a power of vision which might overpass [the] limit [of its walls]...." What she expresses is at once the acceptance of society's definition of her role--hence the apology--and a deeper feeling, the surer knowledge, that the role confines her as a human being. "Women are supposed to be very calm generally: but women feel just as men feel; they need exercise for their faculties and a field for their efforts as much as their brothers do; they suffer from too rigid a restraint, too absolute a stagnation, precisely as men would suffer...."[3]

The expression "women's experience," as it is used throughout this book, will refer to a complex of considerations; male definitions of women and the lived experiences of women within, in relation and in opposition to these definitions. "Women's experience" in this sense can be contrasted with two other interpretations of the term. One the one hand, contra the defenders of the Eternal Feminine, it will never refer to "woman's eternal nature" taken alone, to a "true femaleness" which is unaffected by social circumstances. On the other hand, contra some recent feminists, it will not refer to an equal abstraction--what women's experience would or could be, were it free to define itself apart from male culture and education. "Women's experience" means simply this: the experiences of women in the course of a history never free from cultural role definitions.

To lay the basis for a critique of two modern theologians from the perspective of women's experience, this chapter will develop the conception of women's experience just outlined by addressing two tasks. First, it will deal with some modern formulations of the Eternal Feminine, some proclamations concerning woman's true nature and essence which set the boundaries of her situation. Here, we shall speak not of women, those multifacted, living, changing creatures, but of woman, frozen eternally, ever the same. Second, it will take up the more difficult task of asking what light the experiences of real women throw on these definitions.

The myths about women are endless as is the variety of their experience--as are the ways either might be approached. To write exhaustively on even one aspect of women's experience would take volumes. I will concentrate, therefore, on just two definitions of women's experience which seem particularly relevant to the theological critique of sin and grace and select a small group of significant writers on each topic. A general introduction to the nature of passivity and naturalness will be followed by discussion of psychological theories concerning women as they relate to these traits. Although the making of Eternal Feminine myths could be documented through many kinds of evidence--textbooks, popular magazines, literature, and so on--psychological theory seems to underlie and lend respectability to many of these other areas and thus shape women's experience in a more fundamental way.[4] When we deal with women's experience in the broader sense, on the other hand, we will turn to the writings of women by and about themselves, for it is only through literature that the dynamic of women's experience can begin to emerge in all its complexity.

## A.  The Eternal Feminine

Returning for a moment to Virginia Woolf's astonishment at the number of books on women, we note that
she finds the "strange phenomenon" of writing books on
the opposite sex is one confined to men.  Consulting
the British Museum catalogue under "men," she finds
nothing.[5]  Simone de Beauvoir makes a similar point
in her preface to The Second Sex.  "A man would never
get the notion of writing a book on the peculiar situation of the human male," she says[6]--and apparently, no
woman would either.

Thus before we even examine any particular myths
about women, we are confronted with a strange fact which
is perhaps the basis of all the myths.  "It amounts to
this:  just as for the ancients there was an absolute
vertical with reference to which the oblique was defined, so there is an absolute human type, the masculine."[7]  No one writes books about men as men because
men as men are not mysterious; they do not need to be
explained.  Why should they?  All books are about men,
i.e. human beings--except those which are about women.
The relationship between men and women, de Beauvoir
suggests, is not quite like that between two electrical
poles.  The man represents both the positive and the
neutral, the woman only the negative.  Thus we use the
term "man" to designate human beings, "woman" to designate women only.  Man is the absolute Subject, the paradigmatic human.  Woman is the "Other."[8]

## Naturalness and Passivity

What is the basis of this lack of reciprocity?
How is it that male human beings come to define and
represent the human norm?  Many answers to these questions have been proposed, some more fruitful than
others, perhaps none finally satisfying.  But in an
article entitled, "Is Female to Male as Nature is to
Culture?" anthropologist Sherry Ortner attempts to explain the Otherness of woman in terms of a category
which will occupy us for the remainder of this work.
She argues that at some level of awareness, every
culture distinguishes between nature and culture; every
culture asserts its superiority to and power over
nature; and every culture sees woman as closer to nature
than men.  "That is, culture...recognizes that woman is
an active participant in its special processes, but sees
her as being, at the same time, more rooted in, or
having more direct connection with, nature."[9]  Woman is
the Other, in other words, because she has cross-

culturally been considered more natural than men.

Ortner accounts for the universal attribution of
greater naturalness to women in terms of determinants
of women's experience which are constant in all or
almost all known cultures. The most important of these
is biology. The fact that "proportionately more of a
woman's body space, for a greater percentage of her lifetime...is taken up with the natural processes surrounding...reproduction" is the central ingredient in
the partial identification of women and nature.[10] Biological factors then seem to lead "naturally" to the confinement of women to certain social tasks which are in
turn valued only as transitional or "lower" stages of
the cultural process. The fact that women lactate,
for example, seems to bind them to children--who are in
turn viewed as closer to nature--and, more generally,
to the domestic as opposed to the public sphere.
Thirdly, the traditional roles of women, imposed because of their biology, foster a psychic structure which
also seems more embedded in nature. The universal dimension of the female psyche relevant here, Ortner
argues, is its relative concreteness. The fact that
women need never unlearn or transcend their primary
identification with the mother leads them to become
"involved with concrete feelings, things, and people,
rather than with abstract entities."[11] The association of woman and nature thus gains plausibility from a
combination of biological, social, and psychological
factors.

It is important to stress, however, as Ortner continually does, that with the obvious exception of
biology, none of these factors is innate. The woman/
nature association is itself a product of culture.[12]
Society is an active interpreter of biological data,
encouraging certain life patterns, and making value
judgements and decisions. The continual cultural interpretation of women's experience is visible from a
number of angles. It is hardly necessary, for instance,
that the care and socialization of children be viewed
as natural functions; they could be seen as cultural
processes of the highest order. The many initiation
rites which imply a boy is not "really" socialized until
he is turned over to his father express a social and not
an obvious "natural" distinction.[13] The operation of
social judgement is also reflected in the fact that
while the identification of woman and nature remains
constant, it means different things in different situations. When the mysteries of life and nature which
woman symbolized were found frightening and perplexing,

13

men set woman up as essential and worshipped her as the Great Mother Goddess, source of life and death. Later, classical Christian writers also identified woman with nature, but in a purely negative sense. She represented sensuality and the flesh, the body side of the body/ spirit duality.[14]

Not only the valuation of the woman/nature identification changes from culture to culture, but also its content. While woman may always appear natural in her biological, social, and psychological nature, what is considered natural varies. Thus, in Western culture, the supposed greater subjectivity and emotionality of woman appears a "natural" part of her psychological makeup. Indeed, this aspect of her nature is closely related to her "natural" social role. Mythically speaking, it is the closeness of woman to the wellsprings of human emotional life, her "instinctual" warmth and sensitivity, which fit her so perfectly to preside over home and family. On the other hand, other cultures view different emotional natures as "naturally" linking woman to the domestic sphere.[15]

In western culture, there is associated with naturalness a second quality which will be of central importance to this work--a quality which, for want of a better term, I shall call passivity. Woman has been taken to be, so to speak, naturally passive, and this in a variety of senses. "Naturally" associated with the domestic sphere, and thus excluded from the public one, she appears as passive, first of all, in relation to the work-world of men. Her active involvement in the concrete world of everyday is invisible to the public eye, and therefore invisible altogether. The work that woman does, moreover, is felt to have value only insofar as it frees others to participate in the public world. But this means that woman understands her own worth only in terms of what she can do for others and is therefore passive in a second sense: she is dependent on others for her own self-definition. Undergirding these social aspects of female passivity is the so-called sexual passivity of woman--in intercourse, pregnancy, and childbearing. According to much psychological theory, this sexual passivity is primary and is the basis of what might, fourthly, be described as woman's "active (psychological) passivity"--her submissiveness, self-abnegation, and what Freudians call her masochism.

The importance of naturalness and passivity in contemporary conceptions of woman's (eternal) nature is

14

nicely illustrated by a recent psychology experiment
with college students. The experiment showed that sex
role stereotypes are clearly defined and held in common
by college men and women--and that many of these stereotypes fall into one of the two broad categories of
passivity or naturalness. These students said that men
are dominant, women submissive; men are aggressive,
women unaggressive. Men are independent, women dependent. Men are active, women passive. Men are unemo-
tional and objective; women are emotional and subjective. Men are worldly and knowledgeable; women are
home oriented and ignorant of worldly affairs. Women
are quiet, gentle, tactful, neat, and religious; men
are loud, rough, blunt, sloppy, and non-religious.[16]

The response of these students, while disturbing,
is not surprising, for the characteristics they asso-
ciate with men and women have been reiterated in count-
less writings on women for at least the last hundred
years. John Ruskin, for example, representative Victorian in this respect, wrote of the differences between men and women:

> Now their separate characters are briefly these.
> The man's power is active, progressive, defen-
> sive. He is eminently the doer, the creator,
> the discoverer, the defender. His intellect is
> for speculation and invention; his energy for
> adventure, for war and for conquest...But the
> woman's power is for rule, not for battle,--
> and her intellect is not for invention or crea-
> tion, but for sweet ordering, arrangement and
> decision. She sees the qualities of things,
> their claims and their places...By her office,
> and place, she is protected from all danger
> and temptation. (17)

Not only did he set woman squarely in the domestic
sphere, leaving the wider world to men, but also he
believed she would find her place there naturally. To
settle her in the home was not to force her into a
limited area against her will but to give her the province to which her own natural bent would, in any event,
lead her. Woman, therefore, unlike men, did not have
to be harshly molded by education but could be given
freedom to follow her own pure impulses. The following
Ruskin passage on woman's education abounds in natural
metaphors:

> She will find what is good for her; you cannot:
> for there is just this difference between the

making of a girl's character and a boy's--you
may chisel a boy into shape, as you would a
rock, or hammer him into it, if he be of a
better kind, as you would a piece of bronze.
But you cannot hammer a girl into anything.
She grows as a flower does,--she will wither
without sun; she will decay in her sheath, as
the narcissus does, if you do not give her
air enough; she may fall, and defile her head
in the dust, if you leave her without help at
some moments of her life; but you cannot fetter
her; she must take her own fair form and way....
(18)

Similar in tone, but more recent, is the following
passage from Ashley Montagu's The Natural Superiority
of Women, written in 1954:

Woman is a more worshipful creature than man
because she understands so much more than man
how much there is in the world to be worshipped,
and this understanding seems clearly to be a
function of her maternal role--whether she has
ever had children or not. There is not the
least doubt that women are by nature maternal,
that men are not, and that it is the essence of
the maternal attitude toward life to be sensi-
tive to the needs of others and to retain the
wonder of the miracle of creation and the miracle of love. (19)

In a chapter of the same book entitled, "Women and
Creativity," Montagu discusses the relevance of
woman's worshipfulness to human creativity. Not surprisingly, he finds that woman is most creative in the
sphere of human relations "in which [she] can creatively
love and be loved." Artistic creativity, on the other
hand, is less essential to her. "Because women live
creatively, they rarely experience the need to depict
or write about what to them is a primary experience,
and which men know only at second remove. Women create
naturally--men create artificially."[20] The genius of
woman is one that prepares her first of all not for
excellence in the world of men--though Montagu would
not deny that women are capable of this--but for the
highest task of all, bringing up her children to be
decent people, teaching men how to be human.[21]

What both Ruskin and Montagu claim is that qualities naturally possessed by woman specially fit her
for her domestic and maternal role. These qualities,

16

which are rooted in female biology, need not be incul-
cated. They are as intrinsic to woman's personal development as childbearing is to her physical being. She
need not be forced to become who she is in any of the
spheres of her life: this is the first sense in which
woman is more natural than man. An added dimension of
woman's naturalness is suggested by Montagu's distinction between "primary" and "secondary" creativity. The
world of men is to some extent an artificial world.
The Victorian experienced its artificiality as the
breakdown of traditional values. It is now a techno-
logical world, a world whose natural beauty has been
desecrated and whose environment has been plundered.
It is a work world which is too frequently cut off from
sources of mutuality, human enjoyment and care. And it
is in contrast to this world that the sphere of woman
and the capacities it favors and nurtures appear natural.

Turning to the notion of passivity in these passages, we find that the word itself does not appear,
but that the ground is laid for later explicit use of
the concept. Thus Ruskin contrasts woman with man the
doer, creator, and discoverer, and Montagu distinguishes
her "primary" creativity from the "secondary" creativity
of men. Though in the context of their work these qualities are idealized, it is not difficult to imagine how
other writers would see this different sort of creativity, this power relegated to a small realm, as in
fact passivity. And of course it is passivity in
relation to the world of men. When the idealizing mask
is dropped and the world of men defined as the world,
this relative passivity becomes passivity per se.

## Sexual Passivity

With Freud, the definition of feminine character
is given precisely this negative turn; Freud defines
femininity in relation to an absolute human type which
is masculine. Despite his own warnings against too
facile an identification of masculinity with activity
and femininity with passivity, he continually equates
them,[22] and he views woman as excluded, both personally
and historically, from the male concern with civilization. The account of femininity developed by Freud and
his followers is worth describing in some detail, for
it is through them that myth becomes a modern, scienti-
fically respectable prescription for proper role behavior. Psychology may not deal directly with social role,
but it indirectly prescribes it. It is within the
framework of what psychology says it means to be a woman
that the modern woman has had to struggle to find herself.

17

For Freud, female naturalness and passivity are linked together because the basic meaning of passivity is sexual; psychology is rooted in biology, social role in biologic destiny. The negative tenor of Freud's feminine psychology is indicated by the fact that penis envy, i.e. lack of a penis, is its central determining factor. According to Freud, the development of mature femininity from childhood bisexuality hinges on the shift of the primary sexual zone from the clitoris to the vagina and the exchange of the original mother-object for the father. While the psychological material with which the little girl begins on her developmental path is not altogether the same as the boy's--even in infancy, she tends to be more passive both sexually and temperamentally--early sex differences are less important than individual differences. The real dividing point between boys and girls in terms of the development of adult sexuality is the castration complex and the different meaning it has for each sex. "The discovery [sic] that she is castrated is a turning-point in a girl's growth." "[She notices] the penis of a brother or playmate, strikingly visible and of large proportions, at once recognize[s] it as the superior counterpart of [her] own small and inconspicuous organ, and from that time forward fall[s] a victim to envy of the penis."[23] The key to normal feminine development, Freud says, lies in the correct elaboration of this traumatic experience, for the central features of feminine sexuality and psychology are the results of penis envy. The centrality of envy in the mental life of woman, her sense of inferiority and shame, her greater vanity and narcissism than men are all attributable to it.

The most important result of penis envy for Freud, however, is the development of feminine passivity. Penis envy plays a key role in the girl's turning from "active," "masculine," clitoral sexuality, to adult, "passive," "feminine," vaginal sexuality. According to Freud, the discovery of the penis should deflect the girl rather violently from the clitoral masturbation she had hitherto enjoyed. Humiliated by the discovery of the superior male organ, she concludes that she cannot possibly compete with the little boy and may as well give up the attempt. "Thus the little girl's recognition of the anatomical distinction between the sexes forces her away from masculinity and masculine masturbation on to new lines which lead to the development of femininity."[24]

Often in renouncing clitoral masturbation, Freud

18

says, the girl renounces a certain amount of activity as well. Her turning to the father, which should occur at this point, is then accomplished with the aid of primarily "passive instinctual impulses." What sends the child to her father now is the wish for the penis that her mother had denied her. The mother is blamed for sending her into the world ill-equipped, and the child looks to her father for satisfaction. But this turning to the father is not the goal of her development. The true "feminine situation" is established only if the girl's libido slips into a new position and the wish for a penis is replaced by the wish for a baby. It is with this purpose that she takes the father as love object. The mother thus becomes a rival for the father's love; castration anxiety finds its temporary resolution in the oedipus complex. If the girl's later development is also normal, it will take the direction of a further repression of activity while the clitoris will hand over its sensitivity and importance to the vagina.[25]

## Passivity in the World of Men

Thus, according to Freud, the chief task of female development is the achievement of normal, adult, passive femininity, where the term "passive" refers to woman's sexual role. Freud did not argue directly from the appropriateness of passivity in the sexual sphere to its appropriateness in other areas of female behavior.[26] On the other hand, penis envy does find its final resolution in domesticity, and a corollary to the development of correct feminine sexuality is woman's inadequacy to the demands and tasks of (male) civilization. The problem, Freud says, is that in the girl the oedipus complex follows the castration complex, while in the little boy, the process is reversed. The oedipus stage is the first discernible in the little boy's development. It is abandoned and repressed under the threat of castration,--a threat made real to him the first time he sees a naked girl--and a severe super-ego is set up as its heir. "The authority of the father or the parents is introjected into the ego and there forms the kernel of the super-ego...."[27] In the girl, on the other hand, the oedipus complex is a kind of haven from penis envy. The fear of castration which provides the motive for the breakup of the complex in the boy is absent in the little girl; she has already accepted castration as a fact. There is, therefore, nothing to occasion the dramatic destruction of the oedipus complex in her. She may abandon it slowly when the wish for a child by her father is never fulfilled,

19

may gradually repress it, or its effects may linger on in her mental life. "In these circumstances, the formation of the super-ego must suffer; it cannot attain the strength and independence which give it cultural significance...."[28] These reflections lead Freud to the following remarks:

> I cannot escape the notion (though I hesitate to give it expression) that for women the level of what is ethically normal is different from what it is in men. Their super-ego is never so inexorable, so impersonal, so independent of its emotional origins as we require it to be in men. Character traits which critics of every epoch have brought up against women--that they show less sense of justice than men, that they are less ready to submit to the great necessities of life, that they are more often influenced in their judgements by feelings of affection or hostility--all these would be amply accounted for by the modification in the formation of their super-ego which we have already inferred. (29)

In _Civilization_ and _its Discontents_, Freud explains the lesser cultural contributions of women not in individual-psychological terms, but in historical-psychological terms which clearly presuppose the close relation between woman and nature. At the outset of civilization, he hypothesizes in that book, it was probably families who formed the first work units. Man's need for human helpers to improve his lot on earth, his sexual impulses, and woman's need for protection together provided the foundations for human communal life. With the development of civilization, however, the originally unambiguous relation between love and civilization became clouded, and the two gradually came into opposition. This opposition expressed itself first of all in the conflict between the claims of the family and the larger community, and then in the opposition of women to civilization. "Women represent the interests of the family and of sexual life." As the work of civilization devolved increasingly upon men, it necessitated instinctual sublimations on their part of which women were incapable. Since men did not have unlimited psychical energy, the energy they employed for cultural aims, they withdrew from women. Moreover, their constant association with other men often estranged them from their duties as husbands and fathers. Thus women, though they originally laid the ground for civilization with their claims of love, were increasingly forced into the back-

20

ground by it and became increasingly hostile toward it.[30]

Freud's theories represent a value reversal of the views expressed in the passages from Ruskin and Montagu. In Freud's work, woman's nature and role are defined in relation to male standards which are taken as absolute. The "constitutional passivity" of the little girl which develops into the sexual passivity of the young woman, and the ineffectiveness and hostility of woman in the development of civilization are both defined in relation to male norms. From this perspective, many of the qualities Ruskin and Montagu praised appear as deficiencies. On the other hand, the role and character which all three men envision/prescribe for real women is substantially the same. Thus we are confronted with the problem of evaluating two different mythological styles. Sharing a common view of what woman is and ought to be, one judges her "place" on its own terms, the other in relation to the values of the "world."

## Masochism or Active Passivity

In the followers of Freud, there is a tendency to turn away from his negative manner of expression. While their views of woman and her role are not fundamentally different, they define feminine psychology as an expression of woman's special way of being, rather than as a non-male way. Helen Deutsch, for example, redefines passivity, which still remains the primary characteristic of femininity, to mean "activity directed inward," while "feminine masochism" is defined along similar lines as the interior parallel to masculine aggression.[31]

The concept of feminine masochism is worth examining since it is closely related to passivity but takes that notion further. Freud offers a definition of feminine masochism in "The Economic Problem in Masochism,"[32] but Deutsch develops the idea more fully, particularly in its relation to female passivity. According to her, their origins are "intimately connected," with factors in woman's psychic, physical, and social life leading in this double direction. First, the inadequacy of the clitoris as an outlet for the little girl's active-aggressive tendencies leads her to give up those impulses requiring an active organ. The inhibited activity then "normally" undergoes a turn to passivity, which is, in any event, in keeping with the girl's constitutional predisposition. At the same time, the direction taken by her internal sexual development is reinforced by her environment which also exerts

21

an inhibiting tendency on her active-aggressive drives. Not only does it reject them, but it offers her a bribe for renouncing them. The girl's father, on behalf of the environment, offers her love and tenderness for the renunciation of activity and particularly aggression. "In this renunciation the aggressive forces that are not actively spent must find an outlet, and they do this by endowing the passive state of being loved with a masochistic character."[33]

The implications of feminine masochism for women's lives is not entirely clear since this type of masochism is not to be confused with conscious masochistic perversion. According to Deutsch, the latter form of masochism constitutes a danger for woman, but since every stage of reproductive function is associated with pain, she needs a healthy dose of feminine masochism to be adjusted to reality. Intercourse is associated with defloration, defloration with rape; childbirth is painful and dangerous. Endowing these painful experiences with a pleasurable character is necessary to the preservation of the species. But it does not exhaust the "passive-masochistic psychic energies" which woman must integrate without endangering her personality. This integration may take a variety of forms: loving and self-abnegating service to a person or cause, participation in abstract ideological movements through which one continually suffers disappointments, and so on.[34]

Perhaps the nature of feminine masochism becomes clearest not through psychological texts, but in thoughts like the following by Phyllis McGinley:

> By and large...the world runs better when men and women keep in their own spheres. I do not say women are better off, but society in general is. And that is, after all, the mysterious honor and obligation of women--to keep this planet in orbit. We are the self-immolators, the sacrificers, the givers, not the eaters-up of life. (35)

> Who has taught them [young girls today] that they are tools, not handlers; creatures subject to the caprices of fate and not mistresses of it? Have they learned what a woman chiefly needs--a terrible patience, a vast tolerance, forgivingness, forbearance, an almost divine willingness to forget private wants in the needs of her family? (36)

The concept of feminine masochism extends our view of female passivity. Though woman most often appears as passive in relation to some male activity, there are times when her passivity is portrayed, so to speak, more actively. Here it appears not as an inability to do something or as an exclusion from some realm, but as active submission or self-denial. Woman is active precisely in losing herself. In McGinley, of course, we have not only a description of woman's nature, but a moral imperative. She ought to be self-denying for the good of the created order.

## Passivity in Self-Definition

One last aspect of feminine passivity requires consideration. This aspect is articulated by Erik Erikson, a psychologist who wishes to give woman's place and experience their due rather than defining them in relation to male norms. Long observation of the use of space in the block constructions of pre-adolescent children convinced Erikson of the relevance of the body's groundplan not only to the treatment of space by the two sexes, but to the elaboration of sex roles throughout life. He thus emphasizes the existence for the female of a "productive inner-bodily space" whose reality is surer that that of either a missing penis (Freud) or genital trauma (Deutsch),[37] and thereby places the Freudian theory of female sexual development within a much broader scheme. Indeed, he sees the original conclusions of psychoanalysis as very limited. If we assume the importance for girls of a "productive interior," he says, then theoretical emphasis must shift from penis envy to childbearing potential, from contempt for the mother to sense of solidarity with her, and "from a 'passive' renunciation of male activity to the purposeful and competent activity of one endowed with ovaries and a uterus...."[38]

Novel as this formulation of feminine psychology may sound, however, it quickly leads to some familiar conclusions.

Young women often ask [says Erikson], whether they can "have an identity" before they know whom they will marry and for whom they will make a home. Granted that something in the young woman's identity must keep itself open for the peculiarities of the man to be joined and of the children to be brought up, I think that much of a young woman's identity is already defined in her kind of attractiveness and in the selectivity

of her search for the man (or men) by whom she
wishes to be sought. This, of course, is only
the psychosexual aspect of her identity; and she
may go far in postponing its closure while train-
ing herself as a worker and a citizen and while
developing as a person within the role-possibil-
ities of her time...But a true moratorium must
have a term and a conclusion: womanhood arrives
when attractiveness and experience have succeeded in selecting what is to admitted to the
custody of the inner space "for keeps." (39)

We can understand this as a truism, of course; i.e.
as men and women we reveal something of our identities
in the people we seek and attract and must be open
enough to grow and change in our encounters with others.
But if we interpret Erikson in any other way, it becomes clear that he has simply rejected the Freudian
conception of feminine passivity for a more subtle one.
He wants to avoid saying that woman is sexually passive
or passive in relation to the world of men (though, in
fact, "inner space" may determine her passivity in both
senses), but he envisions her as passive in the
most fundamental sense of all. A woman does not define
and create her own identity, but is defined by her
husband and children in a sense in which they are never
defined by her.

In other words, though Erikson claims to be saying
something new, the implications of his theory for real
women are quite traditional. The "somatic design" of
women, he claims, harbors "an 'inner space' destined to
bear the offspring of chosen men and, with it, a
biological, psychological, and ethical commitment to
take care of human infancy."[40] What does this mean if
not that the body plan of woman predisposes her to a
certain social role, to a life apart from the masculine
world of "outer space," but to a life defined by the
participants in that world? True, this states negatively what is stated positively as "Woman's is the
world of inner space," but the reality is in both cases
the same. What happens, we must ask, if a woman does
not choose to admit anyone to the custody of the inner
space "for keeps"? Who is she then? Does that mean
that for her womanhood and personhood never arrive?

## Naturalness

The idea that the body's groundplan is central to
personal development, taken in another direction, leads
to the concept of woman's naturalness. Erikson suggests

24

that both woman's role and many of her psychological
characteristics flow naturally from her anatomical
structure.  This is most obviously true of her maternal
role, but it is also true of certain qualities associated with it.  Psychologist David McClelland claims
that recent research enables us to list feminine characteristics related to body experience, characteristics
which are not just the negatives of male characteristics.
He says, for example, that woman is interdependent:
she is more concerned than men both with relationships
and with what goes on around her, modifying her behavior
accordingly.  Woman's style is contextual.  She cares
about people.[41]

> Girls...learn early that they are penetrated in
> the sexual act, that the often painful experi-
> ences of menstrual flow and childbirth are
> difficulties that lead to pleasure and happi-
> ness, that to bear a child--the purpose for which
> their body is obviously constructed--they must
> relate to another, who will support them during
> childbirth and their somewhat dependent state
> thereafter, etc.  So there may be common learn-
> ing experiences based on anatomical facts that
> help create some of the psychological reactions
> observed more often among women--their interest
> in interdependence, their idea that they must
> give up one thing to get another, etc. (42)

McClelland's point is not that male experience is unrelated to body structure.  Both he and Erikson would certainly say that it is.  In Erikson's experiment, the
boys' block structures corresponded to the morphology
of their "external," "erectible," and "intrusive"
organs, and McClelland suggests that the phallic
tumescence-detumescence cycle fixes for the boy the
association of rise, pleasure, and assertion.[43]
But in the case of the boy, if anatomy suggests anything,
it suggests a direction or a style of doing things.  It
does not, as the girl's anatomy does, define the thing
that is done.  If anatomy is viewed as destiny, or even
as a co-determinant of it, it therefore fixes the girl's
destiny in a more precise way than the boy's.  What she
does appears as the more natural outcome of what she is.

## Naturalness, Passivity, and Matriarchal Consciousness

The relation between the female body and feminine
psychology or consciousness has been developed by
Jungian psychologists, and in a way which clearly
brings together the traits of naturalness and passivity.

25

Erich Neumann, suggesting once again that psychological traits are related to bodily experience, remarks that attitudes of receptivity and acceptance have characterized woman from the beginning of time. Menstruation, pregnancy, and the endurance of childbirth bring about bio-psychological changes in woman which demand long term adaptations and adjustments. A woman must learn, for example, that many important factors surrounding the birth of a child--its character, sex, health--are not in her power to determine but must be awaited and accepted.[44] Undergoing these experiences thus fosters in her a form of consciousness which Neumann calls "matriarchal," the essential features of which are a receptiveness to experience and a qualitative relationship to time.

A second dimension of woman's experience nurtures these qualities as well. Neumann shares Ortner's view that the primary relationship of identification with the mother is constitutive for feminine development.[45] Unlike the male child, who experiences the mother as a "non-self," the little girl need not learn to differentiate herself from her mother in order to develop her own sexual identity. Indeed, she discovers herself through identification with the mother, and this process of self-discovery "leads to a primary strengthening of all those relationships which take the course of identification."[46] While physically, this tendency toward identification finds its fullest expression in pregnancy, it also intensifies the psychic effects of woman's body experiences. Relating through identification, woman receives and deals with those realities which meet her in the concrete everyday world.

Feminine consciousness, according to Neumann, begins with what emerges surprisingly, uncontrollably from the unconscious, with the <u>Einfall</u> or hunch.

> For matriarchal consciousness, understanding is not an act of intellect, functioning as an organ for swift registration, development and organization; rather it has the meaning of a "conception." Whatever is to be understood must first "enter" matriarchal consciousness in the full, sexual, symbolic meaning of a fructification. (47)

The ego makes its contribution not by willing a content into existence but by accepting it and coming into harmony with it. It circumambulates the content, broods over it, contemplates it. It guides itself by the

26

unconscious processes, abiding them, allowing them to
ripen until they are complete and comprehension is born
out of the unconscious. The ego "lets things happen"
not because it cannot act but because action is
inappropriate.

> It functions as a kind of total realization in
> which the whole psyche participates, and in
> which the ego has the task of turning the libido
> toward a particular psychic event and intensi-
> fying its effect, rather than using the exper-
> ience as a basis for abstract conclusions and
> an expansion of consciousness. (48)

There are dangers in this quality of consciousness,
Jungians point out. A woman can simply passively
follow the stream of images and feelings which invade
consciousness without ever actively relating to and
concretizing them. Or her tendency to self-realization
can get "entangled in mere naturalness." Since "matriarchal consciousness is written into a woman's body,"
she can live only externally what a man must experience
spiritually. The whole of her capacity to realize a
conception may be acted out in physical, literal conception and birth. She may never live her femininity
psychologically, and thus may find her life becoming empty
and meaningless as the outer actuality changes, as her
children grow and leave home. This is woman's particular danger--her sin, as we will refer to it later on.[49]

On the other hand, the submission of the self to
what invades consciousness, Jungians claim, can also be
creative and transforming. The feminine style of
spiritual transformation is that of seeking out and
accepting those aspects of the spirit which are manifest
in the rejected parts of the psyche, the depths of
everyday personal events, the hidden places in the
feelings. In the same way that the feminine style of
ego activity involves a "letting things happen,"
"transformation of the ego is often seen as achieved
through sufferance, through the accord of the self to a
greater will...."[50] A woman's "suffering" the changes
that occur to her body thus takes on a deeper symbolic
significance.

> In all decisive life situations, the feminine,
> to a far greater degree than the nothing-but
> masculine, is subjected to the numinous ele-
> ments in nature, or, still better, has these
> "brought home" to it. Therefore, its rela-
> tion to nature and to God is more familiar and

> intimate, and its tie to an anonymous trans-
> personal allegiance forms earlier and goes
> deeper than its personal tie to a man. (51)

For the feminine ego, it is said, the spirit always
makes itself known through physical events and processes.
The result of seeking the spiritual in the material is
the union of what patriarchal consciousness considers
two "opposites." For the feminine, the spirit is always
born out of the flesh and remains united with it. In
this sense, the mother of Jesus might be considered the
paradigm of the feminine style of spiritual transformation. Mary does not create but receives the reality
that the angel promises--"be it unto me according to
thy word"--and it transforms and is revealed in her
whole being, spirit and flesh.

In fact, the argument continues, the psychological
experience of receiving a new content or numinous element and being taken over by it is symbolized by the
physical processes of penetration, fructification, and
birth. The numinous element fills and changes psychological space, growing within it, until "it [the numinous element] assumes concrete form and autonomous
activity which are manifest now in the way one adapts
to the world and to others."[52] The symbolization of
feminine spirituality in sexual terms suggests once
again that for the feminine, the spiritual is not di-
vorced from sexuality and everyday life but is expressed
through it and represents a deepening of it. In the
end, the highest form of feminine wisdom "is not abstract or disinterested knowledge, but a responsive
wisdom that comes from loving participation in a relationship."[53] "Woman's wisdom is non-speculative, it is
close to nature and life, bound to fate and to living
reality...It is related to this actuality as nourisher,
helper, comforter, and lover, and leads it beyond death
to ever renewed transformation and rebirth."[54]

## Conclusions

This limited survey of writings about women serves
to suggest some elements of the myth to which the modern
woman is asked to conform. She is told, first of all,
that there is a special continuity between female biology, i.e. her nature in the most fundamental sense, and
her cultural and psychological roles. The character
traits she exhibits and the social tasks she is asked to
perform are products not of the interaction of nature
and culture, but of her "being" in all times and places.
Woman is not quite like men in this respect, for although

they too are expected to live and act in ways which are more or less harmonious with their bodily nature, male roles also involve clearer learned elements, more obvious choices. Woman's life, in contrast, seems a more fully _natural_ outgrowth of who she _is_.[55]

Perhaps partly because of the seeming lack of conflict and decision in the process of female development, woman is also defined as more passive than men, and that in several senses. Her sexuality, which is seen as passive, seems to limit her life choices to the domestic arena, while at the same time the public world defines her existence and value. Involved in the processes of her body and the multitude of concrete tasks confronting her every day, she learns to accept and integrate what confronts her, to respond to situations rather than establish them. Where she does initiate, it is mainly on behalf of others; she acts largely to deny herself. Her role is an outgrowth of her biology, her psychology the fruit of her biology and role. Naturalness and passivity are not, of course, the only traits attributed to woman, but they are two central ones--and they are thoroughly interrelated.

## B.  Women's Experience

The relationship between the actual experiences of women and these manifold definitions of women's experience is quite complex. Women have passively conformed to expectations of them. They have lived the expected in such ways as to deepen and enrich it and make it new. They have struggled within and against others' definitions of them. If, as I suggested at the beginning of this chapter, there is no women's experience apart from cultural interpretation of it, how does one understand the relation between women's experience and the prescriptive generalities of the Eternal Feminine? When women's experience confirms cultural expectations, how does one determine the reasons why? What is the path from ideology to the complexities of individual and communal experience?

These questions are crucial both for a full understanding of women's experience and for a theological critique based on it. If no analysis of women's experience can leave out women themselves, a theological critique must ask not only whether theology has taken account of women's experience, but how. Is theology to be another voice on the side of traditional expectation? If so, legitimately or illegitimately? If illegitimately from what standpoint can this illegitimacy be demonstrated? The construction of such a standpoint, the development of a more rounded view of women's experience, is a matter not of stripping layers of patriarchal falsification from an authentic core of women's experience, but of building a viewpoint from a variety of perspectives, adding layer of complexity to layer of complexity.

## Empirical and Anthropological Data

Abjuring any single simple view of women's experience, we are left, however, with the task of carefully weighing the possible contribution of any particular perspective to a balanced approach. Empirical studies of feminine behavior, for example, which seem to provide clear and incontrovertible clues to the nature of women's experience, are complicated by precisely the relation between expectation and experience we are trying to disentangle. We have suggested the particularly extensive and deep-seated nature of social prejudices concerning female behavior. But then the fact that experimenters' expectations have been shown to influence their findings[56] makes empirical studies of women's behavior especially difficult to evaluate. Thanks to Freud, for instance, women had been reporting the experience of two kinds of orgasms for generations before Masters and Johnson proved that all female orgasms follow the same physiological pattern. Perhaps the only valuable empirical evidence is precisely that which contradicts our expectations--in which case the surprising lack of experimental support for much of Freud's theory of feminine development would be particularly significant.[57]

Anthropological investigation, though it deals with only certain kinds of questions, is more clearly useful in that it sets the place of culture in the elaboration of sex roles in sharp relief. The great variety of sex role patternings found in different societies, some flatly contradicting others, definitely suggests the relativity of any particular pattern. Both the value placed on the primary sex differences between men and women and the secondary differences expected to follow from them vary from society to society. Thus the conviction of Western culture that it is male activity and temperament which are most valuable and that the two go together are put in a broader context by Margaret Mead's studies of primitive societies. Mead finds that though a basic configuration of female development is fairly widespread, it is elaborated in very different

30

sex roles and temperaments which are not necessarily related to each other. In two of the three societies she studies in Sex and Temperament, men and women have different roles but are expected to have the same temperament. In one, they both act the way we expect women to act, in the other, the way we expect men to act. In the third society, men and women are expected to behave differently, but in ways which reverse our stereotypic pattern.[58] From society to society, sometimes a particular function is assigned to one sex and sometimes to the other. Sometimes it is women who are thought of as infinitely vulnerable and needing cherishing, and sometimes men. Some societies think of women as too weak to work out of doors; some assign them heavy burdens. Women can even be taught that having children means having their bodies invaded and destroyed and can learn not to want them. Every detail of the female body can be reinterpreted by culture. The clues to sex membership that a child's own body provides are insufficient to determine a particular course of development. The child is always interacting with adults' highly patterned feelings about the experiences it undergoes.[59] "Around the core of differences between men and women...a vast superstructure of myth has been built by emotion, by desire, need, and fear."[60]

## Women's Situation

Anthropological studies like Mead's are important because they so clearly demonstrate the role of cultural expectation in shaping women's experience. They thus make us aware that we can probe the content of women's experience only within a definite cultural context. For if cultural variation in sex roles means anything, it means there is no universal "women's experience," but only the experiences of women in particular societies and particular social groups.[61] The study of specific groups may shed light on general patterns of interaction between cultural expectation and women's experience, but such general understanding can only be a product of specific cultural analysis.

Simone de Beauvoir's The Second Sex is an account of the creation of woman out of one cultural situation-- the modern, European middle class. In her book, the struggle of women within and against a particular cultural context begins to emerge in some of its complexity. The development of women, as de Beauvoir pictures it, always occurs under the shadow of male generalizations and expectations concerning them, with the result that the story of women's lives becomes the story of conflict

31

between efforts toward autonomous existence and the necessity of being-the-other, between vocations as human beings and obligations as women. To every task that a woman performs as a person, to every independent choice she makes, is added the burden of also being a woman. If, under the circumstances, the reality of feminine existence is not entirely different from that described by purveyors of the Eternal Feminine, this is not because woman has an "eternal nature" but because she is defined as having one. This definition does not lead to her fulfillment but undermines her full humanity.

The central dilemma of women's lives, as de Beauvoir sees it, is that women do not shape their own experience, but allow their life choices to be made for them by others. Pleasing their fathers, lovers, husbands, defining themselves through them and through their children become ways of achieving justification at different stages of women's lives. Trained from childhood in the art of enchanting others, charming a man becomes the goal of a woman's existence. Marriage is her fate written in the heavens from the time she is twelve. From puberty, the life of the young girl becomes a period of waiting for The Man who will be her destiny. Marriage is the only career which gives a woman both social status and the possibility of sexual fulfillment. Everyone around her sees her future in it, and so does she herself. At the age of thirteen, when boys are going through an apprenticeship in violence, girls give up their rough games. At the same time, they often lose a good deal of intellectual and artistic ground in relation to boys. Not only are they not encouraged to pursue these things, but they must also be women. The adolescent girl is taught defeatism; her lot is independent of her efforts. It is not by increasing her human worth that she will make friends, become "popular," and finally get a man, but by modelling herself on male dreams.

Marriage achieved, the woman finds that her life, rather than just beginning, is almost over. The things which are to occupy her time are never fully satisfying. She is called upon not to help build a better world but to spend her days endlessly and repetitively repelling the enemy--dirt. She is permitted a flight from herself as she contends with the things around her. As a career, housework is tiresome and empty. It stays always on the level of the general and inessential. The same tasks must be done over and over again. They take on meaning only as part of a fuller life or only when linked up with others who transcend themselves.

Even motherhood, the promised ultimate fulfillment, does not finally get women out of this dilemma. At first, since the pregnant girl takes the place of her own mother, motherhood seems to promise complete emancipation. But the child itself, enriching as it may be, cannot form the limits of its mother's horizon. She can never do more than create a situation which the child as an independent being must transcend. If she invests all possibility of fulfillment in the child, her own transcendence is still by proxy; she is still dependent on another for her own satisfaction.[62]

Feminine psychology, including the traits of naturalness and passivity, is a product of this total feminine situation which includes expectations both as to role and psychology. The psychology of the adolescent girl, for example, must be seen as emerging from a context in which the young person, able neither to accept the destiny which is forcefully impressed upon her, nor to reject it entirely, struggles with it in a number of ways. She may turn against herself--indulge in scornful laughter, strong language, neurotic symptoms, acts of self-mutilation--or plumb the conflicts which disturb her for self-enrichment. Thus she may become more attentive to her feelings than boys of her own age; her inner life is often more richly developed. She can show great psychological insight. Her sensitivity may find an outlet in poetry. She does not act, but she observes, feels and records. She throws herself into things with passion. Empty and unlimited, she wants to attain the All. For this reason, she especially worships nature, for it includes all that exists. Moreover, with it, she is a free person. Away from the society which defines her, "She finds in the secret places of the forest a reflection of the solitude of her soul and in the wide horizons of the plains a tangible image of her transcendence." Sometimes she may seek a reality beyond nature, losing herself in mystic ecstasies.[63] Young girls' magazines which seek contributions from their readers are often filled with dark poems and stories, searching the realities of nature and God, love and death.

Likewise, many other characteristics associated with women, while partly mythical, are in part quite natural outgrowths of their situation. To accuse women of mediocrity, laziness, and frivolity is simply to point out that their horizons are closed; domestic duties do not call for the cultivation of excellence. To say that women are servile is to recall the fact that the successful manipulation of others is their chief

access to power, and masculine support their chief means
to and reason for living. If women are noted for their
subjectivity, this is because "there is a whole region
of human experience which the male deliberately chooses
to ignore because he fails to think it: this experience
woman lives."[64] If women take exception to male logic,
it is not only because it is inapplicable to their experience but because in men's hands logic becomes a means
of coercion. The woman whose husband praises chastity
at a party and then goes home and asks his neighbor's
wife to commit adultery, the woman whose man outlaws
abortion and then asks her to have one when her pregnancy inconveniences him, knows masculine morality and
logic as hoax and fraud. Like the young girl, the
woman too can turn from all that confuses and defines
her to experience herself in relation to nature as a
free being. Trapped as she generally is by the people
and things around her, it is ecstasy to find herself on
a hillside, alone, fully conscious, and ruler of all
she sees. Before the mysteries of the natural order,
her husband's supremacy fades away, and she finds herself a free individual, living not for others but for herself.[65]

## Literary Confirmation

Adding now a final layer to our vision of women's
experience, we find Simone de Beauvoir's account of
womanhood confirmed and deepened by recent literature
by and about women. The work of Doris Lessing is particularly illuminating in this regard. Her five volume
Children of Violence, while probing the realities of
personal existence in a violent century, painfully and
perceptively charts the life history of the modern
woman. Many of the themes discussed by de Beauvoir--
the special agonies of female adolescence, the learning
to be-for-others, the stultifying nature of traditional
marriage--are concretized by Lessing in the person of
her heroine Martha Quest. Martha is certainly not all
women. For one thing, Lessing is too concerned with
the relationship of her characters to historical events
to have created a heroine easily lifted out of context
and proclaimed archetypal. For another, there are many
aspects of Martha's character which are, on the one hand,
clearly individual and on the other, clearly universal
(as opposed to specifically feminine). But to note
these things is not to deny her usefulness for our purpose. Indeed, we might say that since no woman is all
women, it is precisely Martha's individuality and universality which reveal the limits of any definition of
women which regards them solely as woman. It is

precisely through Martha's particularity that she lays
bare aspects of women's situation passed over by de
Beauvoir's generalized description.  In Martha, we have
an image of a twentieth century woman-person struggling
to define herself out of a stunted past and within a
violent present.  Between the lines of her personal
quest, we find truths about women's experience which
Martha herself finds lacking in the novels of the past.[66]

The first part of Martha Quest, the first volume of
the Children of Violence series, begins with a super-
scription Simone de Beauvoir might easily have adopted
for parts of The Second Sex:  "I am so tired of it, and
also tired of the future before it comes."[67]  As the
book opens, the heroine--"adolescent, and therefore
bound to be unhappy; British, and therefore uneasy and
defensive; in the fourth decade of the twentieth century, and therefore inescapably beset with problems of
race and class; female, and obliged to repudiate the
shackled women of the past"--sits reading Havelock
Ellis on her porch steps, listening to the talk of her
mother and a neighbor, "[playing] the part 'young girl'
against their own familiar roles."[68]  Since she resents
and despises their conventionality, her being there is
at once a form of self-punishment and a challenge.  At
odds with herself and the world, Martha needs to pro-
voke them in order to measure her distance from them,
in order to believe in the possibility of her own
escape from the suffocating world they represent.  The
two generations, Lessing suggests, are acting out some
timeless impersonal battle for mothers' and daughters'
voices which Martha will, in turn, enact in the mother
role in her own middle age.

In the present, however, when the real possibility
of escaping the African farm where she was raised presents itself, Martha does not take it.  A week before
the matriculation exam which is to be her "passport to
the outside world," she gets pink eye and decides that
her eyes are too weakened to take the test.  Lessing
thus introduces a pattern which will characterize Martha
through middle age and which is of central concern to
this work--a failure to take responsibility for herself,
a failure to make decisions at crucial points in her
life.  She realizes the terrible importance of the
"matric" to getting off the farm which "more than anything in the world she [wants] to leave," but this knowledge itself paralyzes her.  "She [feels] as if some
kind of spell [has] been put on her."[69]  So begins her
drifting into situations which she knows are impossible
but which she cannot take responsibility for changing.

Quite in line with de Beauvoir, it is only on her forbidden walk down the lovely quiet road between the town and her home, between the prying eyes of the people at the station and the nagging that awaits her, that Martha feels "quite free." There, standing on a rise, the country spread out before her, she experiences a "slow integration" with the things around her.

> ...She, and the little animals, and the moving grasses, and the sunwarmed trees, and the slopes of shivering silvery mealies, and the great dome of blue light overhead, and the stones of earth under her feet, became one, shuddering together in a dissolution of dancing atoms. (70)

She understands herself as "reluctantly allowed to participate" in a basically inhuman order, feels it demanding that she dissolve and yield to its necessity. But the moment over, the vision gone, she returns home to yield only to anger and resentment, to begin the great battle with her mother once again.

When Martha, through the agency of a friend, finally leaves the farm to take a job in the city, "the spell" increases its power over her. Claimed by the son of a family friend as soon as she moves into town, she pliantly adopts herself to what he wants her to be. The critical part of herself, "the watcher" as she calls it, finds him, the people and the life to which he introduces her, empty and repellent. But this knowledge has nothing to do with her capacity to act or to take responsibility for what she knows. Indeed, she experiences no relation at all either between knowing and acting responsibly or between action and its effects. When she is promoted at the office after having gone to school to learn shorthand, "she [feels] an altogether unreasonable astonishment that the work she had put in at the Polytechnic had, in fact, lifted her one degree up the ladder towards efficiency; as if the process of painfully learning a thing could have nothing to do with her for herself."[71] Certainly, her success with her new friends has nothing to do with who she is at all, but with her ability to switch into the "charming manner," into the "new skilled vivacity which [is] part of her equipment, as girl about town." Even this manner is not something she tries to learn. "It had offered itself to her...."[72] Martha Quest is filled with images suggesting Martha's passivity. Donovan brings her new self into being; she submits herself to him; she is caught in a current which she cannot resist. There is no Martha Quest as a responsible, willing being.

36

> She expected they would sit by themselves, if
> she expected anything at all--for this way of
> hers, submitting herself to a person or a
> place, with a demure, childish compliance,
> as if she were under a spell, meant that she
> did not consciously expect or demand; she
> might dream about things being different, but
> that, after all, commits one to nothing. (73)

Martha's problem is that there is no one she can
commit herself to be. The fact she fears and rejects
her mother's life does not mean any positive possibility appears open to her in its stead. "She would
not be like Mrs. Van Rensberg, a fat and earthy house-
keeping woman; she would not be bitter and nagging and
dissatisfied, like her mother," she thinks to herself
at the beginning of Martha Quest. "But then, who [is]
she to be like? Her mind [turns] towards the heroines
she [has] been offered, and [discards] them. There
[seems] to be a gap between herself and the past..."[74]
Either all the novels about young, idealistic heroines
who turn out to love babies and dull marriages are
lies, or Martha is a new type of woman born into the
world. If somewhere there exists a woman "who [combines]
a warm accepting femininity and motherhood with being
what Martha [describes] vaguely but to her own satisfaction as 'a person,'" Martha has yet to find her.[75]
Wanting to be neither a woman trapped by her own frus-
trated intelligence into constant resentment nor a woman
at peace with the domestic life, what is left for her to
be "but fierce and unhappy and determined?"[76] Or what
is left for her to do except to drift, to be pulled
into a pattern, which, if feared and hated, is at least
easily available and thoroughly known?

In the same way, therefore, that she drifted into
being the charming young woman, Martha now drifts into
marriage and motherhood. Meeting a young man who seems
a bit more intelligent than most, who reads the New
Statesman and has his own dissatisfaftions with the present, Martha adopts him as a fellow spirit. He fills
the emptiness that sends her starting up, restlessly
during the night "feeling that there [is] something she
ought to be doing."[77] And somehow, though she does not
want to marry him--"she would rather die" than marry
Douglas--"it [is] decided they [will] marry."[78] Regret-
ting the decision the next day and resolving to tell
Douglas it is all a mistake, Martha discovers that the
town is already out in force to welcome her into the
fellowship of the married. Simply by announcing their
intention to marry, they set in motion some mysterious

impersonal process which sweeps them along in its jubil-
ant path.

Shortly after her marriage, Martha, with cool detachment, ascribes it to the impending war (WWII).

> Well...not to get married when it is so clearly
> expected of us was rather more of an act of de-
> fiance than I was prepared to commit. Besides...
> the international situation positively demands
> it. Who one marries is obviously of no impor-
> tance at all...In short, I got married because
> there's going to be a war. (79)

If Martha is speaking truthfully here, then the sense
of urgency created by impending violence has become the
normal atmosphere of this century, for she is by no
means the only recent heroine to fall into marriage.
It seems, however, as if the pre-war atmosphere as
Lessing describes it--and, perhaps, the violent world
in which we now live--are factors additional to the
pressures already created by the universal expectation
that young women will marry. At least, that is how
other contemporary women authors depict the situation.
Margaret Drabble, for example, has her heroine Jane in
The Waterfall think back about why she married her
estranged husband. "I liked having a safe dependable
reliable man to go around with and kill time with...
After a year, we became engaged. I don't think he proposed to me; we drifted sensibly into marriage, as
people do."[80] And yet knowing she would not have married just anyone who asked, she probes her reasons
further.

> Love, may be: I did think that I loved him,
> but I don't like to think that love might die:
> so I prefer not to believe that I married for
> love. I felt protective towards him, respon-
> sible...I felt in a way that having accustomed
> him to my company and taken away that loneli-
> ness, I owed him myself. (81)

Margaret Atwood's Marian, too, after her first instinc-
tive flight from her "nicely packaged" boyfriend, succumbs to the warmth of a car in a thunderstorm and
agrees to marry him.

> The decision was a little sudden, but now I've
> had time to think about it I realize it is
> actually a very good step to take. Of course,
> I'd always assumed through high school and college

38

that I was going to marry someone eventually
and have children, everyone does.  Either two
or four, three is a bad number and I don't
approve of only children, they get spoiled too
easily. (82)

Marian finally flees again, but only after "becoming"
the fiancee to an extent which surprises even herself.
Each of these women's marriage choices is really
quite limited, for how can a woman choose freely, asks
de Beauvoir, when she does not feel free not to marry?[83]

   To have or not to have children is not really a
choice either as portrayed by these novelists, and this
is true not only of the decision whether to have children but when to have them as well.  For Drabble's
characters, birth control has something of the quality
of a bad joke.  "'You don't decide to have children,'"
one of them comments.  "'They decide to be born.'"[84]
All of her married heroines--and one of her unmarried
ones--have unplanned pregnancies.  Clara in Atwood's
The Edible Woman, despite her best intentions, is on
her third.  And Martha, though she does not want a
baby any more than she wanted to get married, finds
later she was already pregnant at her wedding.  Each
of these characters seems to be overcome by the fated-
ness of motherhood.  One must have children some time,
after all, so why not when they choose to happen?

   Martha, married and pregnant at the ripe age of
nineteen, finds the borders of her life narrowing in on
her.  While her husband Douglas, with the town's other
young men, becomes increasingly absorbed in the coming
war, she gives herself to the lassitude of her own heavy
body.  As was the case during her adolescence on the
farm, it is only in relation to nature that she experiences real freedom.  One rainy afternoon when "the boys"
are off drinking, preferring male company to theirs,
Martha and a pregnant friend in defiance of the "prohib-
itions and firm masculine attitudes" of their husbands,
drive to the veld near the nursing home where they will
give birth, undress, and plunge out into the rain.
Running naked through the wet waist-high grass, rocking
in the muddy water of a pothole observing the animals
that make it their home, feeling her moving infant
"protected from the warm red water by half an inch of
flesh," Martha is able to transcend her resentment at
being just "the wife of one of the lads."  Back in the
car, the friends are embarrassed, "But there [is] no
doubt they [are] both free and comfortable in their minds,
their bodies [feel] relaxed and tired; they [do] not care

now that their men [prefer] other company to theirs."[85]

These moments of transcendence, however, are rare. Her husband's year of military service over, Martha settles into a new house and a brief period of traditional marriage. She is now a member of the fraternity which celebrated her intention to marry, of a "set" of young couples, of a group of women who are pregnant or who have just had a child, who proudly seek for small ways to save money, who cultivate the household arts. "It [is] the time of these women which [supports] the whole edifice [of their comfortable lives]; their willingness to sink their youth in acquiring multifarious small talents...."[86] It is with relative ease that Martha becomes one of them. This is another period of her life in which her instinct toward compliance enables her to be someone whom, on another level of herself, she despises. Her pantry, with its lovely well-stocked shelves becomes her favorite room in the house. She skimps on lunches to save money to the end of the month, spends hours pickling and preserving, makes all her daughter's clothes on her sewing machine. If, through everything, she feels that three quarters of her true being is standing on the sideline waiting to be called into action, the other women of her set have their own not dissimilar complaints. When Martha finally determines to leave her husband, each of these women speaks to her admiringly, expressing the wish for the courage to do the same, while older women tell her that all women feel the same way, that she can learn to adjust. Her mother-in-law lies crying in the darkness, "her own life...made to look null and meaningless because Martha would not submit to what women always had submitted to."[87] What finally distinguishes Martha from the others is not the reality of her daily experience of marriage, but her decision (perhaps the first real decision of her life) not to give in to it, not to accept it as her fate on earth.

Up to this point in the Children of Violence, Martha has followed the path of woman's life laid out for her before her birth: stormy adolescent, attractive young woman, wife, mother. And yet at the same time, it is as if the "real" Martha is only trying on the sole mythology, the only model available to her, as if it were a process necessarily gone through before she can move on to anything else. She moves through the prescribed stages of "women's experience," but they do not describe her; they do not fit her comfortably. There is always a conflict between the passive compliant Martha who enacts a socially predetermined role and "the

40

watcher," the core of her self that feels totally alienated from the life she is living. A deep layer of
unhappiness lies just under the surface of her life.
Lessing suggests that this unhappiness, if felt more
sharply by Martha than by other women, is by no means
unique to her. Almost all Lessing's women characters
experience a discord between themselves as women and
as what Martha calls "persons."

On the other hand, if we are to describe fairly
the ways in which women experience themselves, it must
be said that there are many women who do not feel this
discontinuity. The very things which Martha sees as
digressions from her development as a human being are
viewed by others as important sources of satisfaction
and fulfillment. And indeed, since most women do not
leave their husbands, we should expect that they would
find daily rewards in homemaking and childrearing roles.
If then the qualities fostered by and necessary to
these satisfactions are responsiveness more than initiative, flexibility more than single-mindedness, subjectivity and sympathy more than objectivity and judgement,[88] these qualities should not be denigrated but
appreciated and valued.

Lessing does not so much deny the worth of either
the feminine role or the qualities it fosters as suggest that they take on value for Martha only when she
begins consciously to use them in the service of herself. We might say that women's traditional tasks and
characteristics are not problematical per se but become
so when they are not chosen--when they are not viewed
as some of numberless human possibilities, when there
is no expectation that responsiveness in one realm will
be balanced by initiative in another, when there is no
time and space to look objectively at what first needed
a subjective and immediate response. Such choice and
opportunity is always absent for women when certain
roles and qualities are defined not as aspects of any
whole adult life or personality but as the specific
domain of women, while opposite roles and qualities belong to men. But as Lessing's work so clearly shows,
if the traditional feminine role nourishes certain qualities to the detriment of others, both more and less than
stepping out of the role is required for a woman to become whole. Martha's drifting does not end with leaving her husband, but when she finally does transcend her
drifting, she does so not in opposition to her experiences as a woman but through them.

Initially, Martha steps out of one mythology only

to try on an alternative one--communism.[89]  This new
stage is offered to her not as a woman but as a citizen of the twentieth century; still, she works through
it in her woman's way.  Martha chooses to be a communist in a way she never chose to marry, but the decision having been made, she is carried along by its mo-
mentum.  This is a period of real growing and learning
in her life; yet she does not fully control its direction.  Joining the "left" group in town, she is issued
a whole new set of emotions, ideas, friends, which, if
closer to the "real" Martha, do not come from her.  In
a sense, she has simply defined new boundaries for her
drifting.

Part of what she now drifts into is a second, albeit quite different, disastrous marriage, this time
with the leader of their communist group, Anton, a
stiff, arrogant German refugee.  Their relationship
begins through an "accident."  He nurses Martha while
she is sick, thereby establishing a claim on her which
she cannot clearly define but which nevertheless seems
absolute.  She feels caged in by him, by his inhuman
logicalness, by his sexual ineptitude.  At one point
she thinks, "and it [is] a moment of illumination, a
flash of light:  I don't know anything about anything
yet.  I must try to keep myself free and open, and try
to think more, try not to drift into things."[90]  Yet
immediately after this, when problems with his refugee
status force them to decide whether to marry or to
split up, she decides to marry him.  Her "reasons" are
many:  she owes it to him as a fellow communist; it is
a mere formality; personal feelings don't matter in the
Party.  But she sees her life as "something dark and
unhappy and essentially driven."[91]

Besides "the communist," Martha has another role
to enact during the period that she is thus exploring
and drifting; this role peculiar to women's experience.
In her earlier enactment of the stages of a woman's
life, her image of the ideal love had always detached
itself from the particular men with whom she was involved and floated, "like the painted picture of a sten-
cil floating off paper in water," above them.[92]  It is
only during this period, living with Anton but estranged
from him, that Martha finds a lover and becomes "the
woman in love."

There is a type of woman [says Lessing] who can
never be, as they are likely to put it 'themselves' with anyone but the man to whom they have
permanently or not given their hearts.  If the

42

man goes away there is left an empty space filled
with shadows. She mourns for the temporarily
extinct person she can only be with a man she
loves; she mourns him who brought her 'self' to
life. She lives with the empty space at her
side, peopled with the images of her own potentialities until the next man walks into the
space, absorbs the shadow into himself, creating
her, allowing her to be her 'self'--but a new
self, since it is his conception which forms
her. (93)

This is Martha. All through her relationship with Anton
and well before it, she endures her dissatisfactions with
her life and with the men she knows and marries by telling herself that she is waiting for that "real" man who
will come along and take her by the hand "and make her
be what she [knows] she could be."[94]

If Simone de Beauvoir is accurate, however, in describing the woman in love as one who justifies her dependence by making her beloved the center of reality
and value,[95] Martha's love affair with Thomas, the
Jewish Polish refugee who fills the empty space, is and
is not paradigmatic of women's experience. On the one
hand, she begins her affair with Thomas precisely out
of the need for someone who will make her what she
knows she could be. Before she meets him, Martha feels
herself living self-protectively and precariously in a
house with half a dozen rooms. He is "the roof," the
"fire burning in the center of the empty space," who
unifies them.[96] By adding a new room to her life, the
loft in which they meet to make love, she brings an end
to a period of holding herself together, a period of ar-
ranging before each appointment the Martha she has to
present as she rushes from person to person, job to job.
The loft is the center from which she now lives. And it
is this center not because through her relationship with
Thomas she achieves a new wholeness, but because in relation to him, everything else fades into unimportance.

But Thomas is not simply the Prince Charming who,
through her surrender to him, fulfills all Martha's
fondest dreams and sets her life aright. Her relationship with him is also more than she bargained for.

...No, it was too strong, it was not what she
wanted, it was too much of a wrench away from
what was easy: much easier to live deprived,
to be resigned, to be self-contained. No, she

did not want to be dissolved. And neither did
he.... (97)

Martha refers here not to a final form of passivity and
self-denial, a dissolution of herself into Thomas, but
to a dissolution of both of them into currents stronger
than themselves. If Thomas becomes her hold on reality
and the center of her life for a time, he also puts her
in touch with unlooked for and little understood aspects
of herself which enrich her even after he leaves and
which enable her to endure without him.[98] This period
of dependence becomes a key to later self-exploration
and discovery. One wonders whether Simone de Beauvoir
herself experiences a similar tension in love between
the transcendent and the ordinary in women's experience. "[Sartre's] mere existence justified the world,"
she writes.[99] And yet she obviously creates her own
value and reality beyond him.

In any event, Martha's relationship with Thomas
represents one of the stages in her life in which her
experience as a woman, rather than luring her from her
development as a person, merges with and forwards it.
In the first four volumes of the Children of Violence
series, such experiences of transcendence--the relationship with Thomas, the two moments on the veld, the
awareness of "the watcher"--are brief, flickering, only
partially understood and quickly forgotten. In The
Four-Gated City, however, these concealed moments come
together and gather in importance until the book is
about them and the whole series may be read backwards as
Martha's hidden journey toward a "non-passionate sense
of inner completion."[100]

It is impossible, in a context like this, to do
justice to the multi-themed complexity of this last,
sprawling novel. Too many of it numerous significant
characters and wide-ranging social concerns are simply
not relevant here. What does concern us are the connections between Martha's explorations of non-ordinary
experiences so important in the scheme of the novel and
her experiences as a woman. In the first four novels,
Martha's relationship to social definitions of women's
experience was a mixture of acquiescence, despair, and
struggle. In The Four-Gated City, the experiences she
had previously seen as hindering her development, consciously used, become the base for her journey into the
realm of extraordinary reality. Martha begins to live
certain common elements of women's experience in such a
way as to make them new.

44

At the end of <u>Landlocked</u>, Martha had reserved a
berth on a boat to England and was waiting to begin her
voyage "home." <u>The Four-Gated City</u> begins toward the
end of several weeks of her "drifting and bobbing"
around a gloriously indifferent London. Almost immediately, we are introduced to the city's gift to her--
access to a heightened awareness analogous to her adolescent experience on the veld, but deeper, and more
enduring. Wandering endlessly through the streets of
London, Martha discovers that if she walks enough, eats
lightly, sleeps little enough, "then her whole self
[clears], [lightens], she [becomes] alive and light and
aware." She discovers herself as "nothing but a soft
dark receptive intelligence," a "lit space," the
watcher.[101] If from this space she can move backwards
through time to become Martha Quest, Martha Knowell,
Martha Hesse, she is, at the same time, detached from
all these identities. "...She [is], nothing to do with
Martha, or any other name she might have had attached
to her...."[102]

While Martha desires to explore further the boundaries of this special awareness, she nevertheless recognizes the necessity of first working through her past
experiences. As she puts it, "she [has] debts to
pay."[103] Before she can return to the vision offered
her, she must first live ordinarily and responsibly for
some period ahead, integrating the years of foolish,
careless drifting. The insight that she must move on to
responsibility leads her to take a job as the secretary
to author Mark Coldridge. Having no money and no place
else to go, she moves into his house, intending to stay
for only a few months, and remains for twenty years.

It is ironic that Martha, who felt she had to leave
her own daughter, should become the mother to a whole
house of children not her own, but this is what gradually happens during her first years with the Coldridges.
After the death of Mark's sister-in-law Sally-Sarah,
Martha finds herself taking increasing responsibility
for running the household and caring for the children in
it. Indeed, there comes a time when she finds herself
"a middle-aged person, deputy in the center of a house,
the person who runs things, keeps things going, conducts
a holding operation," "a kind of special instrument sensitized to mood and need and state."[104] This is a period
of her life, like the time just before she met Thomas,
when she is a focal point for the people and events
around her. But unlike that earlier period when she was
a focus simply because of her availability, her present
capacity to hold people and things together comes from a

dearly bought reserve of strength within her. Each time
she argues with Sally-Sarah's son Paul or tries to cope
with Jill and Gwen, Mark's two adolescent nieces, the
detached, silent watcher observes parts of Martha fight-
ing earlier versions of herself. This time it is not
an affair--which she deliberately rejects--but her acute
watchful consciousness of all the processes unfolding
around her which enables her to survive the period as a
unity.

This is an important time in Martha's life, one
which helps her to define and integrate her own past
self, to "pay her debts" and finish her unfinished
business. "To [work] through, to [stand] firm in, that
storm which is the young ones' adolescence [is], after
all, to [be] made free of one's own."[105]  It is now
Martha's turn to play the outraged mother struggling
with the daughter she herself was  sitting on the
porch steps of the Quest home, to call the children down
to supper, to deal with Paul's melodramatics and insist
through everything that he do his homework. And there
are rewards to it all even beyond the fact that she
emerges stronger. It is through the ordinary experiences of middle-age and motherhood that Martha is now
able to move on to her explorations of non-ordinary
reality. Thus it is during this period that she begins to hear voices--first Mark's voice, then Paul's.
Words, phrases, thoughts of theirs, in their language,
begin to trickle through her mind. This hearing is in
a sense a natural extension of her role in the house--
her being at the center of things, being in such close
touch with everyone's moods and feelings. Her role as
mother and counselor which demands a constant tuning
into the currents of energy ("dynamics") in the house,
taken just a step further, enables her to tune into the
thought energy of individuals.[106]

It is instructive to compare Martha at this stage
with Virginia Woolf's Mrs. Ramsey who is also called
upon to be the focal point of her home. Mrs. Ramsey
is Ashley Montagu's superior woman, supremely creative
in the sphere of human relations.[107]  Her capacity to
weave the disparate personalities around her into a
unity is analogous to artistic creation. But the moments of eternity Mrs. Ramsey brings into being by sheer
force of personality are static, self-enclosed.

There it was [says Mrs. Ramsey, feeling the
harmony of the party around the table], all
round them. It partook, she felt...of eternity;...there is a coherence in things, a

46

stability; something, she meant, is immune from change, and shines out...in the face of the flowing, the fleeting, the spectral, like a ruby; so that again tonight she had the feeling she had had once today, already, of peace, of rest. (108)

She is one of the women Simone de Beauvoir refers to when she says, "The moments that women regard as revelations are those in which they discover their accord with a static and self-sufficient reality."[109] Perhaps de Beauvoir is right, and it is Mrs. Ramsey who is typical. But Martha is neither so creative as Mrs. Ramsey nor so lucky! Her best efforts succeed only in holding in uneasy tension the many young people who surround her, while grapplings with reality bring a very different kind of peace. The situation in which Mrs. Ramsey finds moments of eternal harmony, Martha finds only a precarious balance and the tools for further self-discovery.

Martha's most intense period of self-exploration begins after the children are grown and after a period of waiting. "And now what's next?" she asks.[110] It turns out that what is next is another of Lynda's (Mark's wife) breakdowns, and the necessity of seeing her through it becomes the occasion for Martha's own thorough exploration of the region of madness. It is now, having paid her debts, that she is ready to return to and explore the region of the "lit space" she experienced during her first weeks in London. The wave lifts her up again, and she must seek out and test unknown and frightening parts of herself.

Much of what Martha discovers during this time has to do with her relation to the century in which she lives and is not relevant here. There are two aspects of her experience, however, which are worth noting. One is that Martha is able to learn from Lynda, to "become" Lynda, only because she opens herself to her, becomes an "instrument sensitized" to her, in the same way she earlier opened herself to the currents in the house. In this she is different from Mark who helps Lynda through many breakdowns without ever allowing himself to be tested by them. Secondly, Martha can drive herself to madness and back only on the basis of strength and understanding acquired through years of ordinary living, and what she learns during this period she relates again to ordinary life. At one moment of too sharp insight in the month she spends with Lynda, Martha, leaving the house for a walk, experiences a communion with nature

47

much more intense than her adolescent moment on the veld.
In contrast to nature's joyous intensity, the people
around her appear as "sleep-walkers," "slugs;"[111] she
returns to the basement vowing never to leave it again.
But this moment passes. Without losing the insight that
it brings, she is able to return once again to the
everyday.

> ...She had learned that one thing, that most
> important thing, which was that one simply had
> to go on, take one step after another: this
> process in itself held the keys. And it was
> this process which would, as it had in the
> past, be bound to lead her around to that
> point where--asking continuously, softly,
> under one's breath, Where, What is it? How?
> What's next? Where is the man or woman who--
> she would find herself back with herself. (112)

## C. Conclusions

In the attempt to understand the nature of women's
experience, we discussed both societal (male) definitions
of women's experience and the experiences of women within them. We might describe their relation by saying
that the definitions of women's experience are both
descriptive within limits and prescriptive of the lived
experiences of women and that their descriptive and prescriptive functions are related. This is the way you
are, a firmly entrenched social mythology tells women,
and this is the way you ought to be. The sum of expectations concerning women in Western society, given
scientific status by the psychological theories we have
examined, is incorporated into the literature of every
field, filters down through popular literature and the
media, and is communicated to every child in endless
ways from the moment it is born. Children are thus
molded in the image of the myth, and the myth is revali-
dated because it becomes an accurate description of the
way things are.

Part of our task was to examine this circular process, to explore the interrelationship of reality and
myth. We did this first by briefly referring to cross-
cultural anthropological studies which demonstrate very
clearly the relativity of specific social elaborations
of male and female roles. These studies, because they
pointed to the importance of specific cultural factors
in the development of women's experience, led us to a
discussion of Simone de Beauvoir's The Second Sex, a

48

book which discusses the western middle-class woman in particular, as a product of her situation.  Do we need to assume some eternal feminine "nature" to explain women's roles and character, de Beauvoir enabled us to ask, or are they adequately accounted for by women's circumstances?  We dwelt at most length, however, on a third type of evidence.  We examined a significant account of the development of a twentieth century woman in order to compare her experience and self-conception with social definitions of her nature and role.  Lessing's discomfort with the options and models available to women enabled us to use Martha both to give content to the idea of women's experience and to see as myth the myth against which she develops.

Martha's experience is never unrelated to external definitions of who and what she should be, but her relationship to what is expected of her goes through several different stages.  First, there is a long period in which she acts out her proper role.  As an adolescent she is moody and rebellious, difficult, but only within the bounds of what can be expected.  In true Eriksonian fashion, she desires a young man who will take her by the hand and define her.  She marries early, has a child immediately, and becomes part of a "set" of young couples.  At the same time she behaves according to form, she exemplifies the passivity which, according to our psychologists, is the chief feminine characteristic. She drifts into situations, molds her personality to others' images and expectations.  She offers her husband "years of feminine compliance, of charm, of conformity to what he [wants]."[113]  Having no positive image of who she wants to be, she falls into the pattern which is most familiar.  Not surprisingly, given her lack of female models, her years of passivity do not end with the one decision to leave her husband.  Her becoming a communist is rather a signal for her drifting in new directions.  Moreover, during this period, she longs more than ever for a man who will make of her what she knows she can be, and in fact, she finds her Prince Charming in Thomas and becomes the "woman in love."  Still, through her whole life in Africa, Martha is conscious that both her drifting and what she drifts into are antithetical to the demands of her authentic self.

In _Man's World, Woman's Place_, Elizabeth Janeway argues that the virtue of a role lies in its appropriateness to the performer.  A useful role fits her comfortably and loosely, without depriving her of creativity and movement, belittling her hope or denying

her humanity."[114]  By this measure, the role and character women are asked to play are mighty poor ones, for
Martha explicitly sees them as conflicting with her
humanity, as preventing her from being who she can and
wants to be.  Lest we think of Martha as an exception,
Lessing offers us an array of women who choose to make
do with what is offered them and, on some level, are
stunted as human beings.  "Everyone feels like this,"
they tell themselves.  "Life is so terrible."[115]  Their
awareness of the gap between their potentiality and the
roles they play makes us aware of the roles as roles
and of the ways they limit the growth of the people
who enact them.

In the course of the third stage of her development, Martha transcends the "psychology of the patri-
archate" and finds herself.[116]  Precisely because she
now becomes an individual, her life in London is difficult to categorize.  On the one hand, she seems to have
left traditional expectations concerning women's roles
and nature far behind.  Externally, her life in London
is rather unconventional.  Personally, she has matured;
she is more responsible.  She no longer drifts in the
way she did previously.  Her periods of non-action are
times of purposeful waiting and are followed by appropriate decisions.  On the other hand, Martha's life at
this stage illustrates almost perfectly Neumann's account of feminine consciousness.[117]  She accepts fully
the challenges and responsibilities of motherhood.  If
she has a "female" capacity for sensitivity in relationships, it is most manifest in the Coldridge home.
She seeks out what is manifest in the rejected portions
of the psyche, waits purposefully, abides processes
and lets them ripen, and realizes the spiritual in
ordinary life.  If in the first four volumes of Children
of Violence, Martha illustrated the limits and pitfalls
of the feminine role in Western society, in The Four-
Gated City, she represents its possibilities.

Having thus given content to the idea of women's
experience, we now turn to the question of whether
Niebuhr and Tillich take account of this experience in
the formulation of their thought.  Both theologians believe that theology must speak to the human situation.
Is it the human situation or only the male situation
which their anthropologies describe?  Insofar as they
are concerned with the human characteristics we have
connected with women, where do they place them in relation to other characteristics?  Do they see them as
important or unimportant, valuable or harmful?  Have
these theologians appropriated and do they perpetuate
the mythology of the society in which they write, or do
they speak from a broader perspective?

50

CHAPTER TWO

REINHOLD NIEBUHR

I shall attempt to answer the questions raised at
the end of the last chapter by looking first at
Reinhold Niebuhr's treatment of the doctrines of sin
and grace. My aim is not an exhaustive study of the
doctrines. Rather, the argument concerning Niebuhr
will have two prongs, corresponding to the two "female"
traits of naturalness and passivity. My minor argument will revolve around Niebuhr's stress on the negative aspects of human creatureliness to the neglect of
its positive sides. My major argument will concern
Niebuhr's onesided definitions of sin and grace.[1]  I
will argue that Niebuhr, in claiming that the primary
form of sin is pride and the primary fruit of grace
sacrificial love, focuses on aspects of human experience more likely to be associated with men than with
women in western society, and thus both ignores and
reinforces the experiences of women. While both arguments will rely heavily on the definition of women's
experience developed in chapter one, I will also try to
show that Niebuhr's account of sin and grace is partial
even on his own terms.

A.  Niebuhr's Method

A theologian is particularly vulnerable to criticism for omitting certain aspects of human experience
from his thought when he claims to take seriously the
need to speak to and from the human situation. Niebuhr
makes such a claim. In developing his doctrines of sin
and grace, he continually integrates the insights of
Christian revelation with independent analysis of the
human situation.[2] While the content of this integration
will be our main concern, it will be useful to begin
with some methodological comments on how Niebuhr relates
revelation and experience.

In The Nature and Destiny of Man, the book with
which we will be chiefly concerned, Niebuhr presents
his view of human life by contrasting it with what he
calls the shifting tides of idealism, naturalism and
romanticism in modern views of human nature. The
modern mind, he claims, lacks "a principle of interpretation which can do justice to both the height of human
self-transcendence and the organic unity between the
spirit of man [sic] and his physical life."[3] Wanting
such a principle, the modern mind falls into three
great confusions. 1) It identifies human beings with

either reason or vitality, failing to understand the genuine unity of the two in human life. 2) It provides no real grounding for the human sense of individuality. "It lacks an anchor or norm for the free individual who transcends both the limitations of nature and the various social concretions of history."[4] 3) It is complacent about human evil. It conceives of individuals as capable of overcoming the evil within themselves either by increasing their rational control over it or surrendering to the harmony and serenity of nature. "Modern man has an essentially easy conscience."[5]

These three critical problems in modern interpretations of human nature--the inability to relate vitality and form, to ground individuality and to fully understand human evil--are overcome in an interpretation of the self which knows it as truly understandable only in terms of a "principle of comprehension which is beyond...comprehension."[6] For the Christian, this principle of interpretation is the revelation of God's eternal will in both individual and social-historical experience. Niebuhr refers to these two loci of revelation as personal, individual, or general revelation and historical or special revelation. The two are dialectically related in that individual revelation requires historical revelation for definition and control, while historical revelation depends on individual revelation for its credibility.

Human experience enters Niebuhr's discussion of revelation at two points--as the locus of individual revelation and the testing ground of special revelation. General revelation is simply human self-knowledge viewed from a particular angle.[7] When Niebuhr describes human beings in philosophical language, he says that they are self-transcendent; they have the capacity to stand outside themselves and survey themselves and their world. When he uses religious language, he says, "the soul which reaches the outermost rims of its own consciousness, must also come in contact with God, for He impinges upon that consciousness."[8] The point is the same. This "sense of being confronted with a 'wholly other' at the edge of human consciousness"[9] is personal revelation, and it has three elements which become more sharply defined as they are related to other forms of revelation.

The first element in personal revelation is related to what Schleiermacher described as the feeling of "unqualified dependence." It "is the sense of reverence for a majesty and of dependence upon an ultimate source of being." This sense of reverence is supported by another form of general revelation, one pertaining to the outer rather than the inner world--God's manifestation in his creation. "Faith concludes that the same 'Thou' who confronts us in our personal experience is also the source and Creator of the whole world."[10] Creation is not itself a revealed doctrine, but it is basic to revelation insofar as it expresses the biblical idea of the transcendence and immanence of God and lays the basis for the biblical view of the meaningfulness of history.

The second element of general revelation "is the sense of moral obligation laid upon one from beyond oneself and of moral unworthiness before a judge."[11] This sense of obligation, which is related to the phenomenon of conscience, has its counterpart in historical revelation in the covenant relation between God and his people. Conscience and the biblical-prophetic idea of obligation and judgement stand in the same dialectical relation as general and special revelation generally. The universal experience of being commanded and judged which conscience represents is interpreted by biblical religion to mean that human beings stand in relation to a commanding and judging God. This interpretation is not generated by the fact of conscience itself; it is possible only on biblical presuppositions. But once it is accepted, it proves to be the only full and accurate account of conscience. Thus the general fact of conscience can be fully understood only through historical revelation, but historical revelation is supported by the prior experience of conscience.

The third and least defined element in religious experience is "the longing for forgiveness."[12] It is related to the second element in that the longing for forgiveness follows the sense of judgement. But general revelation knows only the desire for forgiveness; it is only special revelation which knows that judgement is not God's final word to humanity, that God takes human sinfulness into himself in Christ. This final, Christian, revelation is not reversible in the same sense that the doctrines of God as Creator and Judge are. The assurance that God has resources of love transcending his judgement has no initial counterpart in individual revelation. It is validated by human experience, however, after it is revealed.[13]

The doctrines of sin and grace, to which we now turn, are grounded in the second and third elements of general revelation and the special revelation of God as

Judge and Redeemer. Since Niebuhr sees the elements of general and special revelation as dialectically related, as he develops the doctrines of sin and grace, he argues from both human experience and what he calls the "Christian" or "biblical view of man." The partial insights of human experience are fully revealed and defined in historical revelation which is then shown to be true to the facts of human experience.

## B. Niebuhr's Doctrine of Sin

### The Occasion for Sin

John Dickinson, in a thesis on Niebuhr and Freud, distinguishes four elements in Niebuhr's doctrine of sin: the occasion for sin, its preconditions, its dimension, and its directions.[14] Adopting this useful framework and taking its categories one by one, we find the occasion for sin is nothing less than human nature itself. According to Niebuhr, the Christian account of human nature is distinguished from the modern view by the way it relates three elements. First, through its doctrine of the image of God, Christianity affirms that human beings can reach the heights of spiritual self-transcendence. Second, it insists that they nevertheless remain creatures, weak, dependent, and finite, involved in all the contingencies of the natural world. Third, it says that this creatureliness is not in itself evil, but that evil is the inevitable but not necessary refusal to acknowledge creatureliness and dependence.

The first of these three elements is clearly affirmed by the Bible but not defined by it, with the result that creation in God's image has been variously interpreted in the history of Christian thought. Niebuhr takes the _imago dei_ to refer not to rationality but to the human capacity for self-transcendence. "Man," he says, "is a spirit who stands outside of nature, life, himself, his reason and the world."[15]

> Man is the only mortal animal who knows that he is mortal, a fact which proves that in some sense he is not mortal. Man is the only creature embedded in the flux of finitude who knows that this is his fate; which proves that in some sense this is not his fate. (16)

The only rational animal, humans can raise questions about their rationality; which proves they are more than

54

their rationality as well.

> The human spirit in its depth and height reaches
> into eternity and...this vertical dimension is
> more important for the understanding of man
> than merely his rational capacity for forming
> general concepts. This latter capacity is de-
> rived from the former. (17)

Christian thought thus interprets human nature in terms
which include the rational faculties but go beyond them.

At the same time, though, that human beings are
spirit, standing outside themselves, confronted with
endless potentialities, finding their norm in ultimate
reality, they are also creatures bounded by nature,
unable to choose anything outside the bounds set by
their creatureliness. At the same time that the mind
is set in a dimension of depth in such a way as to be
able to apprehend, if not comprehend, the character of
ultimate reality, "this same human reason is itself
embedded in the passing flux, a tool of a finite organ-
ism, the instrument of its physical necessities, and
the prisoner of the partial perspectives of a limited
time and space."[18]

Niebuhr takes an ambivalent view of this human
creatureliness. On the one hand, he echoes the biblical affirmation of it. The Bible, he says, consistently
emphasizes the dependence and brevity of human life but
never deprecates human finiteness. Classical dualism's
identification of evil with the body stands in sharp
contrast to the Christian belief in the goodness of
God's creation. On the other hand, Niebuhr continually
emphasizes the negative, limiting aspects of human
finitude. "Man is a child of nature," he writes,
"subject to its vicissitudes, compelled by its necessities, driven by its impulses, and confined within the
brevity of the years which nature permits its varied
organic form."[19] The "finiteness, dependence, and the
insufficiency of man's mortal life" are part of God's
plan and should be accepted "with reverence and
humility."[20]

The two aspects of human nature--spirituality and
creatureliness--though separated for purposes of discussion, are in fact, unified on every level.

> In its purest form the Christian view of man
> regards man as a unity of God-likeness and
> creatureliness in which he remains a creature

even in the highest spiritual dimensions of
his existence and may reveal elements of the
image of God even in the lowest aspects of his
natural life. (21)

Human freedom is not a second story added to the ground
floor of creatureliness, and every biological fact is
altered by its incorporation in the human psyche.
Thus, for example, it is inappropriate to discuss birth
control in terms of the "naturalness" of childbearing
as if anything in human nature were purely natural,
i.e. not interpenetrated by freedom.  On the other hand,
there is no level of freedom at which humans are free
from the boundaries of their creatureliness.  To consider themselves thus free is a sin.

This curiously ambiguous character of human nature
is the occasion for both sin and human creativity.  The
same capacities which make human life uniquely creative
endow it with unique destructive power.  The freedom of
spirit which enables human beings to use the processes
of nature creatively tempts them to ignore the limits
of human existence and deny the restraints of nature.
The extension of human sovereignty is thus always an
extension of the possibilities for good and for evil.

### Preconditions

If, however, the potentiality for sinfulness is
inherent in human nature as creaturely freedom, the
structure of human nature in itself cannot explain sin,
for the same structure is the presupposition of creativity.  Another explanatory factor is necessary, and
that factor is anxiety.  If human nature is the occasion
for sin, anxiety is sin's internal precondition, and
anxiety is itself an "inevitable concomitant" of human
nature.  Involved as the self is in the natural order,
limited by it in every respect, in its freedom it knows
itself as bound and limited.  It is therefore anxious.
It tries to escape this anxiety either by pretending it
is not limited, by identifying itself with the beyond
it apprehends in the reaches of its freedom (pride), or
by identifying itself with some natural vitality and
thus denying its freedom (sensuality).  In other words,
it escapes anxiety by falling into sin.

Just as human nature is not in itself a sufficient
cause of sin, however, sin it not the necessary outcome
of the anxiety which inevitably follows from human
nature.  Anxiety is not already sin--not only because it
too is a source of creativity, but because, ideally, the

self can always purge itself of the sinful element in anxiety by orienting itself in faith to the security of God's love. Along with the internal precondition of sin, therefore, we must suppose an external precondition. In Christian thought, this external precondition is symbolized by the devil. Christianity assumes that there is a force of evil operative in the world prior to human evil which contributes to human temptation. "The situation of finiteness and freedom in which man stands becomes a source of temptation only when it is falsely interpreted." But this false interpretation does not spring spontaneously from the human imagination.

> It is suggested to man by a force of evil which precedes his own sin. Perhaps the best description of this mystery is the statement that sin posits itself, that there is no situation in which it is possible to say that sin is either an inevitable consequence of the situation nor yet that it is an act of sheer and perverse individual defiance of God. (22)

The individual is not tempted to a simple error of judgement, a mere forgetfulness of human creatureliness and the overestimation of human capacities. Sin is never merely the ignorance of ignorance. It always involves an element of pretense, an effort to obscure ignorance and insecurity. Yet any particular act of pretense is always preceded by the bias toward pretense, by sin positing itself.

## Dimensions

Having considered the "whence" of sin, we must now look more closely at its actual character. Niebuhr begins his discussion of "Man as Sinner" by dealing with what he calls sin's religious and moral dimensions.

> The religious dimension of sin is man's rebellion against God, his effort to usurp the place of God. The moral and social dimension of sin is injustice. The ego which falsely makes itself the center of existence in its pride and will-to-power inevitably subordinates other life to its will and does injustice to other life. (23)

Since it is the failure properly to orient the self in faith to God which results in the perpetration of injustice, the religious dimension of sin is primary. In practice, however, the ultimate religious referent of sin often remains in the background of Niebuhr's

57

writing. He discusses pride mainly in terms of the
types of injustice to which it leads, thus focusing on
sin's moral dimension.[24]

## Directions

As was suggested above, the dimensions of sin manifest themselves in one of two directions. The self can
wrongly seek relief from the anxieties of finite freedom either by denying its finitude in pride or denying
its spirituality in sensuality. One of the more prominent features of Niebuhr's doctrine of sin is his insistence on the primacy of the sin of pride and the
derivative character of sensuality. "Biblical and
Christian thought," he says, "has maintained with a
fair degree of consistency that pride is more basic
than sensuality and that the latter is, in some way,
derived from the former."[25] Niebuhr most definitely
concurs with this judgement.

The power of human pridefulness is a recurrent
theme in Niebuhr's writings. He likens human self-
consciousness to a high tower looking out on the world
which vainly imagines itself to be the world that it
sees rather than the precariously erected narrow tower.[26]
He says that sin is a consequence of human attempts to
usurp God's perogatives. Human history is a contest
between all human beings and God in which God has the
resources of power and mercy finally to overcome human
rebellion.[27] Human pretensions to God-likeness are
possible only because human beings are in fact created
in the image of God. But they wish to make their finite
goodness absolute and infinite. Their evil lies in the
pretense that their good is better than it is. "The
devil is an angel who pretends to be God."[28]

Human pretense and pridefulness are not truths only
for faith, Niebuhr says, but are amply attested in the
world around us. Since he is very concerned to combat
liberal optimism about human nature, one of his purposes in The Nature and Destiny of Man "is to relate the
biblical and distinctively Christian conception of sin
as pride and self-love to the observable behaviour of
men." To this end, Niebuhr distinguishes and discusses
at length three interrelated types of pride: pride of
power, pride of knowledge, and pride of virtue. The
pride of virtue may rise to spiritual pride, which is
both a fourth type and pride in its quintessential
form.[29]

The pride of power takes two forms, one character-

izing the powerful, the other the insecure. While in
the first form, the ego simply does not recognize the
contingent and dependent character of its existence but
assumes its self-sufficiency and self-mastery, in the
second, it seeks power in order to guarantee its security. Here the ego is not initially proud but lusts for
power in order to become so. Great Britain and Germany
might be seen as representing the two types of pride of
power in modern history. Britain's over-strong sense
of security prevented her from taking proper precautions
against Germany, which, in its insecurity, transgressed
all previous bounds in self-assertiveness. The distinction between the types of pride of power is provi-
sional, however, Niebuhr says, since the sense of insecurity insinuates itself into the highest places.

Intellectual pride is analogous to the pride of
power in that it too can represent either unawareness
of the mind's finitude or the attempt to obscure the
conditioned character of human knowledge. "Intellectual
pride is...the pride of reason which forgets that it is
involved in a temporal process and imagines itself in
complete transcendence over history."[30] The history of
western philosophy, Niebuhr claims, is filled with men
who denied their intellectual indebtedness, claimed
finality for their own particular systems, or attributed
ideological taint only to the philosophies of others.

Moral pride makes virtue itself the vehicle of sin.
The self claims that its own moral standards and judgements, its own conditioned virtue, are the final
standards and virtue. In spiritual pride, the final
form of moral pride, the self-deification implied in
moral pride becomes explicit. The self sees its own
standards and values as divinely ordained; it has God
on its side. Spiritual pride is naturally most tempting
to persons or institutions which are in some sense the
bearers of God's word. Thus the history of the church
can be seen as a constant "conflict between grace and
pride," as Niebuhr calls one chapter in The Nature and
Destiny of Man.[31]

While Niebuhr first discusses these four types of
pride in relation to both groups and individuals indis-
criminately, he also distinguishes between individual
and group pride.[32] The differentiation is necessary, he
feels, because groups both claim authority over individuals and are prone to even greater pride and preten-
tiousness. Group egotism finds its most consistent
expression in the pretensions of nations, pretensions
which gain a certain degree of plausibility from the

59

state's actual transcendence of certain individual limitations. National pride, like individual pride, is spiritual in nature, and has similar characteristics. The nation, for example, has a tendency to claim absolute value for the values to which it is devoted.[33]

Having forcefully demonstrated the workings of pride in human life, Niebuhr then tries to show how sensuality is a secondary phenomenon. He defines sensuality in two different ways in Human Nature, and the definition he uses to prove its subordination is narrower than his initial description of the term. At the beginning of his discussion of human sin, Niebuhr says:

> Sometimes man seeks to solve the problem of the contradiction of finiteness and freedom, not by seeking to hide his finiteness and comprehending the world into himself, but by seeking to hide his freedom and by losing himself in some aspect of the world's vitalities. In that case his sin may be defined as sensuality rather than pride. (34)

Later in the same chapter, he writes:

> Sensuality represents an effort to escape from the freedom and the infinite possibilities of spirit by becoming lost in the detailed processes, activities and interests of existence, an effort which results inevitably in unlimited devotion to limited values. (35)

This view of sensuality is quite broad. Along with the sins of sexual license, gluttony, drunkenness, etc., popularly associated with the term sensuality, it would encompass the many more subtle ways human beings have of abdicating their troublesome freedom. It would include, for example, the bureaucrat whose existence and value is defined by the manipulation of certain tasks from nine to five daily as it would include the woman who lives for and through the everyday running of her household.

When Niebuhr sets out to discuss the relation of pride and sensuality, however, he begins with the following statement:

> If selfishness [pride] is the destruction of life's harmony by the self's attempt to center life around itself, sensuality would seem to

60

> be the destruction of harmony within the self,
> by the self's undue identification with and
> devotion to particular impulses and desires
> within the self. (36)

This is a far narrower definition of sensuality, and it
is the one Niebuhr uses for most of his discussion of
sin. Surveying the "Pauline-Augustinian theological
tradition" with this definition in mind, he finds that
Romans I is the usual model for relating pride and sensuality. "Lust...is...a consequence of and punishment
for the more basic sin of pride and self-deification."
Until Adam rebelled against God in the Garden of Eden,
the law of his members was obedient to that of his mind.
The disobedience of his flesh was both a punishment for
his disobedience to God and a further sin. "Sensuality
represents a further confusion consequent upon the original confusion of substituting the self for God as the
center of existence."[37]

As in the case of his analysis of pride, Niebuhr
attempts to back up tradition with empirical observation. What is the precise relation of self-love and
sensuality? Niebuhr concludes that it always represents:

> 1) an extension of self-love to the point where
> it defeats its own ends; 2) an effort to escape
> the prison house of the self by finding a god
> in a process or person outside the self; and
> 3) finally an effort to escape from the confu-
> sion which sin has created into some form of
> subconscious existence. (38)

Niebuhr supports this conclusion with an analysis of
some specific forms of sensuality. The drunkard, for
instance, shows a certain ambivalence of purpose. He
may drink in order to make himself the center of the
world, to experience a sense of power and importance
normally denied him, or, he may drink not to assert his
ego but to escape it. "Anxiety tempts the self to sin;
the sin increases the insecurity which it was intended
to alleviate until some escape from the whole tension
is sought."[39] Sexual passion, to take another example,
necessarily involves both the self and another and is
therefore a particularly good vehicle for both assertion
and flight from the self. The sexual act may be a tool
for dominating the other, or--as the language of much
love poetry will testify--a vehicle for an uneasy conscience seeking to escape itself through deification of
the other. If both domination and idolatry prove
abortive, the passion of sex may offer an escape into

nothingness. "The strength of the passion which makes this momentary escape possible is itself a consequence of sin primarily and of an uneasy conscience consequent upon sin secondarily."[40]  Sex, while not sinful in itself, given sin, is the most vivid expression of the general pattern of sensuality.

## C.  Critique of Niebuhr's Doctrine of Sin

There are many areas of Niebuhr's doctrine of sin we have not touched on--e.g. the non-essential inevitability of sin,[41] the relation of sin and guilt--some of which have received a great deal of critical attention.  But his discussion of human nature and his subordination of sensuality to pride are most important from the perspective of women's experience.  It is not entirely clear why Niebuhr is so insistent on the primacy of pride and the derivative status of sensuality. It is true that pride is deemed prior by an important part of the Christian community.  But Niebuhr does not hesitate to oppose tradition, even where its consensus on a particular doctrine is a good deal stronger, if he feels tradition is opposed to good sense.[42]  In fact, he has often been accused of picking his "biblical" and revealed doctrines on the basis of a prior analysis of the human situation.[43]

In the case of the relation of pride and sensuality, he does not establish the primacy of pride even on the narrow definition of sensuality on which he takes his stand.  The sexual act, for example, may, in any one instance, exhibit the three motifs of domination, idolatry, and escape into nothingness.  But to show that sensuality derives from pride, Niebuhr must prove what he only asserts:  that idolatry always succeeds an abortive attempt at domination.  In fact, empirical evidence would probably suggest that while domination is the predominant motif in some people's sexuality, idolatry is predominant in others--and in still others, the two are thoroughly intermingled. Niebuhr can assert that domination is always the primary sin only on the basis of an a priori commitment.

Even if Niebuhr were correct about the ordering of pride and sensuality, however, this would be only because he has made things too easy for himself.  Initially, he defines sensuality as the attempt to solve the contradiction of finiteness and freedom by denying freedom.  This definition is much more faithful to his analysis of human nature than his definition of sensuality as "undue identification with...particular impulses and desires." Early on in The Nature and Destiny of Man, Niebuhr says, "Man contradicts himself within the terms of his true essence. His essence is free self-determination. His sin is the wrong use of his freedom and its consequent destruction."[44] This statement clearly allows for two possible misuses of freedom: exaltation or abdication of it. In the next paragraph, however, Niebuhr identifies sin with only one of these alternatives. "The law of his nature is violated when man seeks to make himself the center and source of his own life," he says. Not only is there no reason for Niebuhr to focus on this one aspect of human self-contradiction, but in doing so, he violates the symmetry of his account of human nature as creaturely freedom. Were Niebuhr to take seriously his own broader definition of sensuality, however, it would be very difficult for him to insist on pride as the primary human sin.

## Sensuality as "Women's Sin"

This point is crucial because insofar as Niebuhr does insist on the primacy of pride, his doctrine of sin fails to take account of women's experience. The problem is not simply that Niebuhr subordinates sensuality to pride. The flaw in his doctrine of sin lies in the fact that, in subordinating sensuality, he loses sight of it as a significant human sin and one independent of pridefulness. He focuses only on those aspects of sensuality which do seem to follow from pride, entirely neglecting important dimensions of the human flight from freedom. He is thus unable to speak to or evaluate those patterns of human behavior which are particularly characteristic of women.

As we have suggested a number of times, Niebuhr operates with two definitions of sensuality in The Nature and Destiny of Man. In suggesting that sensuality is "women's sin," we will have the broader of these definitions in mind. The argument is not that women are more likely than men to "lose themselves in some aspect of the world's vitalities," but that, given society's expectations concerning them, they are more liable to "become lost in the detailed processes, activities, and interests of existence."[45] A recapitulation and expansion of some of the material in the first chapter will both help support this claim and indicate some of the aspects of a broader definition of sensuality Niebuhr passes over.

63

In the course of defining "women's experience" in chapter one, we saw that women's experiences are continually shaped and formed by social expectation, and that these expectations present themselves as "natural" and "proper." The psychologists, philosophers, writers and others who take it upon themselves to define women's nature and role see themselves not as arbitrarily circumscribing women's lives but as pointing out the path women were created to follow. The roles which women traditionally have been assigned seem to be more clearly dictated by their biological nature than male roles are dictated by "male nature."[46] These expectations concerning women's experience are relevant to Niebuhr's doctrine of sin because they predispose women to certain life patterns. Women are steered toward certain functions from the time they are born and taught to see these functions as expressing their true female nature. It would not be surprising, therefore, if the particular sin of women were the adoption of society's view of themselves to the detriment of their freedom. It would not be surprising, in other words, if sensuality and not pride were the primary female sin.

Simone de Beauvoir makes precisely this point in her introduction to The Second Sex. She suggests that the failure of women ever to rebel against their lot is partially explained by certain advantages which accrue to them from their status as Other. The most obvious advantages, she says, are material ones; as long as they depend on men, women are spared the difficulty of providing for their own physical comfort. But more significant, the "Otherness" of women also enables them to evade the necessity of having to justify and give meaning to their own lives. "Along with the ethical urge of each individual to affirm his subjective existence," de Beauvoir says, "there is also the temptation to forego liberty and become a thing.[47]

> ...What particularly signalizes the situation of woman is that she--a free autonomous being like all human creatures--nevertheless finds herself living in a world where men compel her to assume the status of the Other. They propose to stabilize her as an object and to doom her to immanence since her transcendence is to be overshadowed and forever transcended by another ego which is essential and sovereign. (48)

The imposition of the status of Other upon women represents the external dimension of their predicament. Insofar as women accept this status for its rewards and

64

welcome relief from the burden of freedom, they are guilty of complicity in their own oppression; they sin.[49]

As we saw in chapter one, both the imposition and acceptance of Otherness are perfectly illustrated by Lessing's Martha Quest. If there is any one quality which characterizes Martha throughout the first four volumes of Children of Violence, it is her failure to make choices, to take responsibility for her own life. Lacking models of women who manage to be both women and persons, she finds it much easier to drift into what is known and expected of her than to take the "risk of a liberty in which ends and aims must be contrived without assistance."[50]

The most dramatic example of this drifting in Martha's life is her marriage to Douglas. Lessing repeatedly writes of this marriage in language which suggests that it is the culmination of some impersonal process to which Martha completely abdicates her freedom. "...She [doesn't] like any of the things she [has] become obliged to like by the fact of marrying." A "dragging compulsion [began] to operate when they met, which...made it impossible for her to say no at any stage of the process...." "She [feels] the last three months as a bewildering chaos of emotion, through which she [was] pulled, will-less, like a fish at the end of a string, with the sense of being used by something impersonal and irresistible." Martha lives for years with this man who leaves three quarters of her out of account, has a child by him, establishes a home with him. All the while, she feels that some day something will change, must change, but she cannot plan to change things, cannot see herself as the agent of action. It is finally her father who formulates for her the possibility of leaving Douglas. "...Never had Martha said to herself in so many words that she would leave [him]. She felt she would, some time--but to say it was too frightening and definite."[51]

Lessing clearly feels that the abdication of freedom and responsibility is not just a personal defect of Martha's, for the novelist introduces a host of female characters half caught in, half clinging to the pattern of their empty lives. At different stages of her life, Martha is friendly with two groups of women, both of which spend their days creating a "poisonous web of talk" out of the dissatisfactions of their lives. With the set of civil servants' wives, the conversation revolves around servants and recipes, saving money and "paving the way for comfortable middle age." Or, when

65

one of them, against her better judgement, "starts a baby" again, the talk turns compulsively to doctors and the discomforts of pregnancy, the despair of overweight, cravings and the inconveniences of childbearing. The women of the left she meets later abhor the need for servants rather than complaining about them; they despise not their husbands, but the society which makes their marriages unsatisfactory. They still talk of recipes, but spend time on psychological character analysis instead of scandal.

> And, of course, there [is] a horrible fascination...in the fact that of the younger women there was not one who hadn't sworn, ten years ago: I will not get like that! I won't be dragged in...Just like the frivolous, nonprogressive women of the avenues, they [spend] their day over cups of tea, and [go] home in a sort of dragging, rather peevish dissatisfaction, while in their heads still [runs] on, like a gramophone record that [cannot] be turned off, the currents of their gossip. (52)

Both groups of women complain about their lives without altering the order of their existence. "What [women] look for first of all among themselves," says Simone de Beauvoir, "is the affirmation of the universe they have in common."[53] "Everyone feels the same way," they can now go home and tell themselves. "All husbands are the same." "Life is like that." Thus they assure themselves that taking responsibility for change is futile and unnecessary.

De Beauvoir's categories of transcendence and immanence and the experiences Lessing describes are easily translated into Niebuhr's vocabulary. De Beauvoir's terms transcendence and immanence are quite similar to Niebuhr's terms God-likeness and creatureliness, and Niebuhr's doctrine of humanity can certainly accommodate the insight that human beings may attempt to escape the contradictions of their nature by denying the unlimited possibilities of human freedom. Niebuhr's view of human nature, however, does not ground an equally complex doctrine of sin. In dealing with sin, he seems to forget the burdensomeness of freedom and to concentrate on the exaltation of it. But the patterns of self-contradiction manifest in Martha's behavior cannot be subsumed under the category of pride without being misunderstood and distorted. Martha's sin cannot be seen as the product of over-glorification of the self, for the problem is precisely that she has no self; she

has not yet become a self and will not take the responsibility for becoming one.  Her form of sin must be
comprehended on its own terms, and that means it must
be seen to have its own roots in human nature, independent of pride.

This is not to suggest that sensuality is never
connected with pride or that there are no sources of
pride, even sinful pride, in women's lives.  Phyllis
McGinley, for one, describes the rewards of the traditional feminine role in terms which perfectly illustrate Niebuhr's conception of the "pride of power."

From the raw materials of four walls and a
roof, a shelter over our heads, we will have
made a home by the force of our own personalities...For us the baby will have taken his
first step, repeated his first word.  We will
have heard the schoolchild call "Mommy" as
soon as he puts a foot inside the door, not
so much to have a reply as to be assured that
he is safe, life is ordinary, and that We are
there.  We will have been raised to a dizzy
eminence as final authority, dispenser of
justice, necessary Presence.  A husband, no
matter how willingly he gives himself to the
role of householder or parent, never approaches
such triumphs. (54)

It would be hard to find a better example of what Niebuhr means when he says, "There are...many possibilities
of using the loving relationship of the family as an
instrument of the parental power impulse on a higher or
more subtle level."[55]  Yet a good case could be made
that in the instance of such female pride of power, it
is not sensuality which is derived from pride but quite
the opposite.  It is confinement to the sphere of "four
walls and a roof" and the failure to take responsibility
for becoming people in their own right that leads women
to seize on the only power offered them, and in this
case, to need so much and demand so much from their
children.  Certainly this is true in a more general way
of Martha.  It is the narrowness of her not-chosen life
that leads her to take excessive pride in the small
skills that it demands.

The purpose of these remarks, as Valerie Saiving
says in her article on Niebuhr's doctrine of sin and
women's experience, is not to "[indict]...the feminine
character...[The] purpose, indeed, as far as it concerns women in particular is quite the opposite."  It

is to suggest that theology, insofar as it focuses on the sin of pride, not only neglects women's experience, but adds to the pressures that keep women from being "women and persons" by suggesting that self-assertion and the struggle for self-definition are sins.[56] But pride is only one human sin. Human nature as finite freedom poses a danger but it also imposes a responsibility. Human beings can ignore their finitude, but they can also fail to live up to the obligations of their freedom. The refusal of self-transcendence ought to be, if one uses Niebuhr's categories, no less a sin than pride--a sin against oneself, against other persons, and against God. If pride is the attempt to usurp the place of God, sensuality is the denial of creation in his image.

## The Humanization of Theology

It is ironic in retrospect that Niebuhr wanted to relate his doctrine of sin "to the observable behavior of men" and that all his examples of sinful pride are either individual men or male-governed nations. It would be neither profitable nor true to experience, however, to suggest that women are incapable of pride, or, more important, that sensuality is only a female sin. A critique of Niebuhr's doctrine of sin could be constructed without any reference to women, and indeed, John Raines, in an article in Christianity and Crisis, constructs one. He argues that Niebuhr's category of sensuality needs to be developed and appreciated more fully as one pole of the human predicament. As an apologist for Christianity in a newly emergent United States, says Raines, Niebuhr was concerned with the hypocrisy of the powerful; his is a theology for the strong. His analysis of pride is helpful in understanding neither the revolutions of oppressed peoples, nor the whole trend toward conformity and abdication of responsibility in modern culture. He understood human arrogance but not the passivity and self-loss vitiating human beings from the opposite directions.[57]

Raines' criticisms suggest that in women's experience, we can discern with particular clarity certain features of the human situation which need to be recognized by theology and developed more fully.

Human beings [Raines says] must dare to know themselves as...namegivers in creation (Adam) who are graciously denied the name of God (Moses). Surely it is unexceptionable that under the conditions of modern existence,

human beings cannot long survive unless they
are willing to come into the full demand of...
adult world-responsibility and yet, for all
that, be content to know themselves...as
human. (58)

Women, who "have had the power of naming stolen from
[them],"[59] have a special need and responsibility to
know themselves as namegivers. It is hardly surprising,
however, that deeper consideration of the experience of
half the human race should lead to a humanization of
theology, to a richer appreciation and account of what
it means to be a person in relation to God.

## Sin and Creatureliness[60]

A second area in which the perspective of women's
experience helps pinpoint an inadequacy in Niebuhr's
doctrine of sin is in relation to his undervaluation of
human creatureliness. Creatureliness is a rather negative category in Niebuhr's thought. Human finitude,
while not evil, and while necessarily recognized and
respected, is definitely an unpleasant fact for Niebuhr,
one which sets boundaries to human freedom but does not
endow it with any positive content. Nature and spirit
both play a role in human creativity and destructiveness, but the resources of nature are "more negative."
They are the "presuppositions of....creativity rather
than its active agents," "[They] have negative rather
than positive force."[61]

While this deprecation of creatureliness is not
part of Niebuhr's doctrine of sin proper, it does seem
to have a number of implications for it. First of all,
Niebuhr's concern with the negative side of creatureliness may be part of what leads him to underestimate the
sin of sensuality. Sensuality, broadly understood, is
not equivalent to identification of the self with some
natural impulse or some aspect of the world's vitalities, but this is a part of sensuality. The fact that
Niebuhr ignores the positive features of human naturalness may prevent him from fully apprehending sensuality's temptations. Not seeing human beings as continually, positively involved in the world's vitalities,
he is less likely to view loss of self in some aspect of
these vitalities as a clear and ever present danger.

Second, and this is the reverse side of the first
point, Niebuhr's failure to appreciate the extent to
which human creativity and creatureliness can be or-
ganically related may lead him to exaggerate the demonic

potential of all human action. Presupposing a negative understanding of human creatureliness, he is then constrained to worry about its implications. Just as his view of the relationship between nature and spirit may hinder his perceiving the temptations of sensuality, it may also keep him from seeing the ways in which creatureliness, differently understood, can curb and discourage human destructiveness. A concrete example may clarify this point. In discussing the sin of pride, Niebuhr has occasion to remark:

> Sometimes [the] lust for power expresses itself in terms of man's conquest of nature, in which the legitimate freedom and mastery of man in the world of nature is corrupted into a mere exploitation of nature. (62)

> Greed as a form of the will-to-power has been a particularly flagrant sin in the modern era because modern technology has tempted contemporary man to overestimate the possibility and the value of eliminating his insecurity in nature. (63)

The problem with these criticisms of contemporary exploitation of nature is that they accept the presuppositions upon which such exploitation is based. If human finitude is understood primarily as that which limits human freedom, it becomes a challenge to freedom to extend its limits as far as is possible. The concept of finitude as Niebuhr uses it includes no criteria in terms of which a particular exploitative act can be ruled illegitimate. On the other hand, a human creativity cognizant of its positive relation to human creatureliness on every level might be far less likely to trespass on nature's dominion. What is true in this instance of the pride of power may be true of other types of pride as well. Knowledge, for example, which evolves from the concrete situation of the knower (as is the case with Martha) is far less likely to be taken as universal and absolute truth than knowledge which is abstract and cut off from its roots in experience. Organic harmony between human creatureliness and spirit may not be a simple human possibility, but Niebuhr uses a model of creativity which to some extent presupposes the sin he finds in its exercise.

The perspective of women's experience may suggest some ways around this problem. As we have seen, women have frequently been identified with nature.[64] While this association has been largely detrimental to women,

70

in terms of the formulation of a more adequate view of the relation between nature and spirit, it may also have a more positive side. It could be that women, because they have been associated with nature and natural functions, have necessarily developed a more positive contentful sense of human creatureliness than Niebuhr (men?) and a greater sense of connection with natural processes and needs. If this is so, then women's experience may again provide a corrective to an understanding of human nature which is otherwise onesided.[65]

Pregnancy and motherhood are the two women's experiences which most obviously foster a sense of connection with natural processes--and in several ways. First, the physical experience of pregnancy, while certainly an experience of human creatureliness and limitation, is hardly exhausted by the word limitation or adequately described as the presupposition of some other, more human, experience. "Pregnancy is... at once an enrichment and an injury," says Simone de Beauvoir. A natural process which invades and nauseates the body, it can also be appreciated in its own right. "[The pregnant woman] is plunged...into the mainstream of life, reunited with the wholeness of things, a link in the endless chain of generations..."[66]

Secondly, pregnancy may entail an experience of creaturely dependence which, though again an experience of limitation, also has positive aspects as well. Margaret Drabble's novel The Millstone provides an excellent illustration of this point. When its intellectual, highly independent heroine finds herself pregnant after her first sexual experience, she half-heartedly tries a home-made abortion and then decides to have the baby. For Rosamund, pregnancy and motherhood entail coming to terms with her dependence on and need for other human beings. "I was trapped in a human limit for the first time in my life," she says toward the beginning of her pregnancy, "and I was going to have to learn to live inside it."[67] The book is about her movement from this feeling of being "trapped" to an acceptance and affirmation of her human condition. Her dependence matures her; it opens her to both unknown aspects of herself and to others--and insofar as it fails to do so, we feel not that her experience is negative, but that she has failed to learn from it all that she could have.

Once pregnancy is over and the child is born, the mother becomes involved with human creatureliness in a different sense. She is a participant in the child's

growth and development. She watches and nurtures it
from the helpless infancy it shares with most other
animals through its gradual attainment of independence.
This is not to suggest that the mother is the only one
or the "natural" one to care for the child, or that
childcare is a "natural" activity.[68] But because she
is most frequently assigned this role, the mother will
have the opportunity to appreciate in a concrete way
the constant needs, the natural processes of growth
and change, her child shares with other living things.
The sense of relation to natural phenomena and fullness
of human creatureliness fostered by pregnancy is thus
reinforced by motherhood.

In a slightly different vein, Simone de Beauvoir
argues that (young) women seek out nature because it
gives them a full sense of their freedom.[69] If she is
correct, women's awareness of human relatedness to
nature would be even stronger and would take on another
dimension. Certainly Martha, throughout her life, has
a strong and special sense of connection to the natural
world. When she is feeling buried by convention and
the expectations of others, communion with nature helps
her achieve a sense of perspective, a renewed sense of
freedom and self-centeredness. The peace of nature becomes, so to speak, her peace. This kinship with the
natural world which Martha feels is not rooted in her
body in the same way as the experiences of pregnancy or
motherhood, but it belongs to the same family of experiences. It too signifies a sense of human creatureliness,
a sense of continuity with nature which is much more
than a simple sense of limitation.

Lastly, we may recall Neumann's argument that
feminine appreciation of natural processes has a spiritual analogue. Feminine consciousness, he says, is
concrete consciousness, waiting on and relating to
the meaning of actual events. It is marked by the same
involvement with periodicity, growth, and change as the
experiences of motherhood or pregnancy. Once again,
Lessing's Martha can be used to illustrate this point.
She reaches a sense of herself through "putting one foot
in front of the other." Self-knowledge, she finds, cannot be forced but comes of its own accord after periods
of waiting. Since she learns through self-exploration
and experiences of ordinary life, her knowledge is never
disconnected from any level of her being. "Woman's
wisdom is non-speculative," says Neumann, "it is close
to nature and life...."[70]

Each of these lines of evidence suggests that human

creatureliness is not simply the presupposition of
creativity and destructiveness. The integral relation
between human creatureliness and spirit which Niebuhr
recognizes is more fruitful than he cares to acknowledge. Nature operates within and around us in ways
that give content to our lives, and we may experience
a sense of continuity with nature for which our involvement in its vitalities and forms is not an adequate
explanation. Women's experience, in illustrating the
link between nature and spirit in a particularly dramatic way, once again points us to aspects of the human
situation which need to be an integral part of a whole
theology.[71]

## D. Niebuhr's Doctrine of Grace

Niebuhr's treatment of grace follows a pattern similar to his treatment of sin. He deals first with
essential human nature as it is partly intuited by the
individual in the reaches of transcendence. He then
turns to human perfection as it is fully understood and
defined in Christ, who is not only "truth" but "grace."
He lastly tests his account of grace for its faithfulness to human experience and describes its implications
for experience. Here again, however, the human experience Niebuhr addresses is not women's experience. His
view of grace, like his doctrine of sin, partly neglects
the needs of women and partly reinforces a traditional
understanding of women's role.

## Essential Human Nature

From the perspective of general revelation, the
first clue to essential human nature, Niebuhr says, is
the uneasy conscience of sinners. However often human
beings are tempted and succumb to the temptation of
seeing themselves as the center of reality, they still
cannot regard their pridefulness with an easy conscience.
No matter how sinful individuals may be, the lingering
memory of some previous condition eventually reasserts
itself, reminding them that sin is not their normal
state. Theology has generally located the time and
place of human perfection in the period of history
"before the fall." Niebuhr, however, rejects this approach. He believes that to see the fall as having
occurred at a particular moment in history after which
human nature is somehow changed is to obscure the relation between good and evil in every moment of human life.
The fact is, he says, that "sin neither destroys the
structure by virtue of which man is man nor yet

73

eliminates the sense of obligation toward the **essential** nature of man, which is the remnant of his perfection."[72] Distinguishing between essential human nature and the virtue of conformity to it, Niebuhr argues that the self can act against the requirements of essential nature only by using one of the elements of it, namely freedom. The moment after transgression, the self knows that transgression for what it is; essential human nature reasserts its claim.

The self which knows itself as sinner is the self in its transcendence, the self in the moment in which it looks at the world and itself and recognizes itself as a finite creature whose pretenses result in injustice. Yet the self which knows itself as sinner and the sinning self are not two different selves.

> The "I," which from the perspective of self-transcendence, regards the sinful self not as self but as "sin," is the same "I" which from the perspective of sinful action regards the transcendent possibilities of the self as not the self but as "law." It is the same self; but these changing perspectives are obviously significant. (73)

The "law" which sinners experience in sinning is the law of essential human nature which they have just violated. Niebuhr distinguishes two aspects of this law corresponding to the dual nature of human beings. Natural law is the law dealing with the perfection of human creatureliness. "It...defines the proper performance of [man's] functions, the normal harmony of his impulses and the normal social relation between himself and his fellows within the limitations of the natural order." The theological virtues of faith, hope, and love are the virtues of human nature as spirit, the basic requirements of human freedom. Without faith and without hope--"faith with regard to the future"--the anxiety of freedom tempts people to deny their creatureliness and pridefully vaunt their self-sufficiency. Without love, individuals can neither render perfect obedience to God nor relate to other persons as "unique centers of life and purpose" whose needs cannot be satisfied by any general scheme of justice. These three virtues are experienced as law because their realization is not a simple human possibility. Were they attained, they would render all commandments meaningless. Together, they would lead to "the perfect relation of the soul to God," "the perfect internal harmony of the soul with itself," and "the

74

perfect harmony of life with life."[74]

The distinction between natural law and the law of human nature as spirit is a tentative one, Niebuhr emphasizes. Human beings are creaturely freedom on every level of their being. This means both that there is no part of essential human nature which is uncorrupted by sin, and that the requirements of human nature interpenetrate on every level. On the one hand, natural law has a tentative validity but is subject to corruption. On the other hand, "because man is not merely creature but is also free spirit, and because every moral norm stands under higher possibilities by reason of his freedom, there is no moral standard at which the human spirit can rest short of the standard of 'faith, hope, and love.'"[75]

## Christ as the Second Adam

The uneasy conscience of human beings, their fleeting awareness of their undue pride, their clouded perception of the requirements of human nature as free spirit are all aspects of general revelation. They are "tangents towards the eternal" which are revealed by careful analysis of the moral life. They cannot be completely understood, however, without Christian faith. Individual uneasiness over the contrast between who one is and who one might be enables faith in Christ to find a human "lodging place," but it is Christ who fully discloses both the contradictions of human nature and its ultimate perfection. Christianity expresses this truth by calling him the "second Adam," the perfect norm of human life. Christ as the essential human reveals the true meaning of the perfection "before the fall" which individuals intuit in moments of transcendence. The lost perfection of Adam can be defined only in terms of the perfection of Christ.

Niebuhr distinguishes the perfection of human nature as defined by Christ from the primeval goodness of Adam. Since there is no human existence without freedom, human perfection never consists in a simple "innocency," a harmony of nature with nature in which there is no freedom. Insofar as humans are creatures, harmony with nature is a part of the norm of their being. But human nature can never by truly defined without reference to a higher norm--and this is the perfection of sacrifical love. "Christ as the final norm of human nature defines the final perfection of man in history...the perfection of sacrificial love."[76] "As the essential sin of the first Adam was pride and self-love, so the essential goodness of the 'second Adam' is sacrificial, suffering, and self-giving love."[77]  "The animating purpose of [Christ's] life [was] to conform to the agape of God.  His life culminate[d] in an act of self-abnegation in which the individual will cease[d] to be a protagonist of the individual life."[78]  Such sacrificial love is not, of course, a simple possibility for all humans.  "Love is the law of freedom; but man is not completely free; and such freedom as he has is corrupted by sin."[79]  Sacrificial love is thus not the simple fulfillment of the mutual love which is the "ethical norm of history" but stands in a "three-fold relationship of transcendence" to it.

First, "sacrificial love (agape) completes the incompleteness of mutual love (eros)" which "seeks to relate life to life from the standpoint of the self and for the sake of the self's own happiness."[80]  Mutual love continually becomes entangled in prudential con-siderations precisely because it is mutual.  Concerned that its love be reciprocated, the self is unable to "lose itself in the life of the other," and thus fails to elicit the mutual affection which is its aim.  Para-doxically, only sacrificial love makes genuine mutuality possible, for mutuality must be the unintended conse-quence of any action.  "Thus the harmonies which are actually achieved in history always are partly borrowed from the [eternal norm of sacrificial love]."[81]

Second, "the Cross represents a transcendent per-fection which clarifies obscurities of history and defines the limits of what is possible in historic development."[82]  It is a reminder that sacrificial love is not a simple historical possibility, a strategy guaranteed historical success.  He whom the church recognizes as the Messiah was defeated.  His perfect love is both the ultimate possibility and the contradic-tion of all historic virtue.  "...Mutual love...is the highest possibility of history in the sense that only such love is justified by historical consequences; but... such love can only be initiated by a type of disinter-estedness (sacrificial love) which dispenses with his-torical justification."[83]

Third, the perfect love of the cross contradicts the pretensions to virtue of human beings in history and "reveals the contrast between man's sinful self-assertion and the divine agape."[84]  It reminds humans both that there is no limit to the possibilities for extending the sphere of mutual relations and that efforts to extend it will always be mingled with sin.[85]

76

## Grace as Power and Grace as Pardon

There is another aspect to the work of Christ which is of central concern to Niebuhr. The sinful individual, though aware that there are requirements of human nature as free spirit, is not only unsure of their exact nature but is unprepared to meet them once they are defined. Christianity thus makes the claim that in Christ "not only has the true meaning of life been disclosed but also...resources have been made available to fulfill that meaning. In him the faithful find not only 'truth' but 'grace.'"[86] Christ's atoning death on the cross reveals both the seriousness of human sinfulness and the sovereignty of God whose justice and mercy are one. Just as in faith, human beings can "become aware of the limits of human possibilities," so, in faith they can lay hold of the resources of the God who comes to meet them. "The very apprehension of the 'wisdom of God,' the completion of the structure of meaning, must have connotations of power in it."[87] The relation between the accession of wisdom and power is not fully explicable--wisdom is the prerequisite of power while power is the prerequisite of wisdom--but both, we are promised, are available in Christ.

At the same time, however, that grace represents the divine fulfillment of what humans cannot fulfill themselves, the "'newness of life' [which] flows from the experience of repentance and faith is [always] conscious of a continued incompleteness and a certain persistence of the strategy of sin."[88] Self-love is destroyed in principle by grace, but righteousness is never a human possession. The New Testament, and particularly Paul, is aware that grace has a double aspect. It involves both "the power of God in man," shattering sinful pride and enabling persons to become what they truly ought to be, and "the power of God over man," granting forgiveness for sin which is never entirely overcome. The careful insistence on both sides of the meaning of grace, developed and applied to human experience through discussion of Galatians 2:20, forms the heart of Niebuhr's exposition of the doctrine.

"I am crucified with Christ." "...The old, the sinful self, the self which is centered in itself, must be 'crucified,'" says Niebuhr. "It must be shattered and destroyed."[89] The self in its unity as nature and spirit is self-centered. Following the "natural" law of its own self-interest, it pretends to be acting in the name of something beyond itself. Able

truly to fulfill itself only through loving relations
with others, it continually acts out of self-love.
"The self in this state of preoccupation with itself
must be 'broken' and 'shattered' or, in the Pauline
phrase, 'crucified.'" The self cannot extend its horizons, redeem itself to accountability, merely by an act
of intellect. The failed obligations it acknowledges
in moments of self-transcendence are not simply recti-
fied. Indeed, unless the self is "shattered at the very
center of its being," unless it is confronted in Christ
with the power and holiness of God, its awareness of
its responsibilities becomes just another source of
pride and self-centeredness. Only in Christ does the
vague awareness of God which permeates human life
"[crystalize] into a revelation of a divine mercy and
judgement. In that revelation fear of judgement and
hope of mercy are so mingled that despair induces repentance and repentance hope."[90]

"Nevertheless I live."

The Christian experience of the new life is an
experience of a new selfhood. The new self is
more truly a real self because the vicious
circle of self-centeredness has been broken.
The self lives in and for others, in the general orientation of loyalty to, and love of,
God.... (91)

With the words "nevertheless I live," the Christian experience of new selfhood distinguishes itself from both
demonic possession and the loss of self prescribed by
certain mystic schemes for redemption. While the self
possessed by a race or nation, for example, feels itself part of something greater than itself, in fact
that which possesses the self cannot do justice to it
in the heights of its freedom, and the real self is
destroyed. Christianity insists that the criterion of
the holiness of the spirit is Christ. Through him, "an
historical focus of the divine," God makes himself known
in history without sanctifying any particular finite
value or force in history. The self which cannot be
redeemed through demonic possession also fails to find
salvation in the mystic freeing of one level of the
self from the flux of creatureliness. There is no one
part of the self which can free itself from another and
thus be redeemed. According to Christian doctrine, the
self is a unity, and it is as a unity that it is broken
from beyond and brought to new life.

"Yet not I; but Christ liveth in me." Niebuhr

subjects this key passage in Galatians to a double interpretation. It can refer, he believes, either to the
self's acknowledgement that its new life of grace is
the result of a power not its own, or its awareness
that the life of grace is not an accomplished fact, that
"the new self is the Christ of intention rather than an
actual achievement."[92]  On the one hand, the self, freed
from the bonds of self-centeredness, perceives that it
could never have released itself from the hold of sin
and gratefully acknowledges the work of a power beyond
itself within it. On the other hand, the redeemed self
recognizes the persistence of sin within itself. It
perceives that grace itself can become the excuse for a
new pride and self-righteousness, and is thus thankful
for the divine grace which nevertheless imputes perfection to it.

In asserting that sin lingers on in the life of the
redeemed, Niebuhr does not mean to deny the reality of
the "power of God in man." He simply insists that as
long as the individual remains a spiritual creature involved in the flux of history, the graceful possibilities for orienting life to a center beyond the self are
never unmingled with the possibilities of using the
same fruits of grace as the basis for further self-
assertion. The history of Christianity itself, with its
religious hatreds and fanaticisms, its quest for power
in the name of the love of God, provides excellent do-
cumentation of the gap between God's will for humans and
human self-will. Any individual or social self in any
situation can find infinite possibilities either for
vaunting itself or orienting its life in God. The
family, for example, may be the vehicle through which
the parent expresses love for the child or uses the
child as an instrument of power. The nation may try to
relate itself in harmony to other nations or use them as
instruments of its own aggrandizement. The two sides of
the experience of grace--grace as power and grace as
pardon--are equally real in Christian life.

Since Niebuhr is often accused of dwelling on justification at the expense of sanctification, his insistence on both sides of the experience of grace must be
emphasized. In a chapter entitled "The Conflict Between Grace and Pride," he attacks the Catholic subordination of justification to sanctification. But
his discussion of the Reformation calls attention to
the Protestant tendency to lose sight of the truth of
sanctification in the desire to restore justification
to its proper place.[93]

The Catholic Church, Niebuhr argues, is unable to see that the contradictions of human nature as free spirit are not overcome even on the level of grace. Failing to recognize the continued corruption of the sinner and the opposition of nature and grace on every level of human nature, the Church regards grace as the completion of an imperfect nature, and understands the forgiveness of sins to refer primarily to sins past. The sins which obviously plague the redeemed are considered "venial" rather than "mortal;" i.e. they are not taken as expressions of a basic attitude. But, Niebuhr argues, any doctrine of grace which leads people to think they can face God's judgement with an easy conscience--even where that conscience is a gift of grace--lends itself to becoming the basis for a new and more pernicious self-righteousness.[94]

According to Niebuhr, the genius of the Reformers lay precisely in their recognition that every human effort to escape the contradictions of creaturely freedom is a symptom of pridefulness, an attempt to obscure the conditioned character of human existence. Nothing provides exemption from sin, the Reformers insisted. In the process of articulating this important insight, however, the Reformers, perhaps not surprisingly, lost sight of the other side of the Christian doctrine of grace. The Reformation doctrine of justification, Niebuhr claims, had definite quietistic tendencies. Luther, for example, afraid of works' righteousness, tended to transform the warning "without works" into "without action." "Ideally the doctrine of justification by faith is a release of the soul into action;" says Niebuhr, "but it may be wrongly interpreted to encourage indolence."[95] When later Reformers combined a passive understanding of justification with a highly personal and interior view of sanctification, the quietistic tendencies of Reformation thought were deepened. Thinkers who adopted Luther's view that the redeemed soul ecstatically transcends the contradictions of history tended to ignore the complex relationships between law and grace and the myriad obligations of social life. Where the Reformation was not confronted with these problems, it was, Niebuhr feels, in danger of articulating a doctrine of sanctification too similar to the Catholic one. The conclusion of Niebuhr's discussion of the Reformation needs to be quoted at some length, for it epitomizes the dialectical understanding of grace which is central to his theology.

...Reformation insights must be related to the whole range of human experience more "dialec-

tically" than the Reformation succeeded in
doing. The "yes" and "no" of its dialectical affirmations: that the Christian is
"justus et peccator," "both sinner and
righteous"; that history fulfills and negates the kingdom of God; that grace is continuous with, and in contradiction to,
nature; that Christ is what we ought to be and
also what we cannot be; that the power of God
is in us and that the power of God is against
us in judgement and mercy; that all these affirmations which are but varied forms of the
one central paradox of the relation of the
Gospel to history must be applied to the experiences of life from top to bottom. There
is no area of life where grace does not impinge.
There are no complex relations of social justice to which the love of the Kingdom of God
is not relevant. There are on the other hand
no areas of experience where historical insecurity and anxiety are completely transcended,
except in principle. There are indeed moments
of prayer and, perhaps, ecstatic achievements
of agape in which men are caught up in the
"seventh heaven"; but these moments are merely
an "earnest" of the fulfillment of life and
must not be claimed as a possession. There is,
finally, the transcendence of man over history
and sin by faith. But that is also an "earnest";
and is corrupted like the manna in the wilder-
ness when stored up as a secure possession. (96)

## The Workings of Grace

Despite Niebuhr's attempts to hold together the
two sides of the doctrine of grace, criticisms of his
treatment of sanctification are justified to the extent
that he gives no real account of the operation of
sanctifying grace in the life of the redeemed. As
Paul Lehmann puts it, "The Cross, which is apprehended
and interpreted as the basis of a new wisdom and power,
is not adequately apprehended and interpreted as
operative wisdom and power."[97] Niebuhr has a clear
idea of the nature of the sanctified life--both what
it is and what it is not. But he does not provide any
sense of how sanctification functions, any description
of the process through which it changes and enlarges
human life.

This deficiency in his doctrine of grace may stem
in part from the absence of a doctrine of the church in

The Nature and Destiny of Man. Since he explicitly denies the necessity of a Christian context for the operation of grace, Niebuhr does not discuss the church as an instrument for carrying on the atoning work of Christ.[98] Neither the sacraments, nor Christian faith itself, are the necessary vehicles of grace, he claims. The possibilities for orienting life to a center beyond the self are often fruits of a hidden Christ and a grace not fully known.[99] Neglect of the church cannot be a sufficient explanation for this imbalance in Niebuhr's doctrine of grace, however, for other theologians have explicated grace more fully without necessarily limiting it to the church.[100] The more fundamental problem with Niebuhr's thought is that he lacks a doctrine of the Holy Spirit and therefore a vocabulary for talking about the continued presence of Christ's work in either communal or individual life. The result of this omission is that the account of the relation of the Kingdom of God to the earthly struggle for justice which follows Niebuhr's exposition of grace is not essentially different from his discussion of the human possibilities for good in Human Nature, which is based primarily on general revelation.[101]

This is not to disparage Niebuhr's application of the doctrine of grace to human experience. Toward the end of Human Destiny, he devotes two long and important chapters to relating his dialectical conception of grace to the quests for truth and justice in human life.[102] He finds, of course, that grace is related to nature partly as its fulfillment and partly as its negation. In historical existence, we both have and do not have the truth, while the ideal of sacrifical love fulfills and negates human attempts at achieving justice. Human beings as creaturely freedom dare not claim that their truth is the truth and yet are continually tempted to do so. Apprehension of the truth "in Christ" enables individuals to hope for the revelation of a center of meaning beyond themselves and negates their premature centering of the meaning of life in themselves or the group to which they belong. But this apprehension of the truth is not itself a having or possessing the truth. "...Redemption in the realm of culture and truth is a having and a not-having of the truth; ...the pretension of having it leads to a new lie."[103]

The human struggle for justice is determined by the same dialectic. If the Christian interpretation of life is applied to human society, then "nature" signi-

82

fies historical possibilities for the realization of justice, "grace" the ideal of perfect love. "Love is both the fulfillment and negation of all achievements of justice in history."[104] Ever closer approximations to this ideal in human society will always contain within them possibilities for greater corruption as well.

While such a dialectical conception of grace might well end in the same quietism Niebuhr finds characteristic of much Reformation thought, he himself abjures any such conclusion. The fact that extension of good always entails the extension of possibilities for evil is never, he says, a reason for inaction. On the contrary, Niebuhr insists on the necessity of continually trying to extend the reach of justice in any actual situation. The obligation to struggle for justice is never lessened by the fact that every concretion of the rules of justice will contain contradictions of the love ideal; nor must the transcendence of that ideal ever be made an excuse for complacent acceptance of remediable injustices. Niebuhr applies this principle in many ways, discussing it at length in relation to the laws and principles of justice, but one example relevant to our subject must suffice here. The fact that the ideal of equality is not a simple possibility does not give individuals the right blandly to accept inequality in any form. If there cannot be equality between the sexes because the biological restraints on women are greater, this does not free societies of the obligation to minimize the disabilities of women by allowing them to develop functions other than their maternal one.[105]

## E. Critique of Niebuhr's Doctrine of Grace

Valerie Saiving, in her article on Niebuhr, emphasizes the interdependence of his concepts of sin and love and his analysis of the human situation. Sacrificial love, she says, "is normative and redemptive precisely insofar as it answers to man's deepest need. If human nature and the human situation are not as described by [Niebuhr], then the assertion that self-giving love is the law of man's being is irrelevant and may even be untrue."[106] Niebuhr himself acknowledges the interrelation of these central concepts of sin and love. "The Christian doctrine of grace," he remarks, "stands in juxtaposition to the Christian doctrine of original sin and has meaning only if the latter is an accurate description of the actual facts of human experience."[107]

Given the connection between the two doctrines, it is not surprising that the defects in Niebuhr's doctrine of sin have their counterparts in his doctrine of grace. The central problem with Niebuhr's doctrine of sin is that his insistence on the primacy of pride is unfaithful and irrelevant to much of women's (and therefore, human) experience. This inadequacy in his treatment of sin is, if anything, compounded in the doctrine of grace, for Niebuhr treats grace only as a response to pride, setting aside his analysis of sensuality altogether. Juxtaposition of grace to a doctrine of sin focused entirely on pride leads Niebuhr both to a one-sided understanding of grace and an inadequate treatment of the norm of human life.

## Justification and Sanctification

Niebuhr's discussion of "grace as power and grace as pardon" powerfully illustrates his concern with grace as a response to the sin of pride. Throughout the discussion, he focuses on grace as judgement and describes the working of grace as a "shattering," a "destruction," a "breaking," or a "crucifixion" of the old self. "...The old, the sinful self, the self which is centered in itself, must be 'crucified,'" he says. "It must be shattered and destroyed."[108] This vocabulary speaks directly to a particular understanding of sin. The sinful self is a self-centered self. Looking out on the world and itself, it is constantly tempted to identify itself with the whole which it sees. Aware that love is the law of its being, it is nevertheless constantly betrayed into self-love. Its failures, while stemming partly from human finitude, are also always spiritual flaws, failures of the whole self which cannot be corrected or overcome simply by intellectual enlightenment, by a broadening of perspective. To be cured of self-love, "the sinful self must be destroyed from beyond itself because it does not have the power to lift itself out of its narrow interest." It must be "shattered in the very center of its being" through confrontation with "the power and holiness of God."[109] This description of grace is unbalanced in precisely the same sense as Niebuhr's doctrine of sin. It does not take into account the fact that the structure of human freedom both poses a danger (its prideful misuse) and imposes a responsibility (its full realization)--and that therefore the other side of the shattering of the self must be its reconstitution in responsibility before God.

There are references to the Christian experience

of new selfhood in Niebuhr's writings,[110] but they lack the force and clarity of his statements concerning the destruction of the prideful self. Thus Niebuhr explains the key passage "Nevertheless I live" almost entirely in terms of what it does not mean. "The [new] self lives in and for others, in the general orientation of loyalty to, and love of, God...."[111] This is his positive statement about the Christian life. He then goes on for four pages to distinguish it from demonic possession and mystic loss of self without further describing what it is or how it can be achieved.

This unbalanced emphasis on the destruction of the old self seems to result from the convergence of two problems in Niebuhr's thought. First, it is related to the fact that his description of the operation of grace in Christian life is generally inadequate. Viewed in this light, the problem is not so much that deficiencies in Niebuhr's doctrine of sin are paralleled by problems in the doctrine of grace as that his exposition of sin is generally more powerful. But second, because Niebuhr understands sin primarily as pride, he is not forced to move beyond the shattering of the self in understanding grace. Thus a general weakness in his doctrine of grace is reinforced by a specific problem in the doctrine of sin, and because Niebuhr's doctrine of grace is weak, the narrowness of his doctrine of sin is never transcended.

It is possible to understand the shortcomings of Niebuhr's doctrine of grace solely in terms of the Protestant tendency to subordinate sanctification to justification. It could then be argued that a doctrine of grace which more fully developed the concept of sanctification would necessarily be more adequate to women's experience.[112] This insight is useful to a point but--aside from its unfairness to Niebuhr-- ultimately misleading. It is true that a doctrine of grace which focuses solely or primarily on justification will be inadequate to women's experience. The shattering of the self from beyond is received as grace only where the self's sin is pride and self-absorption. Where sin is not "too much" self but lack of self, such shattering is at least irrelevant and possibly destructive rather than healing. Similarly, the sense that one has been forgiven despite a dearth of good works is freeing and redemptive where the self has struggled long and seen its own efforts come to nothing. Where sin is not the attempt to take everything on the self but the failure to take responsibility, the failure to become a self, pardon addressed to the prideful self has less meaning.

If, however, an unbalanced emphasis on justification is definitely problematic, an adequate doctrine of sanctification does not in itself guarantee a theology's relevance to women's experience. Such relevance depends also on the meaning assigned to sanctification. Niebuhr wants very much to affirm the truth in both Catholic and Protestant doctrines of grace, to maintain the reality of both justification and sanctification in the Christian life. While his correction of the Reformation's unbalanced emphasis on justification may be viewed as a failure, he does convey a strong sense of the norm and direction of the sanctified life. It would be most unfair to portray his theology as deficient in this regard. On the other hand, the treatment of sanctification Niebuhr offers is not particularly helpful. Insofar as he understands the new Christian life as life lived with constant reference to the ideal of sacrificial love, his doctrine of grace is still a response to an unbalanced notion of sin and thus still inadequate to women's experience.

## Self-Sacrifice and Women's Experience

Self-sacrifice is a norm addressed to a self constantly tempted to sinful self-assertion. An ideal partially known to individuals in the reaches of their freedom and fully disclosed on the cross, sacrificial love is dialectically related to the realities of human history. It is at once a violation of the standards of mutuality which are the moral standards of history, and their fulfillment. "A tangent towards 'eternity' in the field of historical ethics, it is nevertheless the support of historical ethics."[113] Never a simple historical possibility, sacrificial love is related to mutual love as the beginning and goal of action. In a world in which mutual love too easily becomes the calculation of mutual advantage, sacrificial love "completes the incompleteness of mutual love" by initiating the movement toward the loved one without reckoning the response, and stands as a reminder of the "sinful admixture" in love's every historical realization.

Insofar as Niebuhr sees self-sacrifice as the universal norm of human existence—a response to the universal sin of pride—his account of grace is distorted in a way similar to his doctrine of sin. Self-sacrifice may be relevant to a self whose primary impulse is toward self-assertion. The concrete example of Lessing's Martha, however, should make clear that the norm of sacrificial love is irrelevant or even destructive for one suffering from the "sin" of self-lack. Martha is inactive; she drifts; she looks to others for self-definition; she fails to take responsibility for her own life. These faults require a very different sort of grace from the shattering of the self and self-reconstitution along principles very different from those Niebuhr envisages. Self-sacrifice, taken alone, cannot be the norm of Martha's freedom. The point is precisely that she has no <u>self</u> to sacrifice. This is why, for example, her marriage to Anton is so disastrous. When he first tells her that the political situation requires either their separation or marriage, Martha is ready to give up her happiness for Anton's welfare. "Andrew could marry Maisie to help her out--that was a good thing to do, everyone feels it," she thinks.114 But her sacrifice, the reader feels, is different. Because it is a decision that grows out of weakness rather than strength, because it is just one more instance of her falling or drifting into things, it is destructive rather than noble and enobling. "It is all very fine to be forgetful of self," says Simone de Beauvoir, "but still one must know for whom, for what."115 Since Martha lacks such knowledge, the love ideal is irrelevant to or in conflict with her becoming a person.

The language of self-sacrifice conflicts with personhood and becomes destructive when it suggests that the struggle to become a centered self, to achieve full independent selfhood, is sinful. In this case, theology is not irrelevant to women's situation but rather serves to reinforce women's servitude. It becomes another voice in the chorus of external expectation defining and confining the way women ought to live. Valerie Saiving states this point very clearly. The woman who belives the theological advocates of sacrificial love, she says, will stifle in herself the desire to be a separate person some part of whose mind, time, and feelings are inviolable. She will devote herself wholly to the needs of her family, trusting (but not demanding) that her fulfillment will come from giving to others. But the realities of her daily experience will, to some extent at least, contradict this trust. She does learn and grow from being the center of family relationships, but she finds also that she requires hours of withdrawal and self-enrichment if these relationships are to be sustained. "She learns, too, that a woman can give too much of herself, so that nothing remains of her own uniqueness; she can become merely an emptiness, almost a zero, without value to herself, to her fellow men, or perhaps, even to God."[116]

Thus during the time in her life when Martha is the "deputy at the center of the house," the arranger of details, the mother of all, she also struggles to protect her life for a pre-breakfast hour of self-exploration or a period of "work" before bed. When, as an extension of her role, she begins overhearing the thoughts of those around her, she finds time at the end of each exhausting day to descend to the basement and pursue with Lynda the meaning of her discoveries. It is the psychic distance she gains from these inviolable spaces which makes this period of being with the children one of real growth for Martha and which enables her to continue giving to them.

Kate Brown, the middle-aged heroine of Lessing's novel, The Summer Before the Dark, examines the results of her failure to have created such spaces of her own. Her children grown and going their own ways, her husband away, she spends a summer of stocktaking and of confrontation with the "cold wind...[blowing]... towards her, from the future."[117] She recollects a morning three years earlier when, caught in a minor downtown traffic jam, she paused to observe the women swirling around her. She saw streets filled with young, unmarried women, girls with babies looking like "play" mothers, all with a casual swinging grace, a confident freedom. Then she looked at her own contemporaries and saw that "they moved as if their limbs had slowed because they were afraid of being trapped by something, afraid of knocking into something; they moved as if surrounded by invisible enemies...The faces and movements of most middle-aged women are those of prisoners or slaves."[118] She, Kate, recalls her own slow metamorphosis from the one condition to the other. The real change came with her second child, she decides, and then the third "to get it over with." "With three small children, and then four, she had had to fight for qualities that had not been even in her vocabulary. Patience. Self-discipline. Self-control. Self-abnegation. Chastity. Adaptability to others-- this above all." If these were ever really virtues, she thinks, "if so, they had turned on her, had become enemies." "At one end of some long, totally involving experience, steps a young, confident, courageous girl; at the other, a middle-aged woman--herself."[119]

These passages from Saiving and Lessing provide a
new perspective through which to view some of Niebuhr's
more specific statements about self-sacrifice.   At
several points in his career, he explicitly took issue
with Erich Fromm's view of love as a "phenomenon of
abundance"--a by-product of the overflow of vitality
from the secure and self-accepting self.  Niebuhr
argues that Fromm's position ignores the reality of the
social existence of the self.  The self must have some
security before it can begin to think of others, Niebuhr
admits.  But it acquires that security not from itself
but from others.  "Whatever spiritual wealth the self
has within itself is the by-product of its relations,
affections, and responsibilities, of its concern for
life beyond itself."[120]  Christianity does not deny the
legitimacy of self-realization, Niebuhr says, but insists that such realization is least found where it is
most sought after; its achievement can only be the
unintended consequence of creative relations with
others.[121]

By the time he wrote Man's Nature and His Communities, Niebuhr seems to have modified somewhat his view
of the relation between pride, self-seeking, and self-
realization.  Jesus said only that consistent desire
for self-fulfillment is self-defeating, he now allows.
Christian thought must not obscure the fact that the
ambitions of vital individuals can contribute to the
creativity of their communities or that the sense of
responsibility and joy such people have in their tasks
may draw them beyond themselves, thus creating the conditions for self-fulfillment.  Through "common grace,"
intended self-fulfillment may be lifted above its intention which is then fulfilled.  But the intricate
relation of self-seeking and giving, is still, Niebuhr
believes, accurately caught by Jesus' paradox:  "Who-
ever seeks to gain his life will lose it, and he who
loses his life for my sake will find it."  Consistent
self-seeking he says, is necessarily self-defeating,
while "self-giving is bound to contribute ultimately
to self-realization."[122]

These modifications of Niebuhr's are welcome, but
they do not go far enough nor do they affect the basic
structure of his throught.  In the name of women's
experience, it must be insisted that it is simply not
true that "self-giving is bound to contribute ultimately
to self-realization."  Unless the self is continually
replenished through the mutuality of its relations,
it can give and give until it is depleted.  This is
particularly a danger where the self is continually

involved in relations, like the mother-child relation,
which are not fully reciprocal. Of course the mother
does grow and develop through her relationships with
her children, but they cannot respond to her on all
the levels that she needs; she grows only in certain
ways and in certain directions. This is why, when
Kate Brown looks at herself after twenty years of heed-
lessly giving to her family, she does not see someone
who through this giving has come into her own, but
someone who is "quite simply...demented."

> An unafraid young creature had been turned,
> through the long, grinding process of always,
> always, being at other people's beck and
> call, always having to give out attention
> to detail, minuscule wants, demands, needs,
> events, crises, into an obsessed maniac.
> Obsessed by what was totally unimportant. (123)

This is not to suggest that the self can give
itself what it needs, can become "abundant" apart from
any relations with others. It would seem rather, not
surprisingly, that people have a variety of needs.
The mother who spends hours of every day giving to
(and receiving from) her children needs to balance
those hours with others of deliberate withdrawal and
still others spent in relationships which are perhaps
deliberately sought for their ability to feed and
replenish her (though there may also be room for giving
within them). Without these other kinds of hours,
self-sacrifice becomes empty because there is no self
doing the sacrificing. Love is most meaningful when
it is a "phenomenon of abundance," but the making
abundant is an ongoing process which involves both
giving and taking.

Grace, then, must have a dimension which corresponds to the sin of failing to take responsibility for
becoming a self, of failing to live up to the potentialities of the structures of finite freedom. Niebuhr
understands grace as the shattering forgiveness of the
self and its consequent ability to approach, albeit
fragmentarily, the "impossible possibility" which is
sacrificial love. Grace must also be understood, however, as the acceptance of the self in its abdication
of freedom and its consequent ability, however fragmentary, to act responsibly toward itself and others.

## The Meaning of the Cross

It is one thing, however, to question the relevance

of the norm of sacrificial love to women's experience
and another to claim that it is not the Christian norm,
that sacrificial love is not the love of the cross.  It
is therefore important to point out that many critics,
writing from a variety of perspectives, have found
Niebuhr's account of agape an unbalanced or distorted
interpretation of Christian love.  Paul Ramsey, for
instance, though he believes Niebuhr's view of love to
be essentially faithful to the New Testament, cautions
Niebuhr not to let his attention to the word "sacrificial" eclipse his attention to the primary word "love."
"Love is mainly intent on the good of another," he
says.  "It is not intent on the overt sacrifice or the
suffering this often entails, any more than it intends
the mutuality that sometimes...follows."[124]  Daniel
Day Williams has had a more substantive, long-standing
argument with Niebuhr on the nature of love.  He is
concerned with the issue we raised: "How is [agape] com-
patible with the loves which constitute human selfhood?"
Williams suggests that the good which Christian love
intends is not a good lying beyond history and thus
beyond the fulfillment of the person who loves (his
characterization of Niebuhr's position), but "a real
community of good in which all life, including my own,
is intended to share."[125]  Still further from Niebuhr,
James Gustafson, in an essay on Christian ethics,
suggests that Christ's sacrificial death on the cross
is primarily a revelation of God's being and not an
example to be emulated.  Emphasizing the uniqueness of
the cross, Gustafson finds that Christ's sacrifice is
not readily translatable into norms for human action.
Christian moral action, he says, must be illuminated
and informed by the total context of Christian revelation, which includes "God's actions in the situations
in which the self exists."[126]

These criticisms, taken together, suggest that
the demands and meaning of Christian existence are open
to diverse interpretations.  Each interpretation is,
of course, answerable to the test of faithfulness to
the New Testament and tradition.  But if theology is
to address a variety of human situations and experiences,
it is surely important that it remain open to a variety
of representations of the Christian life.  Indeed, it
is imperative that those understandings of Christianity
which speak to the experience of women be developed and
propounded--or theology will speak past a good part of
the experience of all.

## F.  Conclusions

In this chapter, it has been argued that although
Reinhold Niebuhr claims to describe human nature,
human sin, and the human need for grace, in fact his
theology is most relevant to the nature and problems
of men in our society, and especially the nature and
problems of powerful men.  The central problem with
Niebuhr's doctrine of sin is his insistence on the
primacy of the sin of pride and the derivative character of sensuality.  Not only is this understanding of
sin in conflict with Niebuhr's own definition of human
nature as finite freedom, for according to his analysis,
human beings should be as liable to the danger of
denying their freedom (sensuality) as of over-
exalting it (pride).  But also, as detailed reference
to Doris Lessing's account of the development of a
modern woman shows, Martha's failures cannot be subsumed under the rubric of pride.  The "sin" which the
feminine role in modern society creates and encourages
in women is not illegitimate self-centeredness but
failure to center the self, the failure to take responsibility for one's own life.  It could be said that
women's sin, so far from being the sin of pride, lies
in leaving the sin of pride to men.

Women's experience called Niebuhr's doctrine of
sin into question in a second area as well.  His
largely negative view of human creatureliness leads
him both to underestimate the temptations of sensuality
and to reinforce the demonic potentialities of human
action.  Since women--albeit largely for cultural rea-
sons--are likely to have a greater sense of positive
connection with the natural world than Niebuhr demonstrates, here too, women's experience points to aspects
of the human situation which his theology needs to
incorporate.

Niebuhr believes that grace must be a response to
the situation of sinful humanity.  The deficiencies in
his doctrine of sin, therefore, mar his account of
grace as well.  He interprets grace entirely as a
response to pride and therefore only as the shattering
and destruction of the sinful self.  The workings of
sanctifying grace in human life remain unclear.  At the
same time, where Niebuhr deals with the direction
and norm of sanctification, he places it in agape, the
sacrificial love of the cross.  But using Lessing's
Martha as a reference point once again, we found that
this norm is relevant only when juxtaposed to the sin
of pride.  When the ideal of sacrificial love is

92

addressed to women's sin, it serves only to reinforce it.

While this chapter has been concerned with the relevance of Niebuhr's thought to women's experience, it must be emphasized that insofar as his theology fails to speak to the situation of women, it fails to speak to the human situation. This was made explicit in the case of the doctrine of sin, but it is equally true of the doctrine of grace. Insofar as the demands and privileges of our mechanized society foster not responsibility and self-centeredness but depersonalization and easy flight from the self, the crucifixion of the self and the norm of sacrificial love are no more relevant to men than they are to women. Both men and women need a doctrine of grace which seriously addresses the self in its abdication of freedom and which clarifies the process through which it comes to stand responsibly before itself, other persons, and God.

Niebuhr's theology is not lacking in resources for or pointers toward a more humanly inclusive theology, and we may end our discussion of his thought by alluding to some of them. It has already been argued that Niebuhr's emphasis on the primacy of pride is in conflict with his analysis of human nature, that that analysis suggests that there are (at least) two dangers, and not just one, inherent in the structure of human life. Niebuhr's characterization of human nature as finite freedom is itself a potential source of the insight that we are as likely to abdicate the responsibilities of our freedom as we are to make ourselves gods. Likewise, there is nothing inherent in the idea of sensuality (even narrowly defined) which suggests that it is secondary to the sin of pride. Niebuhr imposes a predetermined order on the two types of sin when he discusses their relation in experience. That order is no doubt derived from his own experience of the destructiveness of the sins of the powerful.[127] The experience of others might lead to independent development of the category of sensuality.

If there are categories in Niebuhr's theology which would enable it to speak more fully to women's experience, then both his profound concern for justice and his specific statements about the situation of women suggest that these categories should be more fully developed. Again and again in the course of his writings, Niebuhr reminds us that there are infinite possibilities for realizing the norm of love in all personal and social relations, and that the contradictions which hound every step in love's direction must never become

93

excuses for inaction.  He devotes whole books to this
theme and dozens of articles.  His application of the
quest for justice to the situation of women is sometimes ambivalent, but in his article on the ordination
of women, in his response to Karl Barth, and in numerous scattered references throughout his thought, he
demonstrates his awareness of women's situation.[128]  If
he argues that "a rationalistic feminism is undoubtedly
inclined to transgress inexorable bounds set by
nature," he also acknowledges that the effort to define these bounds will inevitably result in the incorporation of male arrogance into the standard.  "The
sinfulness of man makes it inevitable that a dominant
class, group, and sex should seek to define a relationship, which guarantees its dominance, as permanently normative."[129]  Surely this lesson must be
applied to his theology as well.

# CHAPTER THREE

## PAUL TILLICH

Paul Tillich's theology is more complex than
Niebuhr's: he presents the feminist critic with numerous contradictions. On the one hand, a number of
recent feminist writers have turned to Tillich's system
for vocabulary to describe their own experiences and
have found aspects of his thought profoundly liberating.[1] He provides insights into areas of experience
which Niebuhr neglects almost entirely, yielding categories for dealing with many of the realities of
women's experience described in this book. On the
other hand, from the same perspective of women's experience, Tillich's theology is highly problematic. His
many individual statements concerning sin as self-
abnegation and grace as reconstitution of the self tend
to be undercut by the monistic tendency of the ontology
which underlies them. His specific remarks relevant to
women, in other words, are not supported by the context
in which they are set. Elucidation of the tensions in
Tillich's thought and their implications for women's
experience will be the subject of this chapter.

## A.   Tillich's Method

Tillich is a systematic theologian, and for him,
the method of systematic theology is the "method of
correlation." To think systematically is to think
consistently about "a group of actual problems which
demand a solution in a special situation." To employ
the method of correlation means to explain "the contents of the Christian faith through existential questions and theological answers in mutual interdependence."[2]
Tillich's distinction between questions and answers
corresponds to Niebuhr's distinction between general
and historical revelation mentioned at the beginning of
chapter two. For Tillich, general revelation is assim-
ilable to the formulation of existential questions,[3]
while historical revelation belongs to the theological
response to these questions.

What Tillich means by the development of the questions implied in human existence is reasonably straightforward. The Christian message, he assumes, will find
no lodging place in human beings unless it corresponds
and responds to questions they have about the ultimate
meaning and horizon of their lives. It is the first
task of theology, therefore, to try to articulate these

questions by analyzing the human situation out of which they arise. Some aspects of this situation are enduring. Because "man is the question he asks about himself, before any question has been formulated," certain basic questions concerning human nature are expressed mythologically, then philosophically, from early in human history.[4] While the underlying content of these questions remains constant, however, their cast or form constantly changes along with the self-understanding of any individual historical era. The theologian must thus become acquainted with the general questions posed by human existence as they arise in his or her particular "situation." "Situation" in this narrower sense refers to "the totality of man's creative self-interpretation in a special period."[5] It is ascertained through analysis of a period's style as it expresses itself in the philosophical, artistic, political, psychological, and sociological realms.

Because it requires detachment, the task of analyzing the questions implied in the human situation is a philosophical one, Tillich says, even when it is performed by a theologian. The theologian qua philosopher looks at human nature as the key to the nature of existence generally. Knowing that the "object" of theology must belong to being, to reality as a whole, (s)he asks after and describes the structures of finite being through which the power of being expresses itself. The fundamental questions concerning human existence are ontological questions, and the theologian thus frames them in the language of ontology.[6]

The theological answers to the questions implicit in human existence are determined through a complex process. "These answers," says Tillich, "are contained in the revelatory events on which Christianity is based and are taken by systematic theology from the sources, through the medium, under the norm."[7] Since the Bible is the basic document describing the events upon which Christianity is founded, it is the primary source of systematic theology. The Bible has revelatory significance, however, only because it is received as revelation, and its reception as such is part of the original revelatory event. Theology's sources may be viewed as a series of concentric circles, each representing the reception of the central revelation by a wider community. The Bible is the first witness to the revelation which it describes. As such, it is also a document in church history, and the theologian's reading of it is influenced by the whole of church history as well as the specific structures of the denomination to which (s)he belongs.

The contents of systematic theology are received through the medium of experience. This means, on the one hand, that the sources of theology are meaningful only to one who participates in them through experience. On the other, it means that the sources are given to experience and not created by it. Experience does not add anything to Christian revelation. The medium colors and influences the interpretation of what it receives, but it never does so intentionally.

Both the sources and medium of theology are subject to its norm. The norm, which develops through the (largely unconscious) historical interaction of the church and the Christian message, must be described anew for every period. Tillich formulates the present norm in response to the contemporary experience of existential disruption, meaninglessness, and despair. It is "the New Being in Jesus as the Christ as our ultimate concern." This phrasing combines theology's material norm (Jesus as the Christ) with the critical principle that theology must always deal with what concerns human beings ultimately. The total norm, derived from an encounter with the Bible, in turn becomes the criterion of the canonicity of the biblical books, as it is also the criterion for use of all other theological sources.

The necessity of redefining the material norm of theology points to the interdependence of question and answer in Tillich's method of correlation. The answers are not derivable from the questions, but the two are formulated in relation to each other. "In respect to content the Christian answers are dependent on the revelatory events in which they appear; in respect to form they are dependent on the structure of the questions which they answer." Similarly, the varied materials pertaining to the question side of theology are arranged "in relation to the answers given by the Christian message."[8] This interdependence of question and answer represents the danger in Tillich's method which must constantly guard against dissolving either the questions into the answers or the answers into the questions.

### B.  Tillich's Doctrine of Sin

The method of correlation determines the structure of Tillich's theological system.  Each of its parts

contains one section developing an analysis of existence
and another section discussing the theological response
to the problems of existence. The broad division of
Tillich's work is trinitarian: the first volume of his
theology dealing with essential (or created) human
nature and the question of God, the second dealing with
estranged (or fallen) human nature and the question of
Christ, and the third dealing with actual life and the
question of the Spirit. While Tillich's systematic is
obviously best understood when read as a whole, and
while he employs certain technical terms which accumu-
late meanings through use and reuse, its parts do have
a certain independence of each other: the three books
do not form one continuous argument. Reraising the
questions implied in human existence at the beginning
of each section, Tillich both recapitulates a certain
amount of material and modifies his ideas in the course
of his writing.

The doctrine of sin proper belongs to the second
division of the system or to the elaboration of the
questions involved in "existential" (estranged, fallen)
being. In this volume of the Systematic Theology,
"existential" is a technical term referring to the distortions of essential human nature in existence. Oddly,
the concept of existential being, like that of essential being, is an abstraction from the broader ontological category of (actual) life which contains a mixture
of essential and existential elements. Thus while our
discussion of the doctrine of sin will focus on volume
two, we will need to refer to the other books of the
Systematic Theology as well. The essential being which
sin distorts is treated by Tillich in volume one, while
the lived reality of sin is presented only in the course
of his consideration of life (the mixture of sin and
salvation) in volume three.

Sin as Estrangement

Unlike Niebuhr, who dwells mainly on the moral
implications of the religious dimension of sin, Tillich
is concerned with sin almost entirely as a religious
problem. He focuses not on sins as the violation of
moral commandments but on Sin, which he reinterprets in
terms of the concept of estrangement.[9]

Like Tillich's other technical terms, the crucial
idea of estrangement must be understood in terms of
its situation in his system and the way in which it
modifies many of the seemingly straightforward words
that surround it. The key to his notion of estrangement

"lies in the implication that one belongs essentially to that from which one is estranged."[10] We belong to God, our infinite ground, and are estranged from him. Tillich makes this point in many ways and in many places. In his essay "The Two Types of Philosophy of Religion," he writes:

> One can distinguish two ways of approaching God: the way of overcoming estrangement and the way of meeting a stranger. In the first way [Tillich's way] man discovers _himself_ when he discovers God; he discovers something that is identical with himself although it transcends him infinitely, something from which he is estranged, but from which he never has been and never can be separated. (11)

"Man is estranged from himself if he is estranged from God," Tillich writes elsewhere, "and God is estranged from himself if he is estranged from man."[12] The method of correlation itself is a symptom of this unity and estrangement. Human beings can ask about the infinite because they belong to it, but were they not separated from it, they would not need to ask.

## The Fall

A primary way in which theology gives content to the notions of unity and separation and talks about the reality of estranged existence is through the story of the fall. Tillich finds the Genesis narrative a powerful symbolic description of the universal human situation but one which requires partial demythologizing. In order that the story not be taken literally, he refers to the fall as the "transition from essence to existence," a "halfway demythologization." He hopes by this phrase to prevent the fall from being understood as an event in time but to preserve enough of a temporal element so that the fall is seen as a fact and not as a necessary consequence of essential human nature.[13] Tillich means something quite complex by this distinction.

Human beings as the product of God's originating creativity are united with the process of the divine life beyond essence and existence and beyond potentiality and actuality. The essential being and totality of moments in the life process of the individual are still hidden in the creative ground. Tillich calls this state of "non-actualized potentiality" "dreaming innocence," thereby suggesting that it precedes but anticipates

"actuality, existence, and history."[14] The state of
"dreaming innocence," however, is unstable. It drives
beyond itself and in doing so leaves the divine ground
for existence.

The possibility of the transition from essence to
existence rests with human nature as finite freedom.
For Tillich as for Niebuhr, the concept of anxiety
plays a key role in his analysis of the fall. As
Tillich puts it, "finitude and anxiety are the same."[15]
For the self still within the unity of the divine life,
the first consciousness of finite freedom is accompanied
by the experience of a double threat, expressed as
anxiety. The individual self must choose between failure ever to realize its potentialities on the one hand
and loss of innocence on the other. This moment of
"aroused freedom," as Tillich calls it, appears in the
Genesis story in the form of the divine command not to
eat from the tree of knowledge. The prohibition presupposes a split between creature and creator which is
not yet sin but no longer innocence. Pulled between
the desire to actualize its freedom and the demand to
preserve its innocence, the self (Adam) freely chooses
self-actualization. In doing so, it moves outside the
process of the divine life, becoming manifest to itself
"and to other life within the whole of reality."[16]

Three points concerning this decision must be emphasized. First, the moment self-actualization is chosen is the moment in which creation and the fall coincide. "To be outside the divine life means to stand in
actualized freedom, in an existence which is no longer
united with essence. Seen from one side, this is the
end of creation. Seen from the other side, it is the
beginning of the fall."[17] Second, although creation
and the fall coincide in time and space in the sense
that created goodness never exists, they do not coincide
logically. Estrangement does not follow deductively
from the structures of finitude but is the original
fact. "...It has the character of a leap," a leap taken
by finite freedom, "and not of structural necessity."[18]
There is a sense, therefore, in which humanity completes
its own creation through freedom. The act which alienates
the self from its divine ground is human and not divine.[19]
As one critic says, "...The order of finitude owes its
being to God...but not its existence."[20] Third, the
decision for self-actualization is a decision of freedom
in correlation with destiny. To be finite freedom means
to be free within a context, to be free "within the
larger structures to which the individual structure
belongs." The context of the free decision for self-

actualization is the "universal transition from essence
to existence. There is no individual Fall. In the
Genesis story the two sexes and nature, represented by
the serpent, work together." Thus the universe too participates in the tragic character of the fall. "...The
very constitution of existence implies the transition
from essence to existence." "Existence is separation."[21]

## Unbelief, Hubris, and Concupiscence

We are now in a better position to see why the idea
of estrangement becomes the interpretative category for
sinfulness. "The state of existence is the state of
estrangement."[22] The mythical human decision for self-
actualization represents a transhistorical, cosmic
estrangement from the primordial unity of the divine
ground. This universal estrangement is actualized in
the individual experience of estrangement from God, from
other beings, and from the self. Sin and estrangement
are not entirely synonymous. Tillich recognizes that
the former term more adequately expresses the element
of personal responsibility for separation than the
latter. The word sin, however, Tillich feels, is too
often understood in terms of specific sins--that is
"deviations from moral laws"--and therefore must be
thoroughly reinterpreted from a religious perspective.
Estrangement is this interpretative tool. "It is not
the disobedience to a law which makes an act sinful,"
he says, "but the fact that it is an expression of
man's estrangement from God, from men, from himself."
When sin is defined as estrangement, the element of
freedom in sin is not denied, but freedom is always
understood in relation to the polar concept of destiny.
"...It is impossible to separate sin as fact from sin
as act," says Tillich. "...In every free act the destiny
of estrangement is involved and, vice versa...the destiny
of estrangement is actualized by all free acts."[23]

Tillich reinterprets sin as estrangement under
the three traditional categories of unbelief, hubris,
and concupiscence, the meaning of each term being modified by its context in his system. The basic form of
sin is unbelief, or, as Tillich would prefer to say,
"unfaith." Like faith, unbelief "is an act of the
total personality, including practical, theoretical,
and emotional elements."[24] It is none of these elements
alone. Thus unbelief is not, for example, "denial" of
God. The possibility of either denying or affirming God
already presupposes the disruption of the "cognitive
participation" in God without which disruption affirmation or denial would be unnecessary.[25] Unbelief is not

"disobedience." The possibility of disobeying or obey-
ing divine commands already presupposes separation of
the human will from the divine will without which separation law would be unnecessary. And Niebuhr aside,
unbelief is not "self-love." "In order to have a self
which not only can be loved but can love God, one's
center must already have left the divine center to
which it belongs and in which self-love and love to
God are united."[26] Unbelief involves rather a turning
away, an alienation from God in all these respects,
an "estrangement from [him] in the center of [one's]
being." "In his existential self-realization [the
individual] turns toward himself and his world and loses
his essential unity with the ground of his being and
his world. This happens through individual responsibility and through tragic universality."[27]

Turning away from the divine center and turning
toward one's self and one's world are clearly two sides
of the same sin. Tillich calls the first movement unbelief and its obverse hubris. Like unbelief, hubris
is not one sin among others but sin in its total form.
As Tillich discusses hubris, however, there is a continual tension between his reinterpretation of it as
estrangement and the customary (narrower) associations
of the term. His description of hubris veers toward
Niebuhr's description of pride, away from it, and back
again.

Self-consciousness, Tillich says, setting out the
preconditions of hubris in language quite reminiscent
of Niebuhr's, is both the glory of human beings and a
source of temptation to them. Looking at themselves
and their world, aware of both their freedom and potential infinity and their finitude, they are tempted to
make themselves the center of the world. Hubris is the
failure to acknowledge final exclusion from God's
infinity; it is self-elevation into the sphere of the
divine. For Tillich, however, unlike Niebuhr, this
description of hubris is a description not just of the
actual human predicament but of the stage of "aroused
freedom" before the choice for "existence" is made.
In fact, all human actions involve hubris because the
choice for self-elevation is a transhistorical as well
as an individual one. Tillich warns, therefore, against
translating hubris as pride, as if it referred to the
moral quality of certain behavior. "Hubris is not the
special quality of man's moral character. It is universally human; it can appear in acts of humility as
well as in acts of pride."[28] No sooner does he say
this, however, than Tillich proceeds to cite examples

102

of hubris which match almost point for point Niebuhr's description of intellectual and spiritual pride. Hegel's claim to have created a system containing all truth, the Pharisees' identification of their goodness with absolute goodness, and the human tendency to attribute infinite significance to finite cultural creations demonstrate, he claims, the "universally human character of self-elevation."[29]

Concupiscence is the third category under which Tillich discusses the doctrine of sin. Its root is the desire of the estranged self to be reunited with the whole of which it was once a part. Where this desire is aimed at a particular object, it is the basis of love (reunion of the separated). Where the self attempts to draw the whole world into itself, however, desiring without object and without limit, it falls into concupiscence. Tillich rejects the classical reduction of concupiscence to the striving for sexual pleasure, claiming that it can refer to any aspect of the individual's relation to self and world. The quest for sex, food, knowledge, power, material wealth, spiritual values--all are concupiscent if sought without limit or goal. Concupiscence, since it represents the attempt to bring everything into the self, is really a form of idolatry of the self, an attempt to make the self universal on the basis of its particularity. In terms of Niebuhr's classification, concupiscence would be the form of pride characterizing the insecure who seek power, knowledge, or unlimited goodness as a way of disguising their finitude. Despite the traditional association of concupiscence with sensuality, Niebuhr's category of sensuality is more likely related to a type of sin Tillich does not discuss in the Systematic Theology, but which, in an early essay, he calls the sin of weakness.[30]

## Essential Being and the Structure of Destruction

In the first volume of the Systematic Theology, Tillich discusses the nature of being as it is created-- the basic ontological structure of self and world, the ontological elements, and the nature of finitude and its categories. While these structures in their essential state are threatened with disruption and destruction, he says, the disruption and destruction do not occur. The tensions to which being is subject are contained within the transcendent unity of the divine life. Unbelief, hubris, and concupiscence, however, contradict the created structures of essential being. Under the conditions of existential estrangement, "the elements of essential being which move against each other tend to annihilate each other and the whole to which they belong."[31] Alienated from the ground of their being, human beings become subject to "structures of destruction" which disrupt their relations with the world, other human beings, and themselves. These structures, which are a direct consequence of sin as estrangement, are considered by Tillich under the heading of evil.

Nonbeing is dependent on being, Tillich says; disruption is dependent on elements in the structure of being. The basic structure of destruction, therefore, is dependent on the basic structure of finite being, the polarity of self and world. While the term self, according to Tillich, can be applied in some measure to all living beings and may be used analogously even of inorganic things, human beings are the only completely centered selves, and thus the only selves possessing a world. Having a self and having a world go together; the loss of one implies the loss of the other. Created being is potentially subject to self-loss, but under the control of <u>hubris</u> and concupiscence, this possibility can become actual. "The attempt of the finite self to be the center of everything gradually has the effect of its ceasing to be the center of anything." The centered self, threatened "by disruptive drives which cannot be brought into unity," experiences moral conflict, psychological disruption, and loss of meaningful relations with the world.[32] Increasingly limited, the self is held in bondage to an increasingly narrow environment.

The disruption of the self/world polarity in estrangement manifests itself in the disruption of the three pairs of ontological elements which share its polar character. Freedom and destiny, which are not separated in the state of dreaming innocence, under the sway of <u>hubris</u> and concupiscence break apart. Freedom ceases to relate itself to the content provided by destiny and becomes mere arbitrariness, while destiny, unrelated to any deciding center, becomes mechanical necessity. The original unity of dynamics and form undergoes similar disintegration. Dynamics degenerates into formless and uncreative attraction to the new as an end in itself, while form becomes external law, producing either legalism or chaos. Lastly, individualization and participation separate into subjectivity and objectivity. The self, shut up within itself, cut off from meaningful participation, falls under the power of objects which tend to make it into a mere object.

The "structures of destruction" affect too the experience of finitude and its categories. In the original unity of the divine life, the sense of anxiety which attends finite beings' awareness of their finitude is balanced by finite self-affirmation or "the courage to be."[33] Under the conditions of estrangement, however, where the self is no longer related to the ultimate power of being, human beings seem to be given over to their finitude, and anxiety takes on a different character. Anxiety about non-being, for instance, becomes the "horror of death," the "loss of one's potential eternity...experienced as something for which one is responsible..." Time, "experienced without the 'eternal now,'" becomes "mere transitoriness without actual presence." Space is experienced as "spacial contingency," the lack of a definite place to which one belongs.[34]

Other evil consequences of estrangement--suffering, loneliness, doubt--are also characteristics of essential finitude which are distorted in the transition from essence to existence. Suffering, for example, which in the state of dreaming innocence is transformed into blessedness, under the conditions of estrangement lays hold of human beings in a destructive way. A chief cause of suffering is individual "aloneness." While all human beings are alone in the world insofar as they are fully centered selves, in estranged existence a loneliness cut off from full participation seeks escape into a collectivity which can never provide genuine communion. Doubt, another characteristic of essential finitude, becomes in existence a consuming despair of meaning and truth which leads to idolatrous efforts to achieve absolute security and certainty. Despair is the "boundary" to which human beings are driven by all the structures of estrangement. It is the pain of the conflict between what one is and ought to be. It is "the agony of being responsible for the loss of one's existence and of being unable to recover it."[35]

## The Quest for Self-Salvation

One further consequence, indeed the consequence, of the state of estrangement is that "no act within the context of existential estrangement can overcome existential estrangement." The unity of freedom and destiny in every act of existential self-actualization means that "destiny keeps freedom in bondage without eliminating it." Within the realm of finite relations, free acts are possible, "but they do not bring reunion with God." All human attempts to bring about reunion through works of

any sort are simply symptoms of estrangement which in
the end demonstrate their own futility.  The fruits of
legalistic, ascetic, mystical, sacramental, doctrinal,
and emotional paths to self-salvation are failure,
despair, anxiety, self-righteousness, and fanaticism--
but never the salvation that is ought.[36]

## Sin and Life

The distortions of self-salvation, however, like
all distortions, live from the positive which they
distort.  There could be no awareness of estrangement
or desire for salvation were not a saving power at work
even in estranged existence.[37]  The fact that salvation
is always fragmentarily present means that estrangement and evil as discussed thus far have been abstrac-
tions from the broader ontological category of life--
the ambiguous mixture of essential and existential
elements.  Clearly, actual existence is not the same
as existence within the unity of divine life; human
beings are not what they ought essentially to be.  But
it is equally the case that life is not pure separation,
sin, and despair.  The negative elements in life could
not exist without the positive.  Essence and existence,
good and evil, sin and salvation are thoroughly intermingled in actual experience, and this means that sin
and evil never appear in so unambiguous a fashion as
Tillich describes them in volume two.

Tillich sets out the structures and the ambiguities
of life in the third volume of the Systematic Theology.
The quantity and complexity of material he deals with
here (it is by far the longest of the three volumes)
make it impossible to do more than mention some of the
modifications which sin and evil undergo.[38]  Tillich
divides his discussion of the "self-actualization of
life and its ambiguities" into three parts which correspond to the three functions of the life process:  self-
integration, self-creation, and self-transcendence.
The elements of self-identity, self-alteration, and
return to the self are visible in each of these functions.  In the first function, self-identity and alteration are present under the predominance of a self-
identity which is "established, drawn into self-
alteration, and reestablished."  In the second, self-
alteration predominates; "the movement of life goes...
forward in a horizontal direction."  In the third function, the actualization of potential goes in a vertical
direction; "life drives beyond itself as finite life."
Each function of life is grounded in one of the three
polar ontological elements:  individualization and

106

participation, dynamics and form, and freedom and destiny, respectively. And each of the functions of life actualizes itself in one of the spheres of life under the dimension of Spirit; morality, culture, and religion, respectively.

This complex schema allows Tillich to integrate the materials of the first two volumes with a wealth of new ontological, sociological, historical, and cultural analyses. The importance of this integration from the perspective of the doctrine of sin is that he is thus able to show how the structures of estrangement function in a wide variety of life situations, but as only part of the total life process. Self-integration is countered by disintegration, self-creation by destruction, and self-transcendence by profanization, "but the positive and the negative elements are mixed in such a way that a definite separation of the negative from the positive is impossible."[39]

The struggle between self-integration and disintegration, health and disease, characterizes life in every dimension. For personal life, as for life in the organic and psychological realms, the root of this struggle is the necessity of taking new content into the self without disrupting its unity. The self must choose between sacrificing new possibilities for the limited, consistent upbuilding of itself, and sacrificing already realized possibilities for new ones. No sacrifice is unambiguous. When is a self worthy of being sacrificed, and when is a cause worthy of sacrifice? These are moral questions, and complete self-centeredness is actualized only in the dimension of the spirit in the moral act. Only in meeting other selves does the self become aware that it cannot draw the whole world into itself. "The experience of this limit is the experience of the...moral imperative... The self-integration of the person as a person occurs in a community, within which the continuous mutual encounter of centered self with centered self is possible and actual." But even the moral imperative which is the basis of this encounter with others--agape, or "acceptance of the other self by participating in his personal center"[40]--is not a guide to unambiguous self-integration. Agape as law is an expression of human self-estrangement, and the structures of estrangement are evident in every attempt to translate agape into specific action.

The second function of life, self-creativity, is countered by destruction. Every time an old form is broken through toward the creation of a new one, there is a moment of chaos, of no-longer and not-yet form, that may resist or destroy creation. Self-creativity and destruction, form and chaos, growth and decay oppose each other in the processes of all realms of life. Under the dimension of spirit, the self-creativity of life expresses itself in the formation of culture, every aspect of which is ambiguous. Language and technology, the two bases of cultural activity, free humanity from bondage to its environment. But language, at the same time it is liberating, separates "meaning from the reality to which it refers,"[42] and tools threaten to make tools out of those who use them. Those areas of cultural creation most closely allied to language, the cognitive and aesthetic acts, strive for truth and authentic expressiveness but are subject to the same contradiction as language: the split between subject and object is both the presupposition of knowledge and art and the source of their ambiguities. The spheres of cultural creativity which are extensions of the technical act have as their goals "humanity" and justice, the fulfillment of the inner aim of the person and of the social group. But the striving for "humanity" is subject to the difficulty that the determining subject is both separated from its essential being and "can determine [itself] only in the power of what it essentially is,"[42] while group efforts at justice are subject to all the ambiguities of communal transformation.

Unlike the self-integrating and self-creating functions of life, self-transcendence and its contradiction, profanization, can be described only as they are reflected in human consciousness. In this mirror, life is perceived as having greatness and dignity, but also as being small and violable. In existence, the greatness of life leads to the tragic character of life; greatness is united with hubris, eros with concupiscence. Tragedy can be avoided only by avoiding greatness, but the avoidance of greatness involves the tragic loss of one's destiny. Under the dimension of the spirit, the great reveals its dependence on the ultimate; self-transcendence expresses itself in religion. As the self-transcendence of life under the dimension of spirit, religion is ideally a quality of the other life functions rather than an independent function. Since, however, transcendence is resisted by profanization, morality and culture separate from religion, becoming "secular," while religion itself becomes a particular function of the spirit, an object among others.

## Sin and the Demonic

The self-transcendence of life in religion is subject not only to profanization but also to demonization.
"The demonic" is an important category in Tillich's
thought.  It was under this rubric that he first began
to develop a doctrine of sin, and even in the Systematic
Theology, he tends to focus on sin in its demonic forms.
The reality of the demonic is rooted in the tension between the abysmal side of divinity, its form-destroying
nature, and its character as depth and ground.[43]
"Demonry is the form-destroying eruption of the creative
basis of things."  The term refers to that destruction
of form which originates not from without but from the
basis of form itself.  The demonic is "that form of contradiction of essence in which contradiction is united
with the essential and creative powers of life."[44]  "[It]
does not resist self-transcendence as does the profane,
but it distorts self-transcendence by identifying a particular bearer of holiness with the holy itself."[45]  It
is anti-divine rather than non-divine.  Almost any
finite thing can claim divinity and thus become anti-
divine--particular forces within the personality, a
nation, a religion, or special groups and customs
within a religion.  Such demonic claims are always
religious because they are always claims to ultimacy.
Sin and the demonic as thus defined are not equivalent,
Tillich says.  Sin can, and normally does, appear in
non-demonic forms as uncreative weakness.[46]  As a type
of contrariness to essential nature, however, the demonic
is a sub-category of sin.


## C.  Critique of Tillich's Doctrine of Sin

At least one constructive guideline emerged from
our criticisms of Niebuhr's doctrine of sin:  in order
to be relevant to women's experience, a doctrine of
sin must deal with more than self-exaltation.  It must
consider the sin of abdicating freedom, of refusing
the obligation to become a self.  While Niebuhr's
account of human nature, it was argued, supports such
a dual understanding of sin, his doctrine of sin itself is one-sided.  His category of sensuality, which
might potentially include sins of self-abnegation, is
never developed independently of pride, and thus sin is
understood in terms more faithful to the experiences
of men in Western society than those of women.

The problems with Tillich's doctrine of sin have
similar consequences for women's experience but very

different roots. In the many strands of his great
literary output directly or indirectly related to sin,
two conflicting tendencies are discernible. On the
one hand, Tillich is very concerned with self-constitution both as an ontological and an existential problem.
His account of estrangement, therefore, unlike Niebuhr's
doctrine of sin, contains many references to the self's
conflicts about responsible self-creation and to the
ambiguities of self-actualization generally. On the
other hand, the ontological framework within which
Tillich formulates his insights tends to contradict
many of the insights expressed. Since he frequently
equates self-actualization and estrangement on an
ontological level, he is unable to show how self-
actualization on a moral level can do anything but contribute further to the state of sin. Thus, while specific aspects of Tillich's thought are relevant to women's
experience, on a deeper level, his theology is no more
able to speak to that experience than is Nibuhr's.

## The Language of Tillich's Doctrine of Sin

The conflicts in Tillich's doctrine of sin first
begin to surface in the course of his discussion of
sin proper, i.e., as he considers estrangement as unbelief, hubris, and concupiscence. On first consideration, the notion of estrangement seems free from many
of the problems which plague Niebuhr's account of pride.
As a term denoting a disrupted relationship with God.
"estrangement" does not evidently imply that the moral
consequences of this disruption take a particular form.
Moreover, on introducing the section on estrangement and
sin, Tillich immediately states that "man is estranged
from the ground of his being, from other beings, and
from himself."[47] This would suggest that he intends to
deal in some way with the issues of selfhood and self-
relatedness as integral aspects of the concept of
estrangement.

Yet after some preliminary remarks on the concept
of estrangement, Tillich spends most of the section on
sin reinterpreting the traditional categories of unbelief, hubris, and concupiscence in the light of
estrangement. This procedure is problematic for at
least two reasons. First, to reverse the criticism of
those who claim that such reinterpretation distorts
the gospel,[48] it could be said that Tillich's use of
traditional language obscures the novelty of his interpretation of sin. A term like "hubris," for example,
carries centuries of reverberations which Tillich is
at pains to deny. His language and intention are thus

110

in conflict. Tillich is not unaware of this problem; he intentionally decides to "redeem" the classical vocabulary, and for understandable reasons. Yet, from the perspective of women's experience, his decision is regrettable. For insofar as the notion of estrangement might provide a more inclusively human way of comprehending sin, its helpfulness is obscured by its association with less adequate terms.

Still, the associations set off by Tillich's use of traditional language would matter less were he to reinterpret this language thoroughly. In fact, however, he himself draws on the traditional associations of his vocabulary. It has already been pointed out that his reinterpretation of hubris quickly gives way to a more customary use of the term.[49] If hubris is not to be translated as "pride," then at least pride is its most important symptom--and the one Tillich gives most space to describing. The term "concupiscence" too as he uses it falls under Niebuhr's category of pride and thus, like hubris, cannot be considered to develop the concept of estrangement in new directions. The question arising out of Tillich's discussion of sin is therefore this: does Tillich's (understandable) decision to use the classical vocabulary of sin trap him into dwelling on its traditional significations against the deeper intention of his thought, or is his concentration on the traditional forms of sinfulness an index to some more fundamental problem in his theology? We can answer this question most adequately by first looking at those specific aspects of Tillich's treatment of estrangement which are relevant to women's experience and then examining the ways in which his ontology is in tension with them.

## Sin and Human Selfhood

To understand Tillich's treatment of issues respecting sin and human selfhood--issues relevant to women's experience--we must distinguish between two levels in his thought. On the ontological level, Tillich is very concerned with the meaning of the term "self" as it appears in such expressions as self-centeredness, self-elevation, and self-sacrifice. He wants to understand under what conditions selves can exist[50] (to be centered or sacrificed) both within and independently of the divine ground. On the existential level, he is concerned with the disruption of the self under the conditions of estrangement and with the ways the self creates itself, grows, and changes in the course of life. It is on this second level that Tillich

111

does or does not speak to women's experience: theology is relevant to women's experience if it deals with sins of self-abnegation in selves actually existing in the world. On the other hand, the first level is the foundation of the second in the sense that if the existence of centered selves is problematic, their pride or humility, responsibility or irresponsibility becomes problematic as well.

In fact, in the course of his discussion of essential being, Tillich establishes selfhood, in the ontological sense, as a primal reality. The self/world structure is the most basic of the ontological concepts which are the presuppositions of experience; it is given with the essential nature of being. "A self is not a thing that may or may not exist;" says Tillich, "it is an original phenomenon which logically precedes all questions of existence."[51] The ontological elements of individualization and participation, which share the polar form of the basic self/world structure, also characterize being in its essential state. Individualization and selfhood, while conceptually different, are inseparable. Every self is to some extent individualized, though individualization is one with participation in the unity of the divine life.

On the level of essential being, "the concepts which characterize the individual self lie below... differences of valuation: separation is not estrangement, self-centeredness is not selfishness, self-determination is not sinfulness." These things are the presuppositions of estrangement and salvation, of selfishness or any other feeling. "It is time to end the bad theological usage of jumping with moral indignation on every word in which the syllable 'self' appears," Tillich says. "Even moral indignation would not exist without a centered self and ontological self-affirmation."[52]

Essential selfhood, though the presupposition of moral (or immoral) action, does not in itself exist, however. With the transition from essence to existence, the self leaves the divine ground to "stand upon" itself, to actualize the finite freedom which it is. The existing self therefore is not just separated but also estranged, and estrangement has a number of meanings. First of all, the total self is estranged from its essence. Thus estrangement from the ground of being, or sin in its primary form, is self-estrangement, because the self is identical with and belongs to the ground which infinitely transcends it.[53] Once it chooses to leave the divine ground, the self's whole structure becomes subject to existential disruption. Since the initial form this disruption takes is the splitting apart of the self/world polarity, the first and basic result of radical self-estrangement is self-loss. Self-loss in this second sense refers not to estrangement from essence but to "the disintegration of the centered self by disruptive drives which cannot be brought into a unity."[54] "Man is split within himself. Life moves against itself through aggression, hate, and despair."[55]

It would be possible for Tillich to argue the necessity for essential self-affirmation and yet claim, as Niebuhr does, that on the existential level the way to self-affirmation is through self-sacrifice. He does not do this, however. Tillich's recognition of the important role of sacrifice in human life is always balanced by an insistence on the necessity of self-constitution, even under conditions of existential disruption. In his sermon "You Are Accepted," for example, he discusses the effects of self-estrangement in the following terms:

> We are wont to condemn self-love; but what we really mean to condemn is contrary to self-love. It is that mixture of selfishness and self-hate that permanently pursues us, that prevents us from loving others, and that prohibits us from losing ourselves in the love with which we are loved eternally. He who is able to love himself is able to love others also; he who has learned to overcome self-contempt has overcome his contempt for others. But the depth of our separation lies in just the fact that we are not capable of a great and merciful divine love towards ourselves. (56)

True self-love is not possible apart from grace, but this does not mean that striving toward self-love is to be equated with sin.

A number of other strands in Tillich's thought also make clear his interest in self-concern and self-actualization. His discussion of the ambiguities of self-sacrifice in the process of human self-creation has already been mentioned.[57] In that context, he suggests that before a sacrifice can be meaningful either to a self or others, the self must already have a certain strength and integrity. "Self-sacrifice may be worthless if there is no self worthy of being sacrificed," he says. "The other one, or the cause, for

113

which it is sacrificed may receive nothing from it,
nor does he who makes the sacrifice achieve self-
integration by it."[58]  Tillich's handling of justice
toward the self in Love, Power, and Justice is of
similar import.  In that book, he suggests that just as
love of others must be rooted in genuine self-love,
sacrifice in personal strength, so justice toward
others must flow from the self which is able to give
itself its due.  "To be just towards oneself," he says,
"means to actualize as many potentialities as possible
without losing oneself in disruption and chaos."[59]
This definition of justice corresponds to Tillich's
proposal that "humanity," the aim of the cultural act,
is "the actualization of the potentialities of man as
man."[60]  To be unjust to the self, to fail to actualize
one's potentialities, is also to be unjust to others
who are forced to deal with a self which is less than
it could be.

## Human Selfhood and Women's Experience

     The theme of human selfhood in Tillich's thought,
though he discusses it abstractly, is most relevant to
women's experience.  The "sin" encouraged by women's
situation, it has been argued, is precisely the failure
to become a self, the failure to venture responsible
self-creation.  Doris Lessing's Martha Quest, along
with the female protagonists of a whole series of
modern novels, are guilty not so much of prideful self-
elevation as the radical failure to make self-
constituting choices.  They drift into life patterns
which seem to be waiting for them and which, if
dreaded, are also easy and familiar.

     Tillich, more than Niebuhr, provides some of the
categories necessary for understanding and diagnosing
these failings.  His statement, for example, that the
true human problem is not self-love but the mixture of
self-hate and selfishness that renders any true love
impossible illuminates much of Martha's behavior in the
first volumes of Children of Violence.  She fails to
leave the farm, becomes involved with the sportsclub
crowd her first months in the city, marries foolishly,
partly because she lacks alternative models, but partly
because she is ambivalent toward herself.  Who is the
Martha, she seems to ask, who deserves better than she
allows herself?  The feelings of self-doubt implicit
in these larger patterns are explicit in her early relations with the Cohen brothers.  The only friend to
these sons of the town's Jewish storekeeper, adolescent
Martha ignores them for two years when a neighbor teases

114

her about them. She is then surprised when the boys
snub her as she tries to renew the friendship again.
To them, her neglect looks like antisemitism. For her,
however, it is exactly what Tillich describes: a mixture
of selfishness and a self-hate which lets her pretend
that her companionship was unimportant to them anyway.[61]

Tillich's comments on the ambiguities of self-
sacrifice are similarly applicable to Lessing's protagonists. They make clear, for instance, why we per-
ceive Martha's marriage to Anton as an act which dis-
credits both of them, and they explain why Kate Brown's
years of devotion to her family are ultimately self-
destructive.[62] Neither Martha nor Kate is sufficiently
her own person for her sacrifice to be meaningful.
Lacking fully developed selves, they cannot really
give themselves to others or "achieve self-integration"
through the attempt.

Tillich, moveover, provides vocabulary not only
for understanding this neglected side of human self-
disruption but also for judging it. Martha,
he enables us to say--when she does not take the
matriculation exam she can pass easily, when she becomes the empty vivacious "Matty" Donovan offers her,
when she marries Douglas and then Anton against the
watcher's knowing promptings--is guilty of injustice
toward herself. Instead of attempting to actualize as
many of her potentialities as possible, she simply
yields to the easiest and closest of alternatives before her. Confronted with a familiar path which she
does not wish to follow and a more difficult one which
she does, she "chooses" the former. Thus, like Paul,
she experiences a conflict between her real self and a
strange law which controls her. She is self-estranged
or in a state of sin.[63]

Tillich's name for Martha's particular form of
sinfulness, a sinfulness which stems from perverse
inaction, is "uncreative weakness," that contradiction
of essential nature which lacks the unity with the
creative powers of life characteristic of the demonic.
So far from relegating uncreative weakness to a derivative status, Tillich, at least in his early essay on
the demonic, labels it sin in its "normal" form. This
seems to be an opinion he continued to hold, for in
the third volume of Systematic Theology he refers to
another form of weakness, the avoidance of tragedy
through the avoidance of greatness, as "the most widespread of all life processes under the dimension of
the Spirit."[64] A type of sin which may appear most

dramatically in the experience of women is thus recognized by him as universal.

There is one further aspect of Tillich's doctrine of sin which is particularly helpful from the perspective of women's experience. His discussion of the freedom/destiny polarity provides a means of articulating the interplay of social and personal forces which lead to women's sin. His theology enables us to take account of the fact that women's life choices are made in a broad and inescapable social context which defines a female destiny, and that nevertheless these choices are their own. He recognizes that if women cannot be blamed for capitulation to expectations which surround them from birth, these expectations are still actualized in their free decisions. The words "choice" and "free" are qualified by their context without being abrogated. "Estrangement" stresses the destiny side of this paradox, "sin" the freedom side, but "sin as fact" and "sin as act" are inextricably interwoven in every action.

## Sin and Human Selfhood Reconsidered

Tillich, then, does provide categories for understanding and judging those aspects of sinfulness more likely to be associated with women than with men in our society. The question of the significance of his use of traditional vocabulary to describe sin therefore rearises. Does he adopt the terms unbelief, hubris, and concupiscence simply out of respect for tradition, or is his use of the words consonant with some more fundamental pattern in his thought? While there are some reasons to suppose that Tillich's true intentions are betrayed by his use of traditional vocabulary, on the balance, it seems that this is not the case. In too many instances in which vocabulary does not dictate a decision, Tillich apparently chooses to focus on demonic, creative aspects of sinfulness rather than sins of weakness. Thus he turns to examples of hubris as pride immediately after stating explicitly that hubris can be realized in acts of humility. He deliberately discards the term "pride" as a translation of hubris only to replace it with the equally active sounding "self-elevation."[65] His motive, of course, is to find a neutral term which draws attention to hubris as a religious rather than a moral flaw. From the perspective of women's experience, however, "self-elevation" has precisely the same connotations as Niebuhr's terms "pride" and "self-centeredness" and is open to precisely the same criticisms.

116

Moreover, though Tillich seldom draws directly on the vocabulary of sin in his discussion of the ambiguities of life, there too with certain exceptions, he concentrates on the complexities involved in attempted actualization of the life processes. Though he recognizes both the self's obligation to realize itself and its widespread refusal of that obligation, he devotes more attention to the ambiguities of ventured self-realization than to concrete strategies of withdrawal. In his analysis of moral self-constitution, for example, he acknowledges that the self can decline to respond to the commands which come to it from the encountered world. He then turns, however, not to a description of the circumstances and effects of this refusal but to an account of specific ambiguities involved in the fulfillment of moral commands.[66] He appreciates the fact that "uncreative weakness" is a prevailing form of sin, but he devotes very little space to depicting its manifestations.

If even where he is not bound by his adoption of traditional categories Tillich still chooses to dwell on active significations of estrangement, then his emphasis is not simply the outcome of his choice of vocabulary. Rather, his choice of vocabulary must be partly grounded in the substance of his thought. In particular, the theological root of his concern for creative forms of sin would seem to lie in his ontology and more especially in his view of the coincidence of creation and the fall.[67] Since the moment of human self-actualization is also the beginning of the fall, active self-constitution is always simultaneously the realization of estrangement. The failure to act, on the other hand, has no clear ontological claim to be considered sin.

It has already been pointed out that Tillich locates the completion of creation in the finite free human decision against the preservation of dreaming innocence and for self-actualization.[68] Although this final moment of creation does not logically entail estrangement, there is in fact no moment in which existence is both actualized and without sin. As Tillich puts it, "Fully developed creatureliness is fallen creatureliness." "Actualized creation and estranged existence are identical."[69] In other words, the human decision to act against the non-realization of potentiality (dreaming innocence) and for the realization of potentiality coincides with the fall. Now although viewed mythologically the transition from essence to existence is a past event, it is actually not an event

117

in time at all but "a universal quality of finite being" which "sets the conditions of spatial and temporal existence."[70] It is the destiny which is realized in every present free action and in which all such actions are embedded. "In every individual act the estranged or fallen character of being actualizes itself." The conclusion follows that in every act of self-actualization, the element of separation from the creative ground is effective. "Human creation is ambiguous."[71]

The problem with this argument is that it simply leaves out of account sins of self-denial and noncreativity. Indeed, it raises the question as to whether and how failure to be self-actualizing can be considered sinful at all. Tillich clearly means the nonrealization of potentiality to be a manifestation of estrangement. His definitions of justice and humanity suggest this. In his essay on the demonic, he says explicitly that uncreative weakness is sin because it is contrary to essential nature.[72] There is certainly no positive suggestion in Tillich's theology that self-abnegation or nonindividualization are closer to essential nature than their opposites, or are paths to reunion. Yet, for all this, it remains the case that Tillich's identification of the choice for self-actualization with the fall provides no way of explaining how or why uncreative weakness is not, so to speak, a "fall back" toward essence or reunion with the divine ground. It provides no way of explaining why uncreative weakness is sin at all.

Wayne Proudfoot's thesis, "Types of Finite-Infinite Relation and Conceptions of the Unity of the Self," places the problem of the status of self-abnegation in Tillich's theology in a somewhat wider perspective. Proudfoot argues that Tillich is basically a metaphysical monist who recognizes the need to define the relation between finite and infinite, conditioned and unconditioned being, but resolves (or dissolves) the tensions between them on the side of the unique substantiality of Being-itself. Terms which in ordinary usage would be taken to characterize independent selfhood are interpreted by Tillich in such a way as to avoid any suggestion of metaphysical pluralism. Proudfoot points out, for example, that while Tillich formally affirms the correlative nature of the two sides of each of the ontological elements, in every case he gives most emphasis to the unity pole. Thus Tillich's description of individualization and participation "avoids the connotations of autonomy usually associated with 'individualization' by [appealing] to the image of a focus or node in order to portray individualization within an undifferentiated monism."[73] In the monistic context, where participation in the divine ground is the ultimate goal of existence, sin is necessarily defined as the (demonic) attempt to interpolate some idol between the self and God, to claim divinity for some object or individual self. Proudfoot's contention that Tillich must be read as a monist whose ultimate concern is reunion with the divine ground raises the question once again: does nonindividualization or lack of self-determination contribute to this union more or at least detract from it less than do individualization and self-actualization?

## Human Selfhood and Women's Experience Reconsidered

The fact that this question is at once so urgent and so difficult to answer points to a serious tension within Tillich's thought, both sides of which need to be taken seriously. On the one hand, as has been indicated, he provides categories both useful and illuminating for understanding and judging women's experience. On the other hand, his remarks on self-sacrifice, self-love and self-hate, justice and humanity, which represent a wealth of sociological, psychological, and philosophical observation, are set in a framework which is to a large extent in conflict with them. The strong monistic tendency of Tillich's thought and his related identification of self-actualization and fallenness tend to undermine those specific comments which emphasize the importance of self-love, justice toward the self, and so on. They also explain the relatively small amount of space in the Systematic Theology devoted to the sins of weakness.

Tillich cannot dwell on the ambiguities of un-creative weakness, despite his recognition of their prevalence, because his ontology provides him no basis for doing so. But this also means that much in his thought which is applicable to women's experience is thrown into question by its broader context. Though Tillich certainly never says this, the underlying message of his ontology is right in the tradition which sees women as more religious than men.[74] Insofar as self-actualization is associated with sinfulness, the relative "naturalness" of women, their less highly differentiated sense of self, and their failure to pursue self-actualization may all be viewed as marks and guarantors of a close and fervent God-relation throughout life. To subscribe to this tradition is, of course, to favor retention of these characteristics and oppose change. From this perspective,

Martha's pattern of passivity would be interpreted not as injustice toward herself but as piety.  "Women's sin" would be a virtue.  The female destiny of estrangement, as compared with the male, would entail less separation from the original unity of God's life.  To the extent that this is the hidden message of Tillich's ontology, his theology, like Niebuhr's protects and reinforces the status quo.

## A Postscript on Sin and Creatureliness

Since in evaluating his doctrine of sin, we criticized Niebuhr's ambivalent attitude toward human creatureliness, it should be pointed out that--probably because of his monism--Tillich's sense of the interconnection of humanity and nature is much more positive. Unlike Niebuhr, he neither finds human immersion in nature burdensome nor attempts to set boundaries to the ways in which nature affects human life.  "Man and nature belong together," Tillich says, "in their created glory, in their tragedy, and in their salvation."[75]  The transition from essence to existence characterizes the created world as well as humanity. Nature is part of the destiny out of and in relation to which the human species and individual persons emerge. For neither is there an exact moment in time at which one can point to the appearance of distinctly human nature or human responsibility.  "...The universe participates in every act of human freedom" just as "there are analogies to freedom effective in all parts of the universe."[76]  In the third volume of Systematic Theology, Tillich's conception of the relation between humanity and nature finds expression in his rejection of the idea of "levels" of life for the concept of "dimensions." "...The metaphor 'dimension,'" he says, "represents an encounter with reality in which the unity of life is seen above its conflicts."[77]  Insofar as various aspects of women's experience foster a sense of relation and connection to the natural world, this is an area in which Tillich's theology embraces women's experience.

## D.  Tillich's Doctrine of Grace

All that has been said thus far about the structures of being and their disruption, about sin, destruction, and the ambiguities of life belongs to the philosophical task of theology and especially to the development of two of the central questions which arise out of the human situation.  Implicit in the sense of separation from self, others, and God, in the experiences

of meaninglessness, conflict and despair which characterize so much of modern life is the longing for a reality
in which self-estrangement is conquered. Latent in the
experience of the mixture of essential and existential
elements in all life processes is the "quest for unambiguous life."[78] This longing and this quest stand at
the boundaries of human possibility. The questions
raised by human existence cannot be answered by human
existence. No human enterprise, no effort or series
of efforts can overcome sin or ambiguity, for every
free act is embedded in and realizes the destiny of
estrangement. Estrangement is transcended only through
the freely inaugurated action of God--through grace.[79]

The doctrine of grace belongs to theology proper,
to the explication of the Christian understanding of
God's response to human estrangement. This response is
not inferred from the account of existence but given in
the revelatory events upon which Christianity is based
and formulated by theology in response to the questions
arising out of a concrete situation. Tillich's doctrine of grace emerges from his interrelated answers
to the questions of sin and ambiguity, and it is
expressed in terms directed at his ontological analysis
of the human situation.

In the second volume of the Systematic Theology,
speaking to the realities of sin and disruption in all
areas of life, Tillich proposes the "New Being in
Jesus as the Christ" as the statement of the Christian
norm adequate today and the "restorative principle"
of his whole theological system. Representing the
"undistorted manifestation of essential being within
and under the conditions of existence," the New Being
is new both in relation to the "merely potential" nature
of essential being and the estranged nature of existential being.[80] In volume three of the Systematic Theology,
Tillich offers as an answer to the question of the ambiguities of life the symbol of the divine Spirit dwelling
in the human spirit or the "Spiritual Presence."[81]
While, in Tillich's thought, the New Being is the criterion of the presence of Spirit, it is the Spiritual
Presence which creates the New Being in both individuals
and Jesus as the Christ. In a curious reversal of
Niebuhr's theology, the doctrine of the Spirit has a
certain priority for Tillich, and the New Being, though
the norm of his theology, must be understood partly in
its light.[82] "The Spiritual Presence, elevating man
through faith and love to the transcendent unity of
unambiguous life, creates the New Being above the gap

between essence and existence and consequently above the ambiguities of life."[83]

## Salvation, Revelation, and the Spiritual Presence

The interrelation of the concepts of New Being and the Spiritual Presence produces a doctrine of grace which is quite complex and must be approached in several stages. Because of the importance of Spirit in Tillich's thought, to understand the New Being either as an objective state of things or as it is subjectively appropriated, one must first comprehend its manifestation in Jesus as the Christ in the context and in terms of the characteristics of a Spirit-created salvation history. On top of this, when one turns to the description of the historical disclosures of the Spiritual Presence, it turns out that Tillich's critical phenomenological account of revelation in the first volume of Systematic Theology is also relevant to his concept of grace because the histories of revelation and salvation are the same. The New Being in Jesus as the Christ is the criterion of the healing power of the New Being operative throughout history, created by the Spiritual Presence, and experienced in a revelation/salvation correlation.

We may begin unraveling the elements of Tillich's doctrine of grace by turning first to the general characteristics of the Spiritual Presence's operation in history. In Tillich's discussion of revelation and his parallel account of the Spiritual Presence, he distinguishes between the subjective and objective sides of the revelatory/salvific process, calling the former "ecstasy" and the latter "miracle."[84] He subjects both words to radical reinterpretation in the attempt to purify them of theological distortion. The term "ecstasy," Tillich argues, authentically refers to that state in which the human spirit is grasped by the divine Spirit and driven out of itself into a "successful self-transcendence." Held by the ground of being and meaning, the individual simultaneously experiences both the negative or abysmal element in the mystery of being and the power of being conquering nonbeing in which the negative element is at once preserved and overcome. Although the ecstatic experience of the Spiritual Presence does what the human spirit cannot do, namely create unambiguous life, it never destroys or violates finite selves in the process. The human spirit is elevated and preserved by ecstasy at the same time it is driven beyond its essential, rational, structure.[85]

"Miracle," which is the objective correlate of ecstasy or "the ecstasy of reality," has three distinguishing characteristics.[86] It is first of all an event which is marvelous and shaking without being antinatural: like ecstasy, it does not destroy the structure of being through which it becomes manifest. Secondly, a miracle is a "sign-event," an event which points to the mystery of being which preserves and overcomes nonbeing. Thirdly, a genuine miracle "is received as a sign-event in an ecstatic experience."[87] Where an event is not experienced ecstatically, one has the report of a miracle but not the miracle itself. Only that event is revelatory which creatively transforms the one who participates in it.

There is no reality, happening, person, or word which, because of its specific qualities, is either uniquely fit or unfit to be a bearer of revelation/salvation. Dividing the media of the Spiritual Presence into the two basic categories of sacrament and word, Tillich argues that the significance of certain objects (sacraments in the narrow sense) and words (the Bible, for example) is grounded in the possibility of any object or word becoming transparent to and communicating the divine Spirit. The differing attributes of natural phenomena, historical events, groups and individuals will affect the significance of revelation and the way in which relation to the mystery of being is expressed, but anything, accompanied and interpreted by language as the fundamental expression of the human spirit, can enter into a revelatory constellation.

The universal possibility of revelation/salvation is not simply theoretical. Humanity is never abandoned by God to the self-destructive consequences of estrangement. The impact of the Spiritual Presence creating the New Being is continuous throughout history. History as such is not the manifestation of the Spiritual Presence, but the Spiritual Presence is manifest in all history. God's self-revelation is limited neither to the developments of prophetic religion--which Christianity sees as preparatory to the final revelation in Jesus as the Christ--nor even to the history of religions generally, but is effective in "secular" history as well. On the other hand, the presence of the New Being in time and space, while constant and unambiguous, is always fragmentary. With reference to itself the New Being is complete and final, but those who participate in it do so only partially and anticipatively.[88]

## Jesus as the Christ

When we realize that revelation is universal but
fragmentary, and moreover that revelation by its nature
appears final to the person grasped by it, the problem
arises of finding a criterion by which all revelatory
claims can be recognized and judged.  It follows from
the existential character of theology, however, that no
criterion can be articulated outside the context of
commitment to some actual revelatory/salvific constellation.  The criterion of final revelation is always
derived from the revelation a group considers final.
The history of revelation then becomes a history of
events interpreted as revelatory in the light of some
final revelation.[89]

For Christianity, the "final" revelation, "the
decisive, fulfilling, unsurpassable revelation, that
which is the criterion of all others," is revelation in
Jesus as the Christ.  In him, the divine Spirit dwelt
without distortion.  "In him the New Being appeared as
the criterion of all Spiritual experiences in past and
future."  "He is the miracle of final revelation [whose]
reception is the ecstasy of final revelation.  [His
appearance] is the ecstatic moment of human history and,
therefore, its center, giving meaning to all possible
and actual history."[90]

Having located the final revelation in Jesus as
the Christ, Christian theology seeks the criterion of
finality in this event.  It asks what it is about Jesus
as the Christ which makes him the final revelation,
and it answers that a revelation is final if it can
negate itself without losing itself.  "The question of
the final revelation," says Tillich, "is the question
of a medium of revelation which overcomes its own finite
conditions by sacrificing them, and itself with them."
On the cross Jesus sacrifices all that is finite in
himself and thus "becomes completely transparent to the
mystery he reveals."  "The decisive trait in his picture is the continuous self-surrender of Jesus who is
Jesus to Jesus who is the Christ."[91]

In the second volume of the Systematic Theology,
Tillich fills out these general remarks concerning Jesus
as the Christ with detailed descriptions of both Jesus'
being as the New Being and his (Jesus') consequent
struggles with and victory over the forces of estrangement.[92]  As the bearer of the New Being "Jesus as the
Christ [has the quality of the New Being beyond the
split of essential and existential being] in the totality

124

of his being, not in any special expression of it." His
words, his deeds, his suffering, and his inner life--
each of which has been singled out at some point in
church history as the source of his significance--are
important precisely insofar as they manifest the New
Being which he is. Thus the power of his words, for
example, comes from the fact that he is the Word, the
power of his deeds from his essential unity with God.
His followers are called not to imitate his finite life,
which he surrenders in its totality and which points
beyond itself, but his full participation in the New
Being within the contingencies of existence. "To experience the New Being in Jesus as the Christ means to
experience the power in him which has conquered existential estrangement in himself and in everyone who
participates in him."[93]

The biblical picture of Jesus as the Christ, in
all its concrete detail, "confirms [this view of] his
character as the bearer of the New Being."[94]

> According to the [Bible]...there are, in spite
> of all tensions, no traces of estrangement be-
> tween him and God and consequently between him
> and himself and between him and his world (in
> its essential nature). The paradoxical char-
> acter of his being consists in the fact that,
> although he has only finite freedom under the
> conditions of time and space, he is not es-
> tranged from the ground of his being. (95)

This affirmation is central for Tillich, and he devotes
some pages to showing how the New Testament depiction
of Jesus as the Christ is in sharp contrast with the
human situation of sin and disruption.

Much of his exposition in this section is not
particularly original. Tillich notes, for example, that
despite the reality of Jesus' contest with the forces
of estrangement, there are no traces of unbelief, hubris,
or concupiscence in the Gospel portrait of Jesus as the
Christ. Acknowledging participation in God as his infinite concern, Jesus cries out to God who has forsaken
him even on the cross. Scorning self-elevation, he
combines acceptance of the messianic title with acceptance of servanthood and violent death. Renouncing
unlimited fulfillment of finite desires, he rejects
the temptations of Satan in the desert.[96]

Tillich's consideration of the reality of the
temptations of Christ is interesting, for here he

125

reexamines an issue which is also important in defining the nature of the fall: whether the possibility of temptation already presupposes estrangement. Tillich explains Christ's temptations not in terms of dreaming innocence--which is how he explains temptation before the fall--but by distinguishing between desire and concupiscence and arguing that desire need not disrupt unity with God. Since life in unity with God, like all life, is determined by the polarity of dynamics and form, it is not static; it involves tension and "the desire for the reunion of the finite with the finite." "Where there is unity with God, [however]...the finite is not desired alongside this unity but within it."[97] The desire presupposed by temptation is therefore not in itself evil provided it remains within lawful bounds. Temptation has its origins in the fact that one can also desire the finite without God; desire, that is, can become concupiscence. The fact that Jesus does not succumb to the temptation to let desire become concupiscence does not negate the seriousness of his temptation. On the other hand, the seriousness of his temptation does not make his victory over it a matter of contingency. As with all human beings, his concrete decisions are products of both his freedom and his destiny, and like all human decisions, they stand under the directing creativity of God.

## Jesus as the Christ and Salvation

The importance of Jesus' victory over estrangement lies in the fact that it is not simply of individual consequence but brings the New Being to all humanity. The cosmic significance of his life story motivates not only the biblical portrait of Jesus as the Christ with its numerous symbols, myths, and legends, but also the continuing theological interest in and refinement of these traditions. There are many doctrines which play a role in declaring or preserving the message of the universal significance of Jesus' subjection to and conquest of existence. It is the doctrine of atonement, however, which has the task of describing the salvific effects of his relationship to estrangement, both in terms of "the manifestation of the New Being which has an atoning effect and...that which happens to man under the atoning effect."[98]

Tillich approaches the doctrine of atonement by first briefly discussing its history and then setting out six principles which he feels should determine future development of the doctrine.[99] First and most important of these is the principle that atonement is

126

dependent on God alone, Christ being the mediator of God's reconciling act. Second, since God's justice is the structural form of God's love, atonement cannot be viewed as settlement of a conflict between the two. Third, in removing guilt and punishment, God does not overlook "the reality and depth of existential estrangement." Fourth, God's atoning activity should be understood not as the removal of estrangement and its consequences but as God's participation in them. Fifth, the Cross of Christ is the central manifestation of this participation and the criterion of all others. Last, "through participation in the New Being, which is the being of Jesus as the Christ, men also participate in the manifestation of the atoning act of God."[100]

These principles form the basis for Tillich's concluding section of the second volume of Systematic Theology: his remarks on the objective element in regeneration (participation), justification (acceptance), and sanctification (transformation).[101] In discussing regeneration, Tillich is concerned that the power of the Christian message of salvation not be lost through too narrow concentration on the religious situation of the individual. One of the implications of his insistence on the interdependence and interconnectedness of life in all dimensions[102] is the impossibility of separating human redemption from the healing of nature or the healing of the relationship between humanity and nature. For Tillich, regeneration relates to the individual only insofar as (s)he participates in an event which is first of all of cosmic significance. While the saving power of the New Being is dependent on human participation in it, the objective reality of the New Being precedes this participation, "grasping and drawing" the individual into a universally new creation. "Regeneration is the state of having been drawn into the new reality manifest in Jesus as the Christ."[103]

Justification, which presupposes this condition of "being grasped by the divine presence," represents the "in spite of element" in salvation. Objectively, and in accordance with the first principle of atonement, it is an eternal act of God, in no way dependent on humanity, in which God accepts those who are unacceptable and takes into the unity of the New Being those who are estranged. Subjective acceptance of this acceptance, "without which there would be no salvation but only despair," depends on participation in the power of the New Being which makes faith possible. Regeneration and justification are thus two sides of

127

one divine act of reuniting that which is estranged. Regeneration is the actual reunion and justification its paradoxical character. Sanctification, or "the process in which the power of the New Being transforms personality and community" is then distinguished from both these "as a process is distinguished from the event in which it is initiated."[104]

## Faith and Love

Since sanctification is the work of the Spirit, Tillich considers it, along with the subjective sides of regeneration and justification, in volume three of the Systematic Theology. In one sense, the entire fourth part of his system might be regarded as a description of sanctification or "life process under the impact of the Spirit."[105] He deals explicitly with sanctification as an aspect of redemption, however, only in the context of a much larger section on Spirit and the ambiguities of life, a section which must in turn be read in the light of his introductory comments on the character of the Spiritual Presence. Though much of this latter material has been assimilated to our discussion of revelation and the New Being, one section remains to be considered. Tillich's account of the three-fold nature of salvation must be understood in relation to his treatment of faith and love.

Through the work of the divine Spirit in the human spirit, the essential and existential elements of being are reunited, and "ambiguous life is raised above itself to a transcendence that it could not achieve by its own power." "Faith" and "love," words which Tillich reworks as thoroughly as "ecstasy" and "miracle," are the manifestations in the human spirit of this transcendent union.[106] Faith is defined formally or generally as "the state of being grasped by an ultimate concern" and materially as the "state of being grasped by the transcendent unity of unambiguous life" or "the New Being as manifest in Jesus as the Christ." Considered as a material concept, faith exhibits the same tripartite structure as salvation. In its receptive character, it is opened up by the Spiritual Presence; in its paradoxical character, it accepts the Spiritual Presence despite the infinite gap between the divine and human (S)spirits; in its anticipatory character, it expects "final participation in the transcendent unity of unambiguous life."[107] Tillich contrasts his understanding of faith with intellectualistic, emotionalistic, and voluntaristic distortions of the term. Faith is neither belief, nor feeling, nor an act of will, but includes and transforms all these through the power of the Spiritual Presence.[108]

Love is both a consequence of faith and "one side of the ecstatic state of being of which faith is the other." In all its forms, love is "the drive toward the reunion of the separated."[109] As agape, or unambiguous love, it is the state of being taken into the transcendent unity of unambiguous life. Agape, like faith, has the receptive, paradoxical, and anticipatory structure of the New Being. It accepts the love object without restriction, holds onto it despite estrangement, profanization, and demonization, and expects its holiness, greatness, and dignity to be re-established. Also like faith, agape inclues emotional, volitional, and intellectual elements without being identical with any one of them.

Tillich's definition of agape is very different from Niebuhr's, mainly because both theologians define agape in contrast to the significance of sin. While for Niebuhr, therefore, agape is a response to the human situation of pridefulness, for Tillich, is is a response to the situation of separation or estrangement.[110] Tillich does not deny that self-sacrifice can be an element in agape. Love may realize "its uniting power in a special situation by the surrender of special forms of self-realization." But he also writes that "love as the power of reunion...demands venturing self-affirmation as much as venturing self-negation."[111]

Tillich's interest in love as a response to estrangement leads him away from Niebuhr in another way as well. He is as concerned with the continuity between agape and other forms of love as he is with the differences between them. He argues in several places for the oneness and indivisibility of love. Love as the "drive toward the reunion of the separated" characterizes epithymia as "the movement of the needy toward that which fulfills the need," philia as "the movement of the equal toward union with the unequal," eros as "the movement of that which is lower in power and meaning to that which is higher," and of course agape as the movement toward the transcendent unity of unambiguous life."[112] On the other hand, agape so defined is not just the highest form of love. It "enters from another dimension...into all qualities of love." Tillich would agree with Niebuhr that whereas all the other qualities of love depend on various contingent characteristics of the love object, agape affirms the other unconditionally in the center of its being. In

129

this sense it is heedless of self; it desires the ultimate fulfillment of the other as the other despite its
ambiguous mixture of essential and existential elements.
Love thus understood is no more a simple human possibility for Tillich then it is for Niebuhr.  In this way
too, _agape_ differs from the other qualities of love.
It is possible only as a creation of the Spiritual Presence and only in unity with faith.[113]

## Regeneration, Justification, and Sanctification

Tillich's account of the subjective side of regeneration, justification, and sanctification may be
understood as an extension of his treatment of the tripartite structure of faith and love.  In discussing the
New Being as creation, paradox, and process, he develops
more fully the import of and relation between the different elements of faith and love as the two fundamental
Spiritual creations.[114]

If regeneration objectively considered is the
"grasping and drawing" of the individual into a new
state of things, subjectively it is "the event in which
the divine Spirit takes hold of a personal life through
the creation of faith."[115]  The individual, through
the "pattern of participation," enters into the new
reality manifest in Jesus as the Christ and is reborn.[116]
Tillich is quite clear on the priority of the experience of regeneration as creation over justification.
Though he agrees with the Reformers that being born anew
is not the cause of a person's acceptance by God, he
insists that the individual can accept divine acceptance only through the faith which is a creation of the
Spirit.  To put justification before regeneration is
to turn faith into the affirmation of a doctrine.

Justification correctly understood is then the "in
spite of" element in the process of salvation which
finds its human response in the courage to accept acceptance despite being unacceptable.  Though traditionally, of course, justification, has been interpreted as
the forgiveness of sins, this reading can be applied
to Tillich only if his peculiar understanding of human
sinfulness is borne in mind.  Just as the central problem of human life is not sins but Sin, "in relation to
God, it is not the particular sin as such that is forgiven but the act of separation from God and the
resistance to reunion with him."[117]

The act of divine forgiveness has both a negative
and a positive side.  Negatively, it means that any

attempt of human hubris to avoid the pain of surrender
to God's "sole activity in our reunion with him" by
trying to bring about reunion through human works must
be relinquished. The unconditional divine act which
declares the unjust just and unacceptable accepted
turns the individual away from the ambiguities and
uncertainties of human goodness to the infinite goodness of God. To accept this acceptance in the courage
of faith is to give up to God one's religious, intellectual, and moral works. Positively, the divine forgiveness of human estrangement means that justification is
operative not just in the moral sphere, but in every
area of human endeavor and meaning. If no human claim
can bring about union with the divine, no human doubt,
no guilt, and no fate means inevitable estrangement
from it.[118]

Tillich is particularly concerned to relate justification to the anxiety of emptiness and meaninglessness, for these undermine the experience of grace by
rendering questionable the very notions of "God" and
"acceptance." Moreover, it is the boundary situation
of radical doubt which characterizes the modern period.[119]
But if "culpability cannot separate one from God [says
the message of grace] neither can intellectual aberra-
tion."[120] The New Being cannot liberate the individual
from the anxiety of doubt, but it can be present precisely
in the depths of that anxiety. Serious despair over the
meaning of life is positive in its negativity; it must
affirm itself in order to negate itself. When the
image of the Father who judges and forgives has lost
its power, "the God above God," the power of being
accepts those whose doubt makes them unacceptable.[121]

"Based on the experience of regeneration [and] qualified by the experience of justification," the life process of the individual under the impact of the Spiritual
Presence develops as the experience of sanctification.
Tillich offers four criteria of life in the Spirit which
"create an indefinite but distinguishable image of the
'Christian life.'" These principles, which are rooted
in the Spiritual creations of faith and love, are increasing awareness, increasing freedom, increasing relatedness,
and increasing transcendence. They determine a life process which never reaches perfection but which "contains
a movement toward maturity, however fragmentary the
mature state may be."[122]

According to the principle of awareness, the individual in the process of sanctification becomes increasingly cognizant of both the demonic forces struggling

around and within him or her and the divine response to the questions implied in this situation. Such awareness leads to the ability to affirm life despite its ambiguities and to respond sensitively to the demands of the self, others, and the concrete situations in which the self is placed.

The criterion of increasing freedom, which is balanced by that of increasing relatedness, refers to growth in independence from the commanding form and the particular content of the law. Since law is essential human nature confronting the individual in the state of estrangement, fragmentary reunion with true being implies fragmentary freedom from prohibition and command. The Spirit-determined personality is freed from the oppressiveness of the fixed content of the law which cannot adjust to ever changing situations, and empowered both to decide on adequate action in the light of the Spiritual Presence and to resist the internal and external forces which threaten this freedom.

The tendency to isolation which may result from such resistance is offset by the principle of relatedness. "Relatedness implies the awareness of the other one and the freedom to relate to him by overcoming self-seclusion within oneself and within the other one." The divine Spirit, in ecstatically elevating the individual above her or himself, enables her or him to enter into genuine relations with others and achieve mature self-relatedness. In his discussions of sin, Tillich describes the self-hated and self-rejection which follow estrangement from God and increase separation from other people. In the New Being, "self-acceptance conquers both self-elevation and self-contempt in a process of reunion with one's self."[123]

The fourth principle of the New Being as process, self-transcendence, is operative in the other three. Mature awareness, freedom, and relatedness are all achieved through acts of self-transcendence, for sanctification is possible only through the "continuous transcendence of oneself in the direction of the ultimate--in other words [through] participation in the holy."[124] Though such participation is often identified with the life of prayer, in fact it is actual in the full range of secular and religious activities through which the Spirit is experienced.

## The Spiritual Presence and the Ambiguities of Life

We have devoted a good deal of space to regeneration, justification, and sanctification, but Tillich's
treatment of the subjective side of salvation is not
the center of his discussion of life under the impact
of the Spirit.  "Since all the functions of the human
spirit...are conditioned by the social context of the
ego-thou encounter," the divine Spirit is first of all
present not to the isolated individual but to the
social group.[125]  Tillich calls the community living
under the creative impact of the New Being in Jesus as
the Christ the "Spiritual Community."[126]  The central
categories of the Protestant understanding of grace
describe the way in which the individual enters into
and experiences this community.  Tillich considers the
New Being as creation, paradox, and process, therefore,
only in the context of his account of the Spiritual
Presence and the ambiguities of communal life, most
immediately religion.  But because religion is not
separate from culture and morality in the transcendent
unity of unambiguous life, and because the Spiritual
creations of faith and love characterize the community
as well as the individual, his description of regeneration, justification, and sanctification is relevant to
all of Spirit-determined life.[127]

Turning first to a discussion of Spirit and the
ambiguities of religion, Tillich relates the Spiritual
Community to the nature and work of the church.  As the
"Spiritual essence" of the church (or churches), the
Spiritual Community is both wider than the church--which
represents only the manifest religious self-expression
of the Community--and free from its ambiguities.  The
situation of the church is paradoxical.  On the one hand,
it participates in the unambiguous life of the Spiritual
Community.  On the other, it participates in the ambiguities of life in general and religion in particular.
Every quality and task of the church, partaking at once
of its "theological" and "sociological" character,
stands under the great "in spite of" justification.
As a community of holiness, unity, and universality,
as a community of faith and love, and in its constitutive, expanding, and constructing functions, the church
both fragmentarily realizes its essential nature and
continually succumbs to the destructive structures of
existence.  Insofar as the Spiritual Presence is effective
in the life of the church and its members, however, it
conquers religion as a special function of the spirit and
with it the forces of profanization and demonization
which characterize religion as a part of life.

The relation between religion and culture in the Spiritual Community is expressed in Tillich's famous phrase "religion is the substance of culture and culture the form of religion."[128] This means that culture under the impact of the Spirit is "theonomous." It expresses ultimacy of meaning in all the independent forms of the creative process without autonomous form either being suppressed by religion or losing contact with the ultimate. In theonomous culture, language, for example, becomes the "Word of God," witnessing to the union of the one who speaks with what is spoken of. Cognition becomes "revelation," replacing observation with participation. Tools become "bearer[s] of form and meaning," while the potential limitlessness of technical production is subjected to the goal of Eternal Life. Self-determination and thus genuine relations with others become possible, for the self is reunited with itself from the vertical direction. The many ambiguities of justice are fragmentarily conquered under the transforming impact of the Spiritual Presence.

Like culture, morality in the Spiritual Community is also theonomous, manifesting its religious substance not through outside determination (heteronomy) but through free arguing. Theonomous morality is able to resolve the central moral problem of the ambiguity of sacrifice in the process of self-integration. The Spirit takes the personal center into the transcendent unity of the divine life in which the personal center embraces all possible encounters beyond potentiality and actuality. The person can thus judge new possibilities and accept or reject them on the basis of their ability to express essential being, and the self can maintain its identity and alter itself without being either impoverished or disrupted. Though any individual will still have to sacrifice certain potentialities, the Spirit turns the tragic character of this sacrifice into a simple acknowledgement of finitude. Theonomous morality also fragmentarily resolves the ambiguities inherent in the moral law as law through the transformation of love as law into love as creation of the Spirit. In reuniting the existing self with its essence, the Spirit both demonstrates the validity of the moral imperative and provides the motivation for its fulfillment. In overcoming the "oscillation between the abstract and the concrete elements in a moral situation, agape solves the problem of the content of the moral law.[129]

## E. Critique of Tillich's Doctrine of Grace

If in order to be relevant to women's experience,
a doctrine of sin must consider the sin of self-denial,
a doctrine of grace must explain how resources from
beyond the self enable the self to be responsibly self-
creating, to gain reserves of strength it could not
acquire on its own. Niebuhr's doctrine of grace, we
argued, because it is formulated solely in response
to the sin of pride, fails to speak to women's experience. If anything, it reinforces the problems of self-
abnegation which constitute "women's sin." Since
Tillich's doctrine of grace is also a response to the
questions implicit in the human situation, it is not
surprising that in his case, as in Niebuhr's, the
strengths, tensions, and problems in his doctrine of
grace reflect those in his doctrine of sin. There are
many aspects of Tillich's doctrine of grace which have
received critical attention: the precise role of Jesus
as the Christ in his system, the adequacy of his definition of agape, the place he allows forgiveness in the
economy of salvation. Without questioning the importance
of any of these issues, we will focus on the problem in
his doctrine of grace which is most fundamental from
the perspective of women's experience: the same tension between concern for autonomous selfhood and a monistic ontology which marked his treatment of sin.

In criticizing Tillich's doctrine of sin, we
argued that the conflict in his thought between concern
with human self-constitution on the one hand and his
ontology on the other is a conflict within and between
two levels of discourse about human selfhood. The same
is true of his doctrine of grace. On the existential
level,[130] i.e. the level referring to actually existing
selves and therefore most relevant to women's experience,
Tillich's discussion of justification and sanctification
generates a number of categories which deal with the
impact of grace on problems of self-creation and therefore implicitly with the situation of women in western
society. At the same time, certain problems on this
level--his static concept of justification, his vague
discussion of sanctification--signal the presence of
weaknesses elsewhere in the structure of his thought
which turn out to be weaknesses in his ontology. Despite Tillich's efforts to ground and maintain the
ontological autonomy of the finite individual in the
experience of salvation, he tends to define participation
in the divine ground in such a way that the finite self
is lost or negated. But since his concern for selfhood
on the existential level is rooted in his ontology,

135

loss of self on the ontological level means self-loss on the existential level as well. Those categories in his doctrine of grace which are relevant to women's experience are thus unsupported by the total context in which they are set. This pattern of interlocking tensions in Tillich's thought is complex, but we can unravel it by looking first at those aspects of his doctrine of grace which are relevant to women's experience and then analyzing the factors which tend to undercut them.

## Grace and Human Selfhood

Since in the doctrine of sin Tillich identifies the moment of human self-actualization with the moment of the fall, it might be expected that in the doctrine of grace, he would identify salvation with self-negation or self-annihilation, and that his doctrine of grace would thus be inapplicable to women's experience. This is not the case, however. On the contrary, Tillich carefully and explicitly warns against any such conclusion. In defining both the New Being and "ecstatic" human participation in the New Being, he tries to establish the ontological integrity of (redeemed) finite selfhood as the basis of the individual experience of graceful self-acceptance.

The message of the New Being is that salvation is achieved, not through return to essential being as potentiality and thus the sacrifice of realized individuality, but through the actualization of essential being under the conditions of existence. The New Being is essential being given flesh, entered into time and space. It is individuality actualized but not estranged. Through the symbol of the New Being, Tillich attempts to maintain the goodness of unestranged actualized being, including its poles of individualization and centeredness.131

The integrity of finite being is similarly maintained in "ecstatic" human participation in the New Being. The subject/object structure of finite existence is preserved and transcended in ecstasy, never negated or destroyed. "Religiously speaking," Tillich says, "God does not need to destroy his created world, which is good in its essential nature, in order to manifest himself in it."132 Tillich's treatment of faith and love as two sides of the ecstatic movement of the human spirit underlines this point concerning the integrity of created being. As the states of being grasped by and taken into the transcendent unity of unambiguous life, faith and love presuppose the relative independence of that which is grasped and reunited. The elements of

risk and courage in faith indicate the persistence of
autonomous selfhood even as the self is opened up to
that which transcends subject and object. Love, for
its part, presupposes the separation of finite self
from finite self, for it exists only where there is
separation to be overcome. In the realm of finite
beings, this means that the highest form of love is that
between persons, for it preserves the separation of the
self-centered selves which are at the same time reunited.
Tillich suggests moreover, that the continuation of
finite self-centeredness also characterizes human
reunion with the divine ground. Without the self's
essential belongingness to its ground, no reunion would
be possible. But without the "serious otherness" of
beings separated from their ground by freedom, God
would be the principle of love but could not have love
for independent beings.[133]

These definitions of the New Being and participation in it suggest that Tillich strives to preserve the
ontological autonomy of finite individuals in the process of salvation. When he discusses human selfhood
as it actually exists, he also tries to maintain the
integrity of finite selves, describing the ways in
which the ambiguities of self-relatedness are (fragmentarily) overcome under the impact of the Spiritual
Presence.

The religious basis of "mature self-relatedness,"
according to Tillich, is the combined experience of
God's regenerating and justifying grace. While Niebuhr
emphasizes the element of judgement in justification,
Tillich finds judgement less important than the reality
of acceptance. Justification is first of all the unconditional love of God and God alone, accepting the self
despite all that renders it unacceptable, and finding
its response in the human courage to accept acceptance.
The possibility of courage is grounded in participation
in the New Being which precedes the experience of justification. Such courage is the basis of all undistorted human self-love and self-affirmation. Only in
the light and power of a "love from above" can the
individual love him or herself without complacency or
arbitrariness. "The condemning element in justification makes self-complacency impossible, the forgiving
element saves from self-condemnation and despair, the
giving element provides for a Spiritual center which
unites the elements of our personal self and makes
power over oneself possible."[134]

Tillich's lack of emphasis on judgement is related

137

to his understanding of sin. Since sin is not pride
but estrangement from the ground with which the self is
originally united, it follows that the primary meaning
of grace would be reunion. Insofar as sin springs from
human freedom as well as destiny, grace will include
judgement and forgiveness as well as the surrender of
human righteousness to the righteousness of God (the
correlate of Niebuhr's shattering of the self). For
Tillich to interpret justification (onesidely) as judgement, however, would be to accentuate the sense of distance from God which he sees as the basic human problem.

The self-reconciliation which is grounded in regeneration and justification grows and matures in the
process of sanctification.[135] The self gives itself
up to God only to receive itself back again in the
power of essential self-realization. According to the
principle of increasing awareness, life in the Spirit
means the development of "sensitivity toward the demands
of one's own growth" and "toward the grades of authen-
ticity in the life of the spirit in others and oneself."
According to the principle of increasing relatedness,
the ecstatic self-transcendence which conquers loneliness and hostility, opening the self to genuine communion with others, is also the basis of the ability
to sustain solitude and genuine self-appreciation. Able
spontaneously to affirm her or his essential being
"beyond subject and object...the [mature] individual
is more spontaneous, more self-affirming, without self-
elevation or self-humiliation."[136]

Grace, Human Selfhood, and Women's Experience

From the perspective of women's experience,
Tillich's treatment of the individual experience of
grace has two distinctly different sides. On the one
hand, his translation of justification as "the acceptance of acceptance" and his establishment of the
principle of increasing relatedness as a criterion of
sanctification provide the correctives to Niebuhr's
onesided emphasis on the shattering of the self and
self-sacrifice we were looking for in the last chapter.
Focusing entirely on the sin of pride, Niebuhr's doctrine of grace provided no response to "women's sin"
of failing to be responsibly self-creating. Tillich's
account of grace, on the other hand, proclaims a
reality in which all ambiguities of self-estrangement
(in its existential as well as ontological sense) are
(fragmentarily) overcome. Self-contempt, self-
disruption, injustice toward the self--all the categories
in Tillich's account of sin which are relevant to women's

138

experience[137]--are also treated in the doctrine of grace. The experience of justification, as he sees it, grounding the possibilities of love and justice toward the self, can speak to and heal the hostility and self-doubt which undermine the capacity for imaginative action and limit the self's horizons to a few culturally sanctioned roles. Through the process of sanctification or growth in the life of the Spirit, justice toward the self becomes an increasing reality as the self can affirm itself in its essential nature and the ambiguities of sacrifice are conquered. Thus it appears that grace as acceptance, providing the basis for growth in healthy self-affirmation, frees the self so that it may act creatively in the world.

On the other hand, while acceptance potentially frees the self for action, it need not necessarily do so; acceptance, as Tillich defines it, is in many respects a static concept. Indeed, one can detect in his thought an occasional tendency toward that quietism which Niebuhr considers the great danger of the Lutheran understanding of justification. In his great sermon, "You are Accepted," for example, Tillich says, "Do not seek for anything; do not perform anything; do not intend anything. Simply accept the fact that you are accepted."[138] This language actually seems to reinforce sins of weakness in that it implies that the failure to act, the failure to take responsibility is not only acceptable but praiseworthy. This is an exaggeration, of course. But while judgement of the sin of hubris is implied in the very notion of acceptance by God and God alone, acceptance does not speak in the same clear way to sins of weakness. Having failed to show just how and why uncreative weakness is a sin, Tillich also fails to show how acceptance initiates a process in which uncreative weakness is transcended.

The impression of quietism left by Tillich's treatment of justification is compounded by the vagueness of his description of sanctification. His principles of sanctification can be filled in in ways which are most relevant to women's experience, but he himself gives these principles little content. One can read Tillich on self-awareness, self-affirmation, self-relatedness and have no idea of what would constitute a mature self-related or self-affirming action in the world. Such indifference to the details of actual existence is generally characteristic of Tillich's theology, and, in the case of the doctrine of grace, may be aggravated by special factors: a fear that defining grace too precisely will turn it into a work; a hesitance, in the

name of the principle of increasing freedom, to tie
grace to the specifics of law.[139]

Whatever the reasons for it, however, this vagueness is particularly distressing from the perspective
of women's experience because the social nexus out of
which "women's sin" arises makes very clear and specific
demands which are always there to step in where there
is no new "law" to replace them.  The concept of self-
affirmation is potentially liberating, but in a society
in which women's fulfillment is defined as dedication
to the home, there is no reason to suppose that growth
toward self-realization would not immediately be interpreted in traditional ways.  Since women's experience
has such an important social dimension, concrete norms
of social justice might compensate for Tillich's vagueness on the nature of personal sanctification.  In
fact, however, his description of community under the
impact of the Spiritual Presence is equally abstract.
When he discusses inequality as an ambiguity of justice,
for example, he says, "Justice implies equality; but
equality of what is essentially unequal is just as
unjust as inequality of what is essentially equal."[140]
Statements like this, which can be used to legitimate
hierarchal structures, are not very helpful in clarify-
ing the meaning of women's personal self-affirmation as
it might be defined within a social context.  Whatever
connections there are to be made between Tillich's
doctrine of grace and women's experience, he certainly
has not made them.

## Grace and Human Selfhood Reconsidered

We have mentioned some possible reasons for the
vagueness of Tillich's account of sanctification.  The
question now arises as to whether it does not also have
deeper roots in his ontology.  Tillich fails to account
adequately for sins of uncreative weakness, we argued
in criticizing his doctrine of sin, because his identification of creation and the fall provides him no basis
for doing so.  Self-actualization involves estrangement,
but non-actualization is in a kind of ontological limbo.
How does self-realization then become positive in the
doctrine of grace?  Or does Tillich not deal with
sanctification concretely because he remains as ambivalent toward self-realization and its basis, the ontological autonomy of finite beings, as he was in the
doctrine of sin?  Can those aspects of his doctrine of
grace which are relevant to women's experience stand in
all their strengths (and weaknesses), or are they too
undercut by his ontology?

140

To answer these questions, we must first understand certain changes in Tillich's language as he moves from the doctrine of sin to the doctrine of grace. When he deals with self-actualization in relation to sin, he clearly implies that self-actualization itself in any form necessarily estranges one from God. Several aspects of his discussion of grace, on the other hand, suggest that self-actualization is sinful if it separates the self from God--but it need not do so. Thus in describing the fall, Tillich says that humanity, caught between the desire to actualize freedom and preserve dreaming innocence, decides for actualization and becomes estranged. There are not different forms of self-actualization amongst which to choose. Actualization is creation and fall, and it involves humanity in the three characteristics of sin as estrangement-- unbelief, hubris, and concupiscence.[141] In describing the life of the Spirit, however, Tillich says that the anxiety of having to decide between loss of one's essential being and loss of one's freedom is resolved through the realization of essential being in existence. Here he clearly assumes a distinction between self-actualization and estrangement. This same distinction underlies his general description of Jesus as the Christ who is fully human yet shows no signs of any of the marks of estrangement, and his specific defense of the reality of Christ's temptations.[142]

Whether these two attitudes toward self-actualization are contradictory depends on how one interprets Tillich's insistence on the irrationality of the fall. As we have seen,[143] the coincidence of creation and fall is nonlogical in that although there is no moment in time when essential being is actualized without sin, estrangement cannot be deduced from the structures of essential being. If the nonlogical character of the fall is taken to mean that estrangement is only one possible result of the decision for self-actualization, the result which happens to have been realized, then it is entirely comprehensible that essential being also could be realized under the conditions of existence. Tillich makes too many statements which flatly equate existence and estrangement, however, to make such an interpretation plausible.[144] More likely, as Guyton Hammond points out in his book Man in Estrangement, the fall is illogical simply because, as we have said, "one cannot derive the existent universe from an analysis of the essences." It is a fact; it just is. Creation need not be completed (this is its irrational element); but if it is completed, then it has to be

141

estranged.  This is a necessity of life not of logic.[145]

On this understanding of the relation between creation and the fall, there is still logical room for the concept of the New Being, and thus for the affirmation of self-actualization.  But the notion of actualized essential being is absurd in the sense that it contradicts the "order of reality."[146]  In the doctrine of sin, Tillich assumes that actualized being, as actualized, is estranged.  Grace is the response to the situation of sin because it makes the actualization of essential being possible.  But this is to beg the question, because it is a necessity of life that actualized being is always estranged.

The source of this (nonlogical) contradiction may lie in Tillich's failure to reinterpret the fall radically enough.  Traditionally, the fall has been understood as an event in time, resulting in the corruption or distortion of a good creation, while grace is the restoration of creation's original goodness.  For Tillich, creation is good in its essential nature but not as actualized.  According to formula then, one would expect that grace would mean the restoration of essential, potential creation.  Tillich wants to claim, however, that the New Being goes beyond the perfection of (essential) creation in actualizing essential being, but he then defines the relation between creation and estrangement in a way which makes the concept of New Being difficult to understand.  Were he to develop the ontological implications of the felix culpa motif one occasionally detects in his treatment of the fall, this problem might be resolved.[147]  Self-actualization would then be a necessary step toward the genuine perfection of the unity of essential and existential being, and there would be theological grounds for interpreting the failure to be self-actualizing as sin.  In depicting the fall in traditionally negative terms, however, Tillich confuses the notion of the New Being and leaves the impression that genuine salvation would lie in the dissolution of the individual center in the divine life.

The New Being is the central symbol Tillich uses to affirm the existence of actualized, essential being, and indirectly, the existence of actual self-affirming selves.  If the confusions in his attitude toward self-actualization tend to undermine the usefulness of the symbol in establishing the ontological independence of the finite individual, his concept of ecstasy, closely examined, holds up no more firmly.  He says that in the state of ecstasy the self transcends the polar structures

142

of finitude without destroying them, just as he says
that the New Being is the actualization of essential
being under the conditions of existence. But he explains no more clearly in the former than in the latter
case how this is possible. What does it mean to say
that the subject/object structure which is the basic
condition of all thought and experience can be transcended and at the same time preserved? If ecstasy means
going "beyond" (albeit without negating) the most fundamental structures of selfhood, those which determine
all of the experience, in what sense can it be said
that the integrity of the finite self is maintained?

It is not simply the opaqueness of Tillich's concept
of ecstasy which makes it problematic, however. Whatever ecstatic self-transcendence means, it is clear
that in relation to the polar character of the ontological elements, it is not symmetrical. Ecstatic transcendence cannot ground the autonomy of the finite individual
because individualization and participation are not
caught up in a balanced fashion in this higher state.
Transcendence always takes place in the direction of participation.

Tillich sometimes speaks as if this asymmetry were
implied in the very notion of ecstasy. "As ecstatic
experience, faith is mystical," Tillich says at one
point,[148] while the mystical element in faith is precisely the participation of the finite in the infinite
to which it belongs. If ecstasy is thus understood,
the response of the human spirit to the breaking in of
the divine Spirit is by definition weighted in favor of
participation. But even where Tillich seems to identify
ecstasy with faith in all its aspects,[149] faith (ecstasy)
is no more balanced.

The asymmetry of Tillich's notion of ecstasy is
perhaps clearest in his description of the ecstatic
experience of absolute faith in The Courage to Be.[150]
In that book, where he attempts to define faith in such
a way that mysticism and personal meeting, participation
and individualization appear as equal aspects, he still
weights his discussion of faith toward the elements of
mysticism and participation. The character of the
human relationship to the divine ground is determined
by the individualization/participation polarity, Tillich
says. Where participation is dominant, the relationship has a mystical character; where individualization
is dominant, it has a personal character; and where
both are incorporated and transcended, it has the character of faith. Faith is neither mysticism nor personal

encounter. It includes a mystical element in the experience of the presence of the infinite in the finite, and it includes a personal element in the experience of the affirmation of the individual self in the encounter with God as person. So far, so good.

When Tillich turns to specifically describing the nature of absolute faith and the way in which it is revelatory of being, however, the language he uses contains no personal elements.[151] Absolute faith is the experience of the _power_ of _being_ even in the face of nonbeing, the experience of the dependence of nonbeing on _being_, and the experience of the _power_ of acceptance. Faith shows that the self-affirmation of being is one that includes nonbeing, that "nonbeing forces being out of its seclusion [and] forces it to affirm itself dynamically."[152] Faith shows that the divine self-affirmation is the basis of the self-affirmation of finite being. Though Tillich intends these nonpersonal terms to indicate that faith in God transcends personality rather than excludes it, the effect of his language is to suggest that faith is closer to mysticism than to personal encounter. Tillich denies this outright[153] (thus indicating awareness of the problem). The fact remains, however, that whereas the mystical elements of participation and identity are explicit in his language of divine/human relation, the elements of individualization and encounter are not. It is difficult enough to understand how a relationship both transcends and includes the personal. Tillich's language, far from shedding light on the problem, suggests that in fact transcendence of the personal involves (at least partial) exclusion of it.

Since Tillich warns against taking The Courage to Be, an essentially apologetic work, as a dogmatic statement,[154] it is important to note that his language in the Systematic Theology involves precisely the same problems. There too God is described primarily in nonpersonal terms as "being," "power of being," "divine ground," and "divine life," while faith is defined as the "state of being grasped by the transcendent unity of unambiguous life." This phrase, which Tillich uses an endless number of times in the third volume, places the mystical elements of identity and participation at the center of the human experience of the divine. Not surprisingly, therefore, the word "participation" itself continually reappears in his descriptions of individual and communal appropriation of the New Being, but its polar element "individualization" is simply never mentioned.[155] The minimum deduction to be drawn from this is that participation is strengthened by the experience of grace in a way in which individualization is not.

## Grace, Human Selfhood and Women's Experience Reconsidered

Since the problems which arise out of women's experience are directly addressed not by notions which ground the ontological autonomy of the self but by those which deal with self-constitution on a personal or communal level, discussion of the New Being and ecstasy seems to have taken us rather far afield from concrete consideration of women's experience. We are quickly brought back to it once again, however, by the fact that it is meaningless to speak of existential self-relatedness in any form unless the ontological independence of finite selves has first been established. We began the critique of Tillich's doctrine of grace by suggesting that he attempts to define the New Being and ecstasy in such a way as to establish the autonomy of finite beings and thus lay the groundwork for discussion of the individual experience of salvation as ecstatic participation in the New Being. Closer examination revealed, however, that his concepts of the New Being and ecstasy, confused and contradictory as they are, cannot support his treatment of grace as it relates to the development and self-constitution of actual selves. Since participation in the divine life seems to involve loss of self in some undefined way, it makes no sense to speak of grace as strengthening the self's capacity for self-affirmation, justice toward itself, etc. Perhaps this explains the static quality of Tillich's concept of justification and the vagueness of his principles of sanctification: his explicit intentions with regard to these doctrines are in conflict with deeper currents in his thought. In any event, whatever specific applicability ideas such as acceptance or self-relatedness may have to women's experience, Tillich's doctrine of grace, like his doctrine of sin, places these categories in a context which threatens their usefulness.


## F.  Conclusions

Tillich's doctrines of sin and grace, then, are related to women's experience in a complex way and are marked by a fundamental tension. On the one hand, Tillich's concern for the nature of human selfhood generates categories for understanding and judging women's experience. On the other hand, these categories

145

are placed in the framework of a monistic ontology which is in conflict with them.

The strength of Tillich's doctrine of sin from the perspective of women's experience lies in its definition of sin as a religious rather than a moral flaw and its ability to clarify and explain many of the features of women's development in modern society. Tillich's contention that "estrangement" is a more inclusive category than pride is borne out by the fact that his comments on the relation between self-love and self-hate, the ambiguities of sacrifice, justice, and humanity speak to the pattern of underdevelopment of self we find in Lessing's protagonists and provide the vocabulary for understanding and judging it. This is one side of Tillich's doctrine of sin.

Despite the reality of his concern for sins of weakness, however, the neutrality of the term "estrangement" with respect to the "directions" of sin quickly gives way as Tillich's dominant interest in demonic, creative forms of sinfulness asserts itself. This interest stems partly from Tillich's desire to relate estrangement to the traditional categories of unbelief, hubris, and concupiscence, but it also has deeper roots in his ontology and especially his view of the coincidence of creation and the fall. His identification of self-actualization and estrangement makes it difficult to understand how or why the failure to be self-actualizing would be considered sinful at all, and thus undercuts his specific remarks on self-estrangement which are relevant to women's experience.

Not surprisingly, since the questions implicit in the human situation and the Christian answers are formulated in relation to each other, this same tension between concern for self-actualization and a monistic ontology is found in Tillich's doctrine of grace. Just as Tillich deals with self-denial as a sin, so he tries to establish the integrity of human selfhood in the experience of grace--both in terms of the continued ontological autonomy of the self and its growing capacity for self-affirmation and self-relatedness. His treatment of justification and the principles of sanctification, while too vague, provides some basis for understanding how the self-denying self can be freed for action in the world.

Here again, however, the stronger currents in Tillich's thought seem to pull in the other direction. Just as he does not provide the philosophical basis for

146

understanding sins of self-negation in the doctrine of sin, so he does not clearly explain how such sins are affected by the dynamics of acceptance. More important, the concepts of New Being and ecstasy which on the one hand seem to insure the ontological autonomy of finite beings, on the other are replete with problems and inconsistencies the effect of which is to undermine the basis for acceptance and self-relatedness altogether. The symbol New Being seems to sidestep rather than acknowledge and transcend Tillich's identification of estrangement and self-actualization. The idea of ecstasy, insofar as it is comprehensible, is weighted toward the participation side of the individualization/participation polarity. It thus contributes toward undercutting the concept of autonomous selfhood.

The total effect of Tillich's thought then is to place his concern for human self-actualization--a concern which is persistent and genuine--in the context of a vision of human life as a process of separation from and return to the unity of the divine life. Self-actualization is finally comprehensible only as estranged self-actualization which means that the failure to be self-actualizing can never convincingly be defined as sin. And all Tillich's protestations aside, reunion with the divine ground, achieved fragmentarily through grace and finally in the eschaton, seems to involve the surrender of self-actualization altogether.

Tillich's fundamental monism has been examined here in the context of his doctrines of sin and grace. Exploration of his epistomology, his concept of symbol, or his eschatology would have led to the same conclusions.[156] Similarly, while the problems in Tillich's thought have been approached here from the perspective of women's experience, the weaknesses in his theology are weaknesses in understanding human experience in all its variety. If his concentration on demonic forms of sinfulness is open to the same general sociological criticisms as Niebuhr's emphasis on pride, his failure convincingly to establish the preservation of finite individuality in the experience of grace leaves ungrounded the human experiences of unestranged individuation, growth, and change. Tillich is not unaware of these failings in his thought; he tries to deal with them. The predominant strain in his theology, however, remains as Ray Hart describes it:

> Tillich's is a radically God-centered theology. This means not only that being itself and the modes of being are asymmetrically related. It

means as well that modes of actual being are in some sense diremptions of the divine life; and that in the essential state, however eschatological it may be, actual modalities of being are sacrificed in favor of being-itself. The questions of 'estrangement' and 'return' are examined therefore in the context of an essential monism, which is to say that the ontological dialectic between unity and estrangement is weighted in favor of union. (157)

# CHAPTER FOUR

## THEOLOGY AND WOMEN'S EXPERIENCE

In this book, I have set out a definition of women's experience and then used it to criticize Reinhold Niebuhr's and Paul Tillich's doctrines of sin and grace. Although the two men claim to speak to and from universal human experience in formulating their theologies, in fact neither of them addresses fully the situation of women in western society. They do not adequately deal with "women's sin" of self-abnegation, and they do not fully explain how grace relates to the reconstitution of the self-denying self.

As I suggested in the introduction, this argument was formulated with both critical and constructive purposes in mind.[1] I hoped that criticizing theology from the perspective of women's experience would highlight problem areas requiring further consideration and perhaps provide clues as to how theology can more fully reflect women's experience. In this final chapter, I will summarize and reconsider some of the more important issues raised by Niebuhr and Tillich. Although I will not attempt to create a counter-system, I hope to leave the questions raised by this study as sharp as possible. I will then conclude with a discussion of several ways in which future attempts to include women's experience in constructive theology will have to go beyond the issues raised here and the frameworks which Niebuhr and Tillich provide.

## A.  Sin and Grace:  Conclusions

### Sin as a Religious and a Moral Flaw

Turning first to the issues revolving around the doctrine of sin, we find that the word "sin" has taken on a number of different meanings in the course of this work, not all of them in the same realm of discourse, and not all having the same relation to women's experience. The most important difference between Tillich's and Niebuhr's doctrines of sin is that Tillich depicts sin primarily as a religious failing, while Niebuhr sees it as a moral flaw. Although Niebuhr begins his discussion of sin by asserting that its moral dimension is subordinate to the religious attempt to usurp the place of God,[2] as he actually describes the nature of sin in the world, his central (ostensibly religious) category of pride seems to designate a particular moral

failing.[3]  Tillich, on the other hand, reinterprets
sin as estrangement, a concept connoting separation
from that to which one essentially belongs.  All human
existence is sinful, for existence is alienation from
the primordial unity of the divine ground.  What makes
any action sinful is not its moral quality but the
fact that it expresses (or actualizes) estrangement.

As an ontological interpretation of sin, an interpretation which deals with the preconditions of human
existence and action, Tillich's account of estrangement
is pertinent to the human situation, not just the situation of men or of women.  Insofar as existence is
the separation of human life from its divine center,
all persons are in a state of unbelief.  And insofar as
the separation of human life from the divine center
enables human life to become fully self-centered,
hubris is an equal possibility for all.  Unlike Niebuhr,
Tillich seems to provide a definition of sin which is
universally applicable.  He is able to do so, however,
only by discussing sin on a very high level of abstraction.
Estrangement defines all action because (supposedly) it
defines no one action more than any other.  The term
expresses the ontological presupposition of action or,
as Tillich acknowledges, the destiny side of the freedom/
destiny polarity.[4]

As soon as Tillich begins to talk about estrangement as realized in concrete deeds by human freedom
(sin as "act" rather than "fact"), however, he jeopard-
izes the universality of the concept through his
descriptions of the specific qualities of human action.
Estrangement is actualized actively or passively, in
deeds which are self-affirming or self-denying, etc.
The term "estrangement" may (and theoretically does)
characterize this whole range of actions, but its
applicability must be demonstrated through careful
choice of varied examples of unbelief, hubris, and concupiscence and wide-ranging description of the ambiguities of life.  In translating hubris as self-
elevation and selecting examples of hubris most of
which are instances of pride, Tillich connects estrangement with what we have described as characteristics more
likely to be associated with men than with women in
western society.  That this connection is not accidental
but is related to fundamental themes in his ontology
need not be reargued here.[5]  The point is that as long
as Tillich deals with estrangement as a kind of ontological destiny, he treats only the presupposition of
what most Christian theologians would call "sin."  As
soon as he discusses actual sin, he is forced to choose

words from the vocabulary of human action, and thus confront the problem that there are different kinds of actions which may characterize different selves in different situations.

When Niebuhr defines sin in religious terms, he defines it very differently. In fact, Niebuhr objects to Tillich's "ontologizing" the Biblical paradox of fate and freedom, arguing that it leads Tillich to emphasize the fatefulness of sin rather than the nature of human responsibility.[6] For Niebuhr, "the religious dimension of sin is man's rebellion against God, his effort to usurp the place of God."[7] He thus places sin as a religious failing firmly within the context of human action, and in such a way as to denote that sin is active; pride is not simply a matter of failing to orient the self to God, but involves establishing the self in God's place.

The claim that sin always has an active dimension is one-sided, but not in itself in conflict with women's experience. Rebellion against God may amount simply to God-forgetfulness, but absorption in the everyday, refusal to become a self can also represent deliberate flight from responsibility before God and is certainly active in the minimal sense that it involves orientation toward what is not God. From the perspective of women's experience, the main problem with Niebuhr's definition of sin is not his failure to take account of sin's passive components but his insistence that turning away from God means turning toward the self. To call this latter assumption problematic is not to deny that self-absorption or fierce or petty pride can characterize women as well as men. It is not to deny that these traits can even be fostered by women's situation. It is to maintain, however, that for many women pride is a secondary phenomenon following on self-restriction. "Women's sin" is precisely the failure to turn toward the self. The sin which involves God-forgetfulness and self-forgetfulness is not properly called "pride," even where the word is used in its religious sense.

Defining sin's religious dimension as rebellion against God and its moral dimension as pride, Niebuhr not only fails to convey the nature of women's sin, however; he actually turns it into a virtue. If self-centeredness is sin, then the sacrifices of a woman like Lessing's Kate Brown, who constantly attends to the "minuscule wants, demands, and needs" of her family to the neglect of herself, become marks of a life of traditional Christian piety. Indeed, a woman may view and

intend them that way herself. Niebuhr recognizes the
variety of motives that may shape a life of sacrifice.
He is aware of the ways in which self-sacrifice can
represent a subtle bid for power or become a tool
through which to manipulate a family.[8] But for him,
these ambiguities do not indicate a destructive element
in the nature of self-sacrifice. They simply exemplify
the paradoxical nature of grace in human history whereby
the extension of possibilities for good involves equal
extension of possibilities for evil.

If there is any part of Niebuhr's doctrine of sin
which addresses the sins of the self-denying self, it
is his category of "sensuality." Niebuhr most frequently uses the word "sensuality" to mean "the self's
undue identification with and devotion to particular
impulses and desires within the self."[9] This definition,
which he employs to establish the subordination of sensuality to pride, is not relevant to the issue of self-
abnegation. It was argued in chapter two, however, that
Niebuhr occasionally interprets sensuality more broadly,
referring to it as "an effort to escape from the freedom
and the infinite possibilities of spirit by becoming
lost in the detailed processes, activities, and interests
of existence." This definition of sensuality, taken
alongside his description of the possibilities and pitfalls of human nature as finite freedom, suggests that
the term might be applied to the multitude of strategies
through which human beings seek to avoid the responsibilities of freedom.[10] Such strategies might conceivably
include dedication of one's life to another (or others)
or submergence in the time- and choice-consuming details
of daily tasks. Thus a broad interpretation of the
category of sensuality seems to afford a way to judge
self-sacrifice which does not flow from a genuine sense
of self as "women's sin."

## Sin in its Theological Context

If we look at the broader context of Niebuhr's
thought, however, we realize that his doctrine of sin
cannot really be extended in this direction. It is not,
after all, the analysis of human life or general revelation which definitely establishes the responsible use
of human freedom but historical revelation or the action
of God. The coming of Christ discloses both the sovereignty of God over history and the final norm of human
nature within history, and that norm is sacrificial love.[11]
This means, however, that so far from excluding self-
sacrifice, Christian freedom is ultimately defined by it.
The redeemed self, according to Niebuhr, strives to

approximate in all its relations the "impossible possibility" which is sacrificial love. Insofar as the self must be a self in order to sacrifice itself, its selfhood too, he insists, is a by-product of self-sacrifice.[12] From the perspective of women's experience, the value of the concept of sensuality is thus undermined by the wider context of Niebuhr's thought.[13]

It is not only in Niebuhr's case that a particular theological category is affected by the framework in which it is set. Tension between specific concepts and larger context characterizes Tillich's thought as well. In Tillich's case, however, the tension lies within and between two levels of concern for human selfhood rather than between the doctrines of sin and grace. On the ontological level, Tillich provides a universal definition of sin and categories useful for understanding the development of human selfhood. First, sin as estrangement is actualized in acts of self-sacrifice as well as self-affirmation so that the problem of defining self-sacrifice as sin is solved.[14] Second, Tillich's description of the individualization/participation polarity supports Niebuhr's point that full individualization is attainable only through relations with others, without implying that those relations must have a sacrificial character.

On the existential level too, while Tillich shows a preference for creative, demonic forms of sinfulness, he deals with the issues of self-relatedness and self-constitution in the sphere of human action. His treatment of self-love and self-hate, the ambiguities of self-sacrifice, the norms of justice and humanity, and their relevance to women's experience are discussed in chapter three.[15] All these categories demonstrate Tillich's recognition that an underdeveloped sense of self can, like pridefulness, issue from the self-disruption which is a result of estrangement.

Tillich's account of the sins of self-denial is problematic, however, in that it is not clearly grounded in his thought as a whole. His existential concerns are not well integrated with his ontology. Reading some of the sermons in which Tillich deals with the experience of self-estrangement, one has the feeling that his insights relevant to women's experience emerge from particular interests in depth psychology combined with keen observation of the human situation.[16] They can be appreciated for what they are but since they conflict with his identification of creation and the fall,[17] they cannot be forced into a systematic context. His specific remarks are not thereby less important, but they are less useful as the basis of a consistent account of the problems of self-abnegation. Niebuhr's category of sensuality is thoroughly grounded in his anthropology but would have to be combined with a new doctrine of grace to bear fruit from the perspective of women's experience. Tillich's discussion of the ambiguities of self-relatedness, on the other hand, corresponds to elements in his doctrine of grace, but it is difficult to reconcile either of them with the wider context of his theology.

## Sin and Human Creatureliness

Neither theologian, then, provides us with a doctrine of sin, firmly grounded in a coherent philosophical anthropology, which recognizes self-exaltation and self-abnegation as equal dangers of the human spirit. Happily, though, Tillich is helpful in finding a way beyond one deficiency in Niebuhr's doctrine of sin--Niebuhr's generally negative view of human creatureliness. There are at least two difficulties with Niebuhr's conception of human naturalness. First of all, since women have generally been identified with nature, a sharp division between spirit and nature often results in a correspondingly sharp distinction between male and female nature--a distinction which is not altogether absent from Niebuhr's thought.[18]  Second, this view of nature does not provide the basis for appreciating human responsibility toward nature or for adequately understanding the interconnection of human destiny with the destiny of the natural world.

Tillich, moving in a very different direction on this issue, establishes the interconnection of humanity and nature in both ontological and ethical spheres.[19] His category "life," the most inclusive ontological classification of the Systematic Theology, embraces existence in all its "dimensions" from the inorganic to the historical, and in such a way as to emphasize the unity rather than the conflicts between the different realms. The metaphor "dimension" itself is meant to point to the fact that all dimensions are potentially real in any one dimension and are actually real in the historical dimension which is also the human one. Tillich also takes seriously the many biblical passages using natural analogies for human experiences and connecting the tragedy and salvation of nature with human freedom. Human freedom precipitates the transition from essence to existence for nature as well as humanity, and irresponsible use of human freedom within existence

results in the devastation of nature and the alienation
of human beings from the natural realm.[20] Insofar as
the association of women with nature would foster their
sense of connection with the natural world, Tillich
articulates women's experience in this area far more
successfully than Niebuhr does.

## Grace as Justification

If we accept Niebuhr's warning that a doctrine of
grace is meaningful only if the doctrine of sin to
which it responds accurately portrays the human situation, and if we accept Tillich's statement that theological questions and answers must be formulated in relation
to one another, we may make a prediction:  a doctrine
of sin which is inadequate will probably be correlated
with an inadequate doctrine of grace.[21] Certainly this
prediction is accurate in the case of Niebuhr and
Tillich.  Yet because their doctrines of grace impinge
on several related areas of theology (e.g. Christology,
doctrine of the Spirit, doctrine of the church), tracing
the problems with their arguments is a complex task.
We will begin here with the center of the doctrine of
grace and follow as it leads into other areas.

The heart of the Protestant doctrine of grace, the
message that God has declared sinners just despite their
sinfulness, can be developed in (at least) two different
directions.  The theologian can emphasize either the
forgiveness of sin or the forgiveness of sin.  In the
first case, the element of judgement stands in the fore-
ground, the reminder that the sinner is accepted despite
persistence in the strategies of sin.  In the second
case, the experience of God's merciful acceptance is the
central reality.  While both these elements are present
in the thought of both Niebuhr and Tillich, Niebuhr
focuses on the former aspect of justification, Tillich
on the latter.

The importance of justification as judgement in
Niebuhr's theology stems from the fact that grace is a
response to the sin of pride.  The sinful self which
remains locked and centered in itself, unable to enter
into loving relations with others, must be shattered
in the very center of its being through confrontation
with the power and holiness of God.  Finally aware of
its true source and center, the self which trusted only
itself must be "crucified with Christ" and destroyed.[22]
Though Niebuhr also speaks of justification as the
"power of God's love over man, annulling his sin by His
mercy,"[23] the image of the judge standing over against

the self, breaking into its willful self-enclosure, generally prevails. "Without the radical sense of judgement in biblical religion it is always possible [for the self] to find some scheme of self-justification," he says.[24]

Niebuhr's doctrine of grace addresses the self which, through its own self-absorption, contradicts the love which is the law of its being. This is the self which needs to be "broken open" and thus opened up to others. His view of grace does not address the self which may spend its life in service to others but which cannot meet them as subjects because it has not become a subject itself. It is meaningless to say that this self can become a self only through being shattered and turned to others, for its sin is precisely that it has no self to shatter. The self-abnegating self may be in need of grace as surely as the prideful self, but the dynamics of grace must be understood in a different way.

Tillich's interpretation of justification as acceptance provides this necessary alternative interpretation only ambiguously. His doctrine of grace focuses not on a God over against the self judging it, but on the self's participation in that which accepts it despite its unacceptability. The primacy of the participation/acceptance motif in Tillich's thought is underlined by his insistence on the priority of regeneration over justification. The self is able to accept justification (i.e. accept that it is accepted despite being unacceptable) only by virtue of having been taken up into the New Being. Justification is the paradoxical, "in spite of" character of participation in the New Being. If this interpretation of justification seems to threaten the traditional understanding of the forgiveness of sins altogether, it must be remembered that Tillich's doctrine of sin is not concerned with sins but with Sin as estrangement. Grace is therefore primarily reunion.

In relation to women's experience, the positive aspect of this interpretation of justification is the promise of healing it brings to the sin of self-denial. Since estrangement is the source of all self-disruption, one side of the experience of reunion should be the possibility of genuine self-love and self-relatedness. Able to affirm and become itself, the accepted self would be freed for creative action in the world.

But while these elements are theoretically included

156

in Tillich's conception of justification, his doctrine is actually quite static. Unlike Niebuhr, who sees the shattering of the self as opening the self toward something, Tillich does not seem to view acceptance as inherently future oriented. In accepting acceptance, the self surrenders all of its goodness to the sole activity of God in bringing about reunion. Not only can no moral, intellectual, or other work secure the self's acceptance--this is of course the meaning of justification--but no work need follow from it. The self must simply accept the fact that it is accepted. The question arises: is this an appropriate response to the self whose sin is the failure to act, the failure to become a self?

The importance of this issue should not be minimized. One can point to sources of Tillich's quietism which are peculiar to him, correlating his view of justification with aspects of his ontology and deficiencies in his doctrine of sin.[25] The question remains, however, as to whether the Protestant doctrine of justification per se is a response to the sin of pride and therefore more relevant to men's than to women's experience.[26] Where sin is perverse inaction rather than self-assertion, does the message that the self is forgiven despite persistence in sin foster a passivity which is women's real problem? Perhaps one could formulate a doctrine of justification which would judge the failure to become a self and open up into a process of self-actualization (in the way that Niebuhr's doctrine of grace opens up into the possibility of self-sacrifice). Perhaps, however, one must be a bit Pelagian to be faithful to women's experience!

## Grace as Sanctification

Whatever the problems with the notion of justification, balancing it with a strong doctrine of sanctification does not in itself solve the problem of relevance to women's experience. Such relevance depends on the meaning sanctification is assigned. Where, as in Niebuhr's theology, sanctification transforms the prideful self, relating the paradox of grace to a wide variety of situations in the world does not increase grace's applicability to the sins of self-abnegation.

Sanctification for Niebuhr is the "power of God in man," conquering "in principle" the principle of sinful self-centeredness.[27] Where confrontation with the power of God shatters the sinful self, the real self is fulfilled into new life beyond itself. It is now able

157

to live "in and for others, in the general orientation
of loyalty to, and love of, God." Yet it is not the
self which wholly subordinates its will to the will
of God, Niebuhr says, exegeting Galatians 2:20, but
the Christ of intention which lives within it. Within
historical existence, the contradiction between human
self-will and the divine purpose is never completely
overcome. Grace is always simultaneously sanctification and justification--the "power of God in man" and
the "power of God over man," judging and forgiving continued human pridefulness.[28]

Sanctification does not really extend, then, the
realm of experience to which Niebuhr's doctrine of
grace applies. In principle, the "real" self which is
reconstituted after the shattering of the prideful self
is a whole self--a finite free self orienting itself
to God, its source and center of being. In fact, however, just as Niebuhr's doctrine of justification emphasizes the destruction of the self with pretensions to
God-likeness, so the center of his doctrine of sanctification is the self's acknowledgement of its limited
freedom and creaturely finitude. The dynamics of the
responsible use of freedom, the understanding of which
is so important to the sin of failing to become a
self, is more or less ignored. And insofar as an account of freedom can be inferred from Niebuhr's total
position, one has to assume that the norm of freedom
would be sacrificial love.

The narrowness of Niebuhr's doctrine of grace,
springing partly from the fact that grace brings healing
only to the sin of pride, is augmented by another problem. Niebuhr argues that the cross not only discloses
the true meaning of human life, but makes available the
resources to fulfill that meaning. However, he does not
adequately describe the way in which these resources
operate for the self's healing.[29] Niebuhr talks about
the self's acquisition of a power not its own which
enables it to become what it ought to be. But exactly
what this accession of power involves and how it comes
about is never explained, for Niebuhr lacks both a
doctrine of the church and of the Holy Spirit. The
effect of these rather major omissions is to leave the
impression that Niebuhr stresses justification at the
expense of sanctification. His best efforts to balance
the two aspects of grace notwithstanding, what emerges
from his application of the paradox of grace to experience is precisely the continued contradiction of nature
and grace and thus the need for continued judgement.
This in turn increases the difficulties with Niebuhr's

doctrine of grace from the perspective of women's experience.  Despite his insistence on the reality of sanctification, the image of the shattering (and reshattering)
of the old self remains predominant in his thought.

Tillich, in contrast to Niebuhr, can hardly be accused of slighting sanctification or bypassing the
doctrine of the Holy Spirit.  If sanctification is
defined as "life process under the impact of the
Spirit,"[30] the whole fourth part of his Systematic
Theology might be considered an explication of that
doctrine.  Tillich defines the operation of the divine
Spirit in the human spirit in terms of the "ecstatic"
movement of the human spirit which from one perspective
is called faith, from another love.  Under the impact
of the Spiritual Presence, the human spirit is driven
out of itself, into a successful self-transcendence.
It is grasped by and taken into the transcendent unity
of unambiguous life.[31]

The aspect of Tillich's doctrine of sanctification
most relevant to women's experience is the criterion
of increasing relatedness.  The answer to the self-
hate and disruption which characterize the sinful self,
the concept of self-relatedness elaborates the positive
features of the category of acceptance.  Tillich views
self-relatedness not simply as a by-product of relatedness to others, but as an important fruit of the
reuniting power of agape.  Freed from self-humiliation
and self-elevation, the self which participates in the
transcendent unity of unambiguous life is (potentially)
just toward itself and others.

Important as the principle of relatedness is as a
response to self-abnegation, it is partially undercut
by the same tensions which characterize other parts of
Tillich's thought.  Aggravating the static quality of
Tillich's concept of justification, for example, is
the vagueness of his principle of relatedness.  If the
principle provides a basis for the self's new relations
to itself and the world, it does so without defining
the nature of these relations.  Tillich says that "the
principles of sanctification make the basic manifestation of the Spiritual Presence [as faith and love] concrete for the progress toward maturity."[32]  But unlike
Niebuhr, who applies the paradox of grace to numerous
situations in the world, Tillich provides little idea
of what growth in self-relatedness (or any other principle) means in terms of human action.  Since, unfor-
tunately, the forces and pressures which form women's
lives are not abstract at all, general principles are

easily applied in ways which only serve to reinforce the status quo.

Still more important, Tillich's description of self-relatedness, like his analysis of self-disruption, seems to float in his theology. Not only is it unclear just why relatedness should be one of the four principles of sanctification (Are Tillich's categories exhaustive? Are they just interesting? Where do they come from?), but it seems to conflict with Tillich's emphasis on the mystical/participatory aspects of grace. Since the ontological autonomy of finite selves is threatened by Tillich's definition of ecstatic self-transcendence, it makes no sense to describe transcendence as leading to increasing self-relatedness and self-affirmation on the existential level.[33]

## Grace and Christology

The norms of Niebuhr's and Tillich's theologies do not emerge in a vacuum, but express their understanding of Christian revelation. No explication of their doctrines of grace is complete, therefore, which does not touch on their Christologies. For Niebuhr, certainly, Christ is the ultimate criterion of the life of grace. The content of Christ's life and particularly his death on the cross define "the final perfection of man in history,... the perfection of sacrificial love." Sacrificial love is action within history which transcends history in that it is not justified by history; but it is necessary to history in that the mutual love which is the highest historical good is impossible if it is the intended goal of action. Sacrificial love, as the initiator of mutual love, is the "tangent toward 'eternity' in the field of historical ethics" or the "impossible possibility" of human life.[34]

Niebuhr's description of the relevance of the agape of the cross to the Christian interpretation of history, discussed in chapter two, need not be recapitulated here.[35] The interesting feature of his treatment of the cross is its congruity with his understanding of the doctrines of sin and grace. The sacrificial love of the cross is the norm directed at pride and self-centeredness, and through Christ's death the power of human pridefulness is broken. We need not raise the question of which doctrine determines the others. Niebuhr's analysis of sin is certainly colored by his Christian presuppositions; his fascination with certain types of sinfulness undoubtedly affects his Christology; and both feed into his doctrine of grace. The point is that these different areas support one another in such a way that the introduction of changes in the doctrines of sin or grace would need to be tied to an argument for a different understanding of the cross. While a new Christology cannot simply be invented to meet the needs of experience, it is possible to argue that alternative interpretations of the cross both meet the test of faithfulness to biblical sources and are more relevant to a variety of experiences Niebuhr neglects.[36]

Tillich's Christology is also correlated with his doctrines of sin and grace. Like them, it first appears to solve the problems of particularity inherent in Niebuhr's theology, and then on closer examination reveals problems and contradictions of its own. Tillich's Christology gives the impression of universal applicability, for he argues that the most important aspect of the biblical picture of Jesus as the Christ is his continual surrender of himself and everything finite in him. This means that the followers of Jesus too are liberated from the authority of the individual details of his life. Grace does not have the character of imitiatio Christi but of participation in the New Being (the unity of essential and existential being) which is the being of Jesus as the Christ.[37] Since all persons are estranged, it follows that all seek the ontological healing manifest in him.

This Christology, however, is plagued by the same inconsistencies found in other parts of Tillich's system. Aside from the ontological confusions possibly involved in the very notion of the New Being,[38] the weight Tillich gives Jesus' surrender of his finitude is the source of several difficulties. First, it may be a factor contributing to the problematic vagueness of his doctrine of sanctification. The nonbinding character of the biblical picture of Jesus' life means the picture provides no authoritative model for the sanctified life.[39] Second, the concept of surrender, like that of self-sacrifice, is of questionable relevance to the self which has not claimed divinity for its finite selfhood but failed to become a self. Third, the idea of surrender raises the same ontological problems as the concept of ecstasy.[40] Tillich says that the final revelation (i.e. Jesus as the Christ) negates itself "without losing itself,"[41] but since his language leaves the impression that unity with God in some sense entails the dissolution of individual beings, it is not clear what this statement means. Tillich's Christology, like Niebuhr's, supports and is supported by the doctrines of sin and grace and would have to change along with them.

B.　Theology and Women's Experience:　Conclusions

　　　This is the end of our critical study of Niebuhr's
and Tillich's doctrines of sin and grace.　As this book
has argued and this summary of their thought suggests,
they present us with an array of categories and principles which do not add up to a coherent account of sin
and grace addressing both pride and self-abnegation.
Since categories in their thought which are relevant to
women's experience are not supported by the context of
their theologies as a whole, anyone wishing to use
these categories to write theology from the perspective
of women's experience would have to integrate them into
a coherent theological framework of her/his own making.

　　　But the feminist theologian would face an even
larger task than this suggests.　This book, as a case
study of certain doctrines and thinkers, illustrates
only the type of questions a constructive feminist
thinker might want to raise.　Someone sitting down to
write theology from the perspective of women's experience would have to consider both other doctrines that
affect and are affected by the doctrines of sin and
grace, and other aspects of women's experience that
might teach us something about our relation to ultimate reality.　I will conclude this work then, acknowledging its limitations, by mentioning some issues
in each area that warrant further critical and constructive reflection--first a significant doctrine,
then some matters pertaining to women's experience.

The Doctrine of God

　　　The doctrines of sin and grace, because of their
explicit connection with human experience, are immediately
accessible to criticism from the perspective of women's
experience.　These doctrines, however, are indissolubly
connected with the doctrine of God.　On the one hand,
the doctrine of God affects theology's relevance to
women's experience indirectly, for who God is determines
the boundaries, possibilities, and imperatives of human
life, and reflection on the nature of sin and grace always involves implicit and explicit assumptions concerning
the nature of God.　On the other hand, insofar as human
images of God draw on various aspects of male and female
sexuality and sex roles, the doctrine of God reflects and
conveys more directly certain attitudes toward women and
men.

　　　At several points in this study, disagreements between Niebuhr and Tillich concerning the nature of grace

were traced to differences in their doctrines of sin.[42]
Though we left the argument there, these differences in
their views of sin also require explanation. They in
turn can be traced to their fundamentally different
images of the divine/human relation. These images,
which are differently related to women's experience, are
discernible in the doctrines of sin and grace which presuppose them.

The fundamental image of God in Tillich's thought
is perfectly, if unintentionally, captured by Erich
Neumann as he sketches one aspect of the Great Mother
archetype. Neumann writes:

> As elementary character we designate the aspect
> of the Feminine that as the Great Round, the
> Great Container, tends to hold fast to everything
> that springs from it and to surround it like an
> eternal substance. Everything born of it be-
> longs to it and remains subject to it; and even
> if the individual becomes independent, the Arch-
> etypal Feminine relativizes this independence
> into a nonessential variant of her own perpetual
> being. (43)

This Great Mother image corresponds to the emphasis on
unity and reunion so characteristic of Tillich's theology. As Tillich himself suggests in reconsidering the
doctrine of the trinity, the concept of God as ground of
being, symbolically understood, "points to the mother-
quality of giving birth, carrying and embracing, and, at
the same time, of calling back, resisting independence
of the created, and swallowing."[44]

Interestingly, Tillich's conception of the ground
of being as Great Mother is the source of both negative
and positive aspects of his thought in relation to
women's experience. The image controls first of all
his reinterpretation of sin as estrangement. As Tillich
says many times, the notion of estrangement presupposes
that the participation of beings in the ground from which
they are separated—the experience of unity or contain-
ment—is more fundamental than the experience of separation. It is, in fact, the basic reality of human life.
The human decision for self-actualization is identical
with the fall as the origin of estrangement because the
independence of finite beings threatens the hold of
the ground on all that is. The Great Mother is thus
the unifying image of that strand in Tillich's thought
which sees self-actualization in any form as a manifestation of sin. On the other hand, the image is also a

source of those categories in his theology--self-love, justice, humanity--which are most relevant to women's experience. They are generated in part by his need and desire to account for the emergence of finite beings from their containing ground--a need which is rooted in the power of the Great Mother image.

In his doctrine of grace, the priority of regeneration over justification is an effect of the same symbol. The primary quality of grace is not the judgement or forgiveness of a God who is over against the self but participation in the ground to which one essentially belongs. Once again, the mother image both unifies elements in Tillich's thought which suggest that participation involves the surrender of individuality, and engenders opposing categories. Tillich, aware of the problems his image of God involves, insists that participation does not compromise the independence of created beings. God is not a "foolish mother," he says, who keeps her children "in a state of enforced innocence and enforced participation in her own life."[45] Many aspects of his thought suggest otherwise, however. On the symbolic level, the fundamental contradiction running through Tillich's thought may be viewed as a conflict between two different types of mothering. To what extent is God a mother who wills and fosters the estrangement, and thus the growth, of her children, and to what extent is she a smothering mother whose children leave their divine home without permission only to be brought back again into the transcendent unity of unambiguous life?

In strong contrast to Tillich, Niebuhr conceives of the divine/human relation in such a way that the issue of the independence of finite beings never arises: it is presupposed. God is not primarily the ground of being but a creator, judge, and redeemer characterized by will, freedom, wisdom, justice and mercy--a personality confronting human persons who are finite freedom. It is not the unity of the early mother/child relation which defines the relationship between God and humanity, but the greater autonomy of the father/child relation, or the greater distance of king and subject. Niebuhr's God is the "divine king and father" Tillich rejects, the God who repeatedly forgives the stubborn pridefulness of "his subjects and children."[46]

It is in the context of this understanding of the divine/human relation as a relation between persons that sin and grace are described as usurpation of the place of God and subordination of human will to the will of

164

God, rather than as estrangement and reunion. More concerned with the categories of freedom and will than Tillich is, Niebuhr depicts sin more as active rebellion than as tragic destiny. "Sin is the unwillingness of man to acknowledge his creatureliness and dependence upon God and his effort to make his own life independent and secure."[47] Grace, correspondingly, is God's judgement and forgiveness of wayward humanity, and humanity's love of and loyalty to the God who is over against it as its source and center. History is not a process of separation and return to the divine life but a dramatic struggle between humanity and God in which God has the resources of power and mercy to overcome human rebellion. The struggle comes to an end not in reunion but in the establishment of right order in a relation between separate beings.[48]

Niebuhr's theology exhibits a correlation between symbolism and gender of God-language that is not found in Tillich's thought. Both men use masculine pronouns to refer to God, but Niebuhr also images God in terms of authority, power, initiative, and creativity--terms borrowed from the male side of the stereotypic masculine/feminine sex polarity. Congruent with these differences in imagery, Niebuhr conceives of the divine/human relation not along the lines of Tillich's whole/part model but as hierarchal. For Niebuhr, the primary characteristic of the proper human attitude toward God is obedience. "Man...is set under the ordering will of God." "Each individual life is subjected to the will of God. It is obedience to the divine will which establishes the right relation between the human will in its finiteness and the whole world as ruled by God."[49] Although Niebuhr never says this, his view of the relationship between humanity and God echoes the culturally sanctioned relation of male and female in society, humanity playing an essentially feminine role before God.

The problems with this conception of the divine/human relation are both political and more directly theological. Politically, images of God as sovereign male both reinforce notions of male superiority and male dominance current in the social order and limit the power to envisage alternative political structures.[50] Although the political message of such imagery is generally implicit and therefore largely invisible, during recent battles in the Episcopal church over the ordination of women, it was broadcast loud and clear. Priests opposing ordination tapped the hidden message of male God-language to legitimate exclusion of women from leadership in the church. "The Christian cultic minister," said one churchman using a common conservative argument, "symbolizes the fact that the church exists through the initiating act of God as transcending nature, and this symbolism is normally adequately expressed in the male priesthood."[51]

Theologically, imaging the divine/human relation as hierarchal with a male God in the superordinate position may foster a conception of human life which ultimately undermines the relationship to God it seeks to preserve. In discussing Niebuhr's doctrine of grace, we argued that sacrificial obedience, viewed not as an "impossible possibility," but concretely through the lens of women's experience, is destructive of human selves. Sacrifice, not balanced by self-consolidation and creation, can drain selves to the point where they are incapable of entering into genuine relationships with themselves or others.[52] If the model of sacrificial obedience is destructive on an inter-human level, however, it may also be destructive as a model for the human relationship to God. Here too, sacrifice which flows from weakness rather than creativity and strength may hurt the giver and be worthless to the one who receives.[53] The damaging consequences of Niebuhr's doctrine of grace thus can be used to question his image of the divine/human relation which corresponds to it.

The problems with male God-language just described do not flow simply from the use of masculine pronouns but from a total complex of masculine images. Tillich's theology should remind us of this. Despite his (occasionally jarring) references to God the mother as "he," it is doubtful that his doctrine of God could be used to buttress arguments against the ordination of women or for hierarchal structures of any kind. On the other hand, Tillich's theology should provide warning that the difficulties with male imagery will not be solved simply by replacing it with female imagery. If a hierarchal model is stunting to human selfhood, a part/whole model does not allow for the genuine independence of the self at all. From the perspective of women's experience, neither Niebuhr's nor Tillich's doctrine of God can ground an adequate understanding of sin and grace.

These differences between Niebuhr and Tillich on the doctrine of God demonstrate the relevance of the doctrine to the critique of sin and grace. But they also suggest the importance of the doctrine of God to any constructive theology which would want to take

166

account of women's experience. Conceptions of the nature of God shape to a very large extent conceptions of the problems and possibilities of human life, and reflect and convey specific attitudes toward women and men.[54] To what degree does the use of mother images in the doctrine of God necessarily suggest divine resistance to human independence? Does this theme in Tillich's thought (and Neumann's analysis of the archetype) perhaps arise out of a culturally determined and distorted understanding of motherhood? If so, is the image rendered useless by its cultural associations, or can it be combined with an adequate account of the integrity of human selfhood?[55] Are the images of God as male and as person inseparably related? Does the image of God as male person necessarily involve a hierarchal model of the divine/human relation? Does a hierarchal model require that sin be defined as pride, and grace as judgement and obedience? What are other sources of models of the divine/human relation besides the parent/child relation? What problems and possibilities do they involve? These questions, suggested by the theologies of Niebuhr and Tillich, are basic to envisaging alternative conceptions of the divine.

## Sin, Grace, and Community

Remaining within the framework of Niebuhr's and Tillich's thought has been very limiting in that it has led us to speak of sin and grace almost exclusively in individual terms. With the exception of a brief discussion of Tillich's concept of destiny, we have left aside the relation of the doctrines to the social context of human life. It is impossible to do justice to women's experience, however, without taking into account its social horizon. As chapter one should have made clear, "women's sin" is in large measure a product of social, cultural forces. While each woman has to define her own relation to her culture's expectations and in this sense may be said to freely affirm her cultural destiny, the horizon of her struggle with social expectations is set by her society; it provides a fixed range of choices. If women's experience is not determined by cultural definitions, no single woman is free from them. It then distorts experience to speak of "women's sin" either as some flaw inherent in women or as something which "springs up in" or is "chosen" by a significant percentage of women viewed as isolated individuals.

We have sought to avoid the misrepresentation that self-denial is a flaw inherent in women by carefully

167

defining women's experience. The suggestion that self-denial characterizes women as individuals, on the other hand, has to some extent been forced on us by the decision to criticize Niebuhr and Tillich from within their own theological frameworks. Insofar as they deal with sin and grace as individual experiences, we have tried to show that there are aspects of individual experience which they leave untreated. Thus, we have adopted their vocabulary of sin which too often seems to "blame the victim" and which shows too little awareness of the ways in which sin--or "women's sin"--in any event, is a product of social experience. Similarly, grace too has been viewed as something that transforms the individual, as if individual transformation were possible apart from social transformation--and as if grace were not understood individually at the expense of the social context.[56]

This may sound like an odd criticism of Tillich, who defines the individual experience of grace as participation in the universally New Being, and an especially odd criticism of Niebuhr, who is so attentive to the social applicability of Christian thought. Neither theologian, however, defines sin or grace in terms which are fundamentally social. Thus Niebuhr, for all that he continually deals with political realities, is more concerned with the social <u>effects</u> of sin than its social <u>origins</u>. His account of the dynamics of group pride <u>in The Nature and Destiny of Man</u>, for example, does not probe the ways in which individual pride emerges in a social context.[57] Pride is the <u>individual</u> effort to obscure the reality of human finitude, and group pride is first of all an aggregate of <u>individual</u> attitudes which then gains a certain power over the individual. Similarly, Niebuhr quite legitimately understands the sins of pride and sensuality to be rooted in human nature as finite freedom; without his account of human nature, the social context of sin would be incomprehensible. When he explains how sin inevitably but responsibly comes to be actualized, however, he entirely ignores the social dimension of original sin.[58] Pride is not understood dialectically as cause but also product of a competitive society. And more important from the perspective of women's experience, the pride of the powerful is not seen as a cause of sensuality (understood in its broader sense) in the powerless.[59]

Since Niebuhr sees sin as, in the first instance, the individual's turning away from God, he understands grace as the shattering of the individual self and the restoration of its right relationship to God. The nature of this right relation is immediately socially interpreted by him. It is manifest in a life lived with and for others, in a broad tolerance of the "truth" of others, and in the effort to extend the norms and principles of justice in the never-ending attempt to approximate the ideal of sacrificial love. The grace which expresses itself in the social context, however, is not adequately understood as developing in or mediated through a social context. It is the work of God in the individual who is then freed for action in the world. This emphasis on individual experience is party a product of Niebuhr's representation of the divine/human relation as a person to person relation. But his neglect of the social context of the doctrine of grace is reinforced by one aspect of his thought and contradicted by another. On the one hand, Niebuhr's distrust of collective egotism, which he qualifies only in his last book, makes it difficult for him to see the social sphere as a sphere of common grace.[60] On the other hand, his statements that love for others rises partly out of loving and being loved lead one to expect an account of the relation of grace to human relations which is not forthcoming.[61]

Tillich's interpretation of sin as estrangement, for all that it stresses the destiny pole of sin, provides less of an account of the social dimension of sinfulness. While the concept of destiny certainly can be used to illuminate the social factors affecting "women's sin," Tillich himself is concerned with estrangement as <u>ontological</u> destiny. His description of the origins of estrangement, so far from dealing with social context, precedes and grounds the possibility of social relations between finite beings, while his discussion of sin as act considers individual unbelief, <u>hubris</u>, and concupiscence in the same way that Niebuhr considers individual pride. The fact that every act actualizes a universal destiny of estrangement does not alter the individual character of individual action.

The same problem marks Tillich's doctrine of grace. The statement that individual salvation is participation in a cosmic event embracing all dimensions of life seems to be an ontological assertion concerning the nature of the New Being which has no discernible implications for the individual nature of grace. Tillich's insistence that human salvation is linked to the salvation of nature, for example, does not lead him to reflect on the connections between humanity and nature in the state of grace or on the way in which grace might alter human responsibility toward nature. What is more revealing, in discussing sanctification as increasing relatedness, Tillich says that "only a relation which is inherent in all other relations, and which can exist even without them, [can conquer loneliness, self-seclusion, and hostility]."[62] Despite the universal transforming power of the New Being, in other words, it is the participation of the isolated individual in the transcendent unity of unambiguous life which makes relations with others possible; relations with others are not an inseparable element of such participation. Niebuhr too implies that proper orientation toward God precedes genuine relations with others, but he sees grace as immediately manifest in the social order. Perhaps because participation swallows all forms of finitude, Tillich deals with neither the social context nor the social implications of grace.

## Sin, Grace, and Community in Women's Experience

Some ways in which neglect of the social context of sin and grace distorts women's experience may be illustrated through brief discussion of the current women's movement, for the movement is an important source of the communal experience of sin and grace. Becoming involved in the women's movement means moving from isolation as a woman to community. It means moving from defensiveness about one's life choices, to a reluctant recognition of hurt, to a deep and radical questioning of the premises from which one has lived one's life.[63] Through consciousness-raising, women become aware of both the social context of sin and their own collusion with it, and the possibilities for new individual and communal life.

Awareness of the social nature of sin comes through the central experience of the consciousness-raising process--the experience of the bankruptcy of sex-role conditioning and all its supporting institutions, or the "nothingness" of the patriarchal structures in terms of which women have been asked to define their lives.[64] This experience releases anger, the dual nature of which corresponds to the dialectic of compulsion and freedom in the Christian doctrine of sin, but gives sin a thoroughly social interpretation.[65] On the one hand, women are angry at the social structures which define and constrict their lives. The different socialization of boys and girls, the schooling which continues a process begun in infancy, the institutions of church, society, and family all seem to have conspired to prevent women from making meaningful self-determining choices. Getting married, having children, making certain career choices--decisions which at one time seemed to be real, now seem to have been decided by forces entirely beyond individual control. On the other hand, precisely because women recognize the processes of socialization for the first time, they also now for the first time appear as changeable. Anger is directed, therefore, not only at society, but also at the self which failed to see the hollowness of the path laid before it. The individual caught up in destructive social structures feels herself responsible for not having envisioned an alternative life course, for having "chosen" the choices into which she was channeled. Moreover, co-operation with hated social structures is felt to extend into the present. Clear perception of the lost opportunities and confining decisions of the past is just the beginning of a lifetime of questioning and requestioning rejected assumptions which are hard to overcome.[66]

These concurrent feelings of hopelessness and responsibility in relation to past and present might induce despair instead of "conversion" were it not that the experiences are sustained in a communal context, a context of hearing and of being heard. One comes to the experience of nothingness through receiving openly the words and stories of other women and having one's own story in turn received and affirmed by them. Since the need for speech arises out of the shared experience of the breakdown of all old authorities, no one's story is too unimportant to be heard. In and beyond the confrontation with nothingness is an experience of acceptance by and commonality with others which is an experience of grace. Nelle Morton puts it this way:

> Stripped of every old prop, of every necessary measure to shore up the old ego, [each woman is] able to go in all her agony directly to the other women present. In receiving the speaker (who [touches] the quick of their existence) they [hear] the speaker speak for them to the extent that they, in turn, [are] able to receive themselves. They [are] able to relate to one another out of their whole selves rather than partially through the mind alone, or through the emotions alone. (67)

This experience of grace is an experience of "turning" with both individual and social implications. The woman who, having seen the non-being of social structures,

171

feels herself a whole person is called upon to become the person she is in that moment. The discontinuity of the experience of wholeness with her previous development means that she must work slowly and painfully through the concrete changes her new vision entails. Yet she cannot become a new person without working for the transformation of a society in which women and men are socialized into roles which prevent each sex from appropriating the important human qualities of the other. The need for and possibility of personal and social transformation is discerned in the context of community, and the continuing process of questioning, growth, and change remains collective and is aimed at the collective.

The experience of turning, however, changes more than one's attitudes toward self and society; it alters one's relation to the cosmos. Richard R. Niebuhr, in his discussion of gladness in Experiential Religion, conveys perfectly the experience of grace which is also an experience of joy. "Rejoicing," he says, "entails consciousness of liberation into the stream of life, a sense of collectedness, a feeling of union of one's own power with power and energy itself, and finally a sense of effectiveness and of recognition as an agent in a human commonwealth that transcends the present."[68] The experience of the divine/human relation which underlies this feeling of joy is an experience neither of subordination nor participation which threatens the boundaries of the individual self. It is best expressed in words using the prefix "co"--co-creating, co-shaping, co-stewardship; and in non-objectifying process words, aliveness, changing, creating, challenging, opening, confronting, loving, pushing, etc.[69] These words convey the renunciation and transcendence of the self-denial which is "women's sin." The self comes to this experience of grace through the surrender of everything which defined the old self;[70] it does so, however, only to receive itself back again. The experience of grace is not the experience of the sole activity of God, but the experience of the emergence of the "I" as co-creator--albeit through participation in the creativity of God. God comes to be known through community as the one who sustains the self in community. Relatedness to God is expressed through the never-ending journey toward self-creation within community, and through the creation of ever wider communities, including both other human beings and the world.[71]

# Conclusion

I return at the end of this book to a concrete discussion of women's experience in order to reaffirm that
theology will begin to speak fully to this long slighted
area of experience only through conscious appropriation
of women's experience in all its particularity.  The
fact that neglect of women's experience always involves
neglect of some aspect of human experience does not mean
that theology can move directly from preoccupation with
male experience to concern for "universal human experience."  This is in part a historical judgement.  Maleness and humanity have too long been identified for
"the feminine" and women's experience to be incorporated
in the doctrine of God and theological anthropology other
than deliberately.  But one may also ask whether there
is any "universal human experience" and, if there is,
to what extent theology ought to be concerned with it.

In the introduction to this work, I said that I
would not be examining the limits of and warrants for
theological anthropology generally but calling more
specifically for theology's inclusion of women's experience.  It is interesting to note as we conclude, however,
that the significance of the thought of Niebuhr and
Tillich seems to be at least partly rooted in their
(unacknowledged) blending of the universal and particular
in human experience.  If there are structures (or presuppositions) of experience which may be universal, they
are actualized in different ways by different cultures
and different groups within a single culture.  Categories
in Niebuhr's and Tillich's analyses of human nature which
might be considered universal (Niebuhr's finite freedom,
Tillich's ontological elements) form the groundwork for
their discussion of particular features of human experience.  As soon as Niebuhr begins to consider the dangers
of finite freedom, for example, he no longer describes
general features of human nature but the characteristics
of certain (many) human beings.  Tillich's treatment of
the implications of estrangement for human life, similarly, is a description of experience not in all times
and places but in modern western society.  Their accounts
of concrete experience are broader and stronger for being
grounded in analysis of the structures of experience.
But it is the delineation of particular aspects of experience which gives substance to their general analyses,
and which enabled them to speak so powerfully to their
time.

Thus, though it may seem as if calling for theology's
integration of women's experience is just repeating the

error of theological one-sidedness in a new form, the problem with Niebuhr and Tillich is not particularity <u>per se</u>, but the universality of their claims on behalf of the particular. And while the attempt to take account of women's experience will undoubtedly result in new false claims to universality, these cannot be avoided by avoiding the particularities of experience. Theology cannot deal with "universal experience," not simply because human reason is finite (Niebuhr), but also because experience itself is so varied.

Unlike Niebuhr, we have no cause to regret this, however. If there is no universal experience, there are significant human experiences which many groups share and which may be illuminated through concern with particular experience. "The possibilities of a wide extent of universality depend...not on an impossible horizontal impartiality, so to speak, but on the human depth of a definite commitment."[72] Human particularity represents not just limit but also possibility. If Niebuhr does not succeed in showing that pride is <u>the</u> human sin, he does establish it as an important temptation of human finitude, and in such a way that it can be recognized and named wherever it is found. He accomplishes this, moreover, precisely through the detail with which he describes current manifestations of pride. The specificity of his account is not in conflict with breadth; rather, breadth emerges through specificity. This relationship between universality and particularity is not confined to theology proper. It also characterizes the biblical message of sin and grace which is conveyed through the story of a particular people living in a particular place and in a particular situation.[73]

If what is common in human experience can be discerned only through the particularities of experience, it becomes the obligation of groups from which little has been heard to articulate their own experience and contribute their perceptions to a multi-faceted theological exploration of experience. Recognizing that "women's experience" is as varied as human experience, this work has sought to make such a contribution from the perspective of white, western, middle-class women's experience. It represents just a beginning, and the voices of other groups of women have yet to be heard. As Mary Daly says so well, "Women have had the power of naming stolen from us."[74] Discovering and recovering women's experiences will be a slow and difficult process.

174

It is not yet clear how radical the theological implications of this process will be. I have argued here with regard to Niebuhr and Tillich that in order to take account of women's experience, they would have to make substantial changes in their doctrines of sin and grace which would in turn necessitate changes in other areas of their thought. Yet this argument is just one example of the way in which women's experience can be used as a critical tool. Mary Daly, employing it more broadly as a measure of predominant themes in ethics and theology throughout the Christian tradition, contends that one cannot take women's experience seriously and still remain a Christian at all. Whether or not one accepts her conclusions, they are based on a mass of evidence which deserves careful critical sifting.[75]

The theological implications of a serious concern for women's experience are not simply negative or critical, however. There is no area in which criticism from the perspective of women's experience does not lead to at least implicit construction. If it is inadequate to view pride as the human sin, then in the light of women's experience, the sin of failing fully to realize one's freedom, failing fully to become a self, must be seen as equally firmly rooted in human nature. If grace cannot be interpreted either as shattering judgement or the static forgiveness of sins, then women's experience leads us to look for grace in moments of self-creation which point toward a future in which all persons can become whole. The point is that the submerged perspective of women's experience, once brought to expression, precisely in its particularity has the power to direct our attention to previously unexplored aspects of human experience. The implications of this power are not limited to theology, but they certainly have a theological dimension: sin may flourish and grace abound where they have not yet been suspected.

## Introduction

[1]Valerie Saiving Goldstein, "The Human Situation: A Feminine View," Journal of Religion 40 (April, 1960): 100-112. (Ms. Saiving has changed her name since publication of this article.)

[2]Ibid., p. 101.

[3]Ibid., p. 108.

[4]See Rosemary Ruether, ed., Religion and Sexism (New York: Simon and Schuster, 1974) and Elizabeth Clark and Herbert Richardson, eds., Women and Religion (New York: Harper and Row, 1977) for examples of critical work. Examples of constructive work are found in Carol Christ and Judith Plaskow, eds., Womanspirit Rising (New York: Harper and Row, 1979).

[5]Sheila Collins, "Toward a Fminist Theology," The Christian Century 89 (August 2, 1972), p. 789; Mary Daly, Beyond God the Father (Boston: Beacon Press, 1973), p. 100f.

[6]That is, one would first have to argue that Barth does, in fact, speak from human experience and then that he speaks from male experience.

[7]Reinhold Niebuhr, Essays in Applied Christianity (New York: Meridian Books, 1959), p. 93.

[8]Hannah Tillich, From Time to Time (New York: Stein and Day, Publishers, 1973).

[9]Goldstein, p. 101.

[10]John Raines, "Sin as Pride and Sin as Sloth," Christianity and Crisis 29 (February 3, 1969): 4-8; Wayne Proudfoot, "Types of Finite-Infinite Relation and Conceptions of the Unity of the Self" (Ph.D. dissertation, Harvard University, 1971). This latter work has been published as God and the Self (New Jersey: Bucknell University Press, 1976).

CHAPTER 1 - <u>Women's Experience</u>

[1]Virginia Woolf, <u>A Room of One's Own</u> (Harmondsworth, England: Penguin Books, 1945), p. 28f.

[2]The existence of such a social mythology is thoroughly documented by Elizabeth Janeway in her <u>Man's World, Woman's Place</u> (New York: William Morrow and Company, Inc., 1971).

[3]Quoted in Woolf, p. 69.

[4]See Mary Daly on the "mind-gynecologists," <u>Gyn/Ecology</u> (Boston: Beacon Press, 1978), pp. 229, 251-254.

[5]Woolf, p. 29.

[6]Simone de Beauvoir, <u>The Second Sex</u> (New York: Alfred A. Knopf, Inc., Bantam Books, 1961), p. xv.

[7]Ibid.

[8]Ibid.

[9]Sherry Ortner, "Is Female to Male as Nature Is to Culture?" <u>Woman, Culture, and Society</u>, Rosaldo and Lamphere, eds. (Stanford: Stanford University Press, 1974), p. 73.

[10]Ibid., p. 75.

[11]Ibid., p. 81.

[12]Dorothy Dinnerstein takes Ortner's argument a step further, proposing that women seem more natural to us because we are all mother-raised children--a fact which can be changed. (<u>The Mermaid and the Minotaur</u>, New York: Harper and Row, 1976.)

[13]Ortner, p. 80.

[14]De Beauvoir, p. 67; Rosemary Ruether, "Misogynism and Virginal Feminism in the <u>Fathers of the Church</u>," <u>Religion and Sexism</u>.

[15]See p. 31 below.

[16]Paul Rosenkrantz, Susan Vogel, Helen Bee, Inge Broverman, Donald Broverman, "Sex-Role Stereotypes and Self-Concepts in College Students," Journal of Consulting and Clinical Psychology 32 (1968), p. 293.

[17]John Ruskin, "Of Queens' Gardens," Sesame and Lilies (New York: The Macmillan Company, 1954), p. 99f.

[18]Ibid., p. 125f.

[19]Ashley Montagu, The Natural Superiority of Women (New York: The Macmillan Company, 1954), p. 99f.

[20]Ibid., p. 138ff.

[21]Ibid., p. 143f.

[22]For Freud on the difficulties of defining masculinity and femininity, see Three Contributions to the Theory of Sex (New York: Nervous and Mental Disease Publishing Company, 1916), p. 79, footnote; "Femininity," New Introductory Lectures on Psychoanalysis (New York: W.W. Norton and Company, Inc., 1965), pp. 144, 116. For examples of his actual usage, see "The Passing of the Oedipus Complex," Sexuality and the Psychology of Love (New York: Collier Books, 1963), pp. 177, 180; "Female Sexuality," Ibid., p. 197; Three Contributions to the Theory of Sex, p. 79; "Femininity," pp. 118, 130.

[23]Freud, "Femininity," p. 126; "Female Sexuality," p. 187.

[24]Freud, "Some Psychological Consequences of the Anatomical Distinction Between the Sexes," Sexuality and the Psychology of Love, p. 191.

[25]The above account of penis envy is based on "Female Sexuality," "Some Psychological Consequences of the Anatomical Distinction Between the Sexes," and Three Contributions to the Theory of Sex.

[26]Julia Sherman, On the Psychology of Women (Springfield, Illinois: Charles C. Thomas, 1971), p. 108. In fact, in his later career, Freud even recognized that the term "passivity" was inappropriate to certain aspects of female sexuality--without, of course, changing his theory. See "Femininity," p. 115.

[27]Freud, "The Passing of the Oedipus Complex," p. 179.

[28]Freud, "Femininity," p. 129.

[29]"Some Psychological Consequences of the Anatomical Distinction Between the Sexes," p. 193. It is interesting that some of the traits Freud lists here, e.g. woman's lesser sense of justice, are precisely the opposite of what Ruskin and Montagu claim for her. As Simone de Beauvoir remarks (The Second Sex, p. 174), since women exist apart from male myths concerning them, they are always both the incarnation of the myths and their opposite. "There is no figurative image of woman which does not call up at once its opposite." Cf. Dinnerstein on this phenomenon.

[30]Sigmund Freud, Civilization and its Discontents (New York: W.W. Norton and Company, Inc., 1962), pp. 46-51.

[31]Helene Deutsch, The Psychology of Women, 2 vols. (New York: Grune and Stratton, 1944-45), 1: 190f.

[32]Sigmund Freud, "The Economic Problem in Masochism," General Psychological Theory (New York: Collier Books, 1963), p. 192f.

[33]Deutsch, 1: 251.

[34]The above discussion of Deutsch is based on ibid., chapters six and seven.

[35]Phyllis McGinley, Sixpence in Her Shoe (New York: Macmillan Company, 1964), p. 47. Quoted from Janeway, p. 40.

[36]Phyllis McGinley, The Province of the Heart (New York: The Viking Press, 1959), p. 17.

[37]Erik Erikson, "Inner and Outer Space: Reflections on Womanhood," The Woman in America, Robert Lifton, ed. (Boston: Beacon Press, 1967), p. 6.

[38]Ibid., p. 13.

[39]Ibid., p. 19f.

[40]Ibid., p. 5.

[41]David McClelland, "Wanted: A New Self-Image for Women," The Woman in America, p. 176ff.

[42]Ibid., p. 185.

[43]Erikson, p. 10; McClelland, p. 185.

[44]Erich Neumann, "The Moon and Matriarchal Consciousness," Dynamic Aspects of the Psyche (New York: The Analytical Psychology Club, 1956), p. 63.

[45]See above, p. 13; Ortner, p. 81f; Erich Neumann, "Psychological Stages of Feminine Development," Spring (1959), p. 65ff.

[46]Neumann, ibid., p. 67.

[47]Neumann, "The Moon and Matriarchal Consciousness," p. 57f.

[48]Ibid., p. 64.

[49]Ibid., p. 69f; Ann Belford Ulanov, The Feminine in Jungian Psychology and in Christian Theology (Evanston: Northwestern University Press, 1971), p. 179f. Cf. Penelope Washbourn, Becoming Woman (New York: Harper and Row, 1977).

[50]Ulanov, p. 183.

[51]Neumann, "The Moon and Matriarchal Consciousness," p. 62.

[52]Ulanov, p. 186f.

[53]Ibid., p. 191.

[54]Neumann, "The Moon and Matriarchal Consciousness,"
p. 68.

[55]This is quite close to Saiving's argument, but now
we are going to modify it considerably.

[56]See Naomi Weisstein's "'Kinder, Kuche, Kirche' as
Scientific Law: Psychology Constructs the Female,"
Sisterhood is Powerful, Robin Morgan, ed. (New York:
Vintage Books, 1970), pp. 205-220.

[57]Sherman, pp. 67, 87f, 245.

[58]Margaret Mead, Sex and Temperament (New York: Dell
Publishing Company, 1968).

[59]Margaret Mead, Male and Female (New York: Dell Publishing Company, 1968), pp. 38, 230ff, 155.

[60]Janeway, p. 10.

[61]I say particular social groups because expectations
as to sex-role and sex-temperament are not necessarily
uniform even within a given culture. Victorian sex-
role ideals, for example, based on the assumption
that all women were ladies sharing a certain degree
of privilege, ignored the lives of the black and
white poor. Of course, the women in a given society
may share many experiences even as they differ in
others, but that cannot be taken for granted.

[62]De Beauvoir, pp. 252-279, 341-351, 465-495.

[63]Ibid., pp. 306-341.

[64]Ibid., p. 576.

[65]Ibid., pp. 562-585.

[66]I wrote the following section at the same time Carol
Christ was writing "Explorations with Doris Lessing
in Quest of The Four-Gated City" (Judith Plaskow and
Joan Romero, eds., Women and Religion, revised edition,

Montana: The Scholars Press, 1974, pp. 31-61).   Although we deal with very different aspects of the
books, our conversations about <u>The Children of Vio-
lence</u> influenced my thought at many points.

[67]Doris Lessing, <u>Martha Quest</u> (London: Panther Books,
Ltd., 1972), p. 7.

[68]Ibid., pp. 8, 14.

[69]Ibid., p. 30.

[70]Ibid., p. 62.

[71]Ibid., p. 123.

[72]Ibid., pp. 112, 125.

[73]Ibid., p. 165.

[74]Ibid., p. 17.

[75]Doris Lessing, <u>A Proper Marriage</u> (London: Panther
Books Ltd., 1972), p. 229.

[76]Lessing, <u>Martha Quest</u>, p. 131.

[77]Ibid., p. 239.

[78]Ibid., p. 245f.

[79]Lessing, <u>A Proper Marriage</u>, p. 69f.

[80]Margaret Drabble, <u>The Waterfall</u> (Harmondsworth,
England: Penguin Books, 1969), p. 91f.

[81]Ibid., p. 97.

[82]Margaret Atwood, <u>The Edible Woman</u> (Toronto: McClelland
and Steward Limited, 1969), pp. 70, 101.

[83]De Beauvoir, p. 408.

[84]Margaret Drabble, <u>The Millstone</u> (Harmondsworth,
England: Penguin Books, 1968), p. 67.

[85]Lessing, _A Proper Marriage_, p. 152ff.

[86]Ibid., p. 278.

[87]Ibid., p. 370.

[88]See above, p. 33 and Janeway, p. 87.

[89]Christ, pp. 37, 40.

[90]Doris Lessing, _A Ripple From the Storm_ (London: Panther Books, 1969), p. 186.

[91]Ibid., p. 220.

[92]Lessing, _A Proper Marriage_, p. 35. See also _Martha Quest_, p. 203.

[93]Lessing, _A Ripple From the Storm_, p. 46.

[94]Ibid., p. 247.

[95]De Beauvoir, p. 604.

[96]Doris Lessing, _Landlocked_ (London: Panther Books, 1969), p. 37.

[97]Ibid., p. 103f.

[98]Carol Christ pointed out to me the importance of Martha's not falling apart when Thomas leaves.

[99]Simone de Beauvoir, _The Prime of Life_ (New York: Lancer Books, Inc., 1962), p. 255.

[100]Anne Murphy, "A 'Woman's Book,'" an unpublished paper written for Carol Christ at Wesleyan University, 1971.

[101]Doris Lessing, _The Four-Gated City_ (New York: Bantam Books, 1970), p. 36ff.

[102]Ibid., p. 38.

[103]Ibid., p. 40.

[104]Ibid., pp. 353, 352.

[105]Ibid., p. 449.

[106]Christ, p. 46.

[107]See above pp. 16, 17.

[108]Virginia Woolf, To the Lighthouse (New York: Harcourt, Brace and World, Inc., A Harvest Book, 1955), p. 158.

[109]De Beauvoir, The Second Sex, p. 584.

[110]Lessing, The Four-Gated City, p. 449.

[111]Ibid., p. 506f.

[112]Ibid., p. 588.

[113]Lessing, A Proper Marriage, p. 338.

[114]Janeway, p. 82.

[115]Lessing, A Proper Marriage, pp. 368, 354.

[116]Neumann, "The Psychological Stages of Feminine Development," p. 90.

[117]See above, pp. 26-28.

CHAPTER TWO - Reinhold Niebuhr

[1]This part of the argument takes off from Saiving's, "The Human Situation: A Feminine View."

[2]William John Wolf, "Reinhold Niebuhr's Doctrine of Man," Reinhold Niebuhr: His Religious, Social, and Political Thought, Kegley and Bretall, eds. (New York: The Macmillan Company, 1961), p. 232.

[3]Reinhold Niebuhr, The Nature and Destiny of Man, 2 vols. (New York: Charles Scribner's Sons, 1964), 1:122. Volume I is hereafter referred to as Human

<u>Nature</u>. While I have avoided use of the male generic throughout this work, I have not altered direct quotations. Whether or not Niebuhr's use of the term "man" is truly generic is the central question of this chapter.

[4]<u>Ibid.</u>, p. 123.

[5]<u>Ibid.</u>, p. 23f.

[6]<u>Ibid.</u>, p. 125.

[7]Wolf, p. 236.

[8]Niebuhr, <u>Human Nature</u>, p. 127.

[9]<u>Ibid.</u>, p. 131.

[10]<u>Ibid.</u>, pp. 131, 132.

[11]<u>Ibid.</u>, p. 131.

[12]<u>Ibid.</u>

[13]The above analysis of general and special revelation is based on <u>Human Nature</u>, chap. V.

[14]John Mervyn Dickinson, "Aggression and the Status of Evil in Man: A Critical Analysis of Sigmund Freud's Assumptions From the Theological Perspective of Reinhold Niebuhr" (Ph.D. dissertation, Boston University Graduate School, 1964), p. 159. These categories are taken from Niebuhr himself.

[15]Niebuhr, <u>Human Nature</u>, p. 3.

[16]Reinhold Niebuhr, <u>An Interpretation of Christian Ethics</u> (New York and London: Harper and Brothers Pub., 1935), p. 67.

[17]Niebuhr, <u>Human Nature</u>, p. 157.

[18]Niebuhr, <u>An Interpretation of Christian Ethics</u>, p. 66.

[19]Niebuhr, _Human Nature_, p. 3.  Emphasis mine.

[20]Ibid., p. 167.  Emphasis mine.

[21]Ibid., p. 150.

[22]Ibid., p. 181.

[23]Ibid., p. 179.

[24]Mary Francis Thelen, _Man as Sinner in Contemporary American Realistic Theology_ (New York: King's Crown Press, 1946), p. 99.

[25]Niebuhr, _Human Nature_, p. 186.

[26]Ibid., p. 17.

[27]Reinhold Niebuhr, _Faith and History_ (New York: Charles Scribner's Sons, 1949), pp. 121, 125.

[28]Niebuhr, _An Interpretation of Christian Ethics_, pp. 84, 87.

[29]The following discussion is based on Niebuhr, _Human Nature_, pp. 188-203.

[30]Ibid., p. 195.

[31]Niebuhr, _The Nature and Destiny of Man_, 2: chap. V. Volume II is hereafter referred to as _Human Destiny_.

[32]Niebuhr, _Human Nature_, p. 179.

[33]In his last book Niebuhr balances his view of the excessive egotism of groups with a study of how the group can be a sphere for common grace.  His view of the demonic potentialities of group pride still stands, however.  (_Man's Nature and His Communities_, New York: Charles Scribner's Sons, 1965, p. 106ff.)

[34]Niebuhr, _Human Nature_, p. 179.

[35]Ibid., p. 185.

187

[36] Ibid., p. 228.

[37] Ibid., pp. 230, 233.

[38] Ibid., p. 240.

[39] Ibid., p. 235.

[40] Ibid., p. 237.

[41] Dickinson, p. 178.

[42] See his modifications of the doctrines of original sin and original righteousness, for example. Human Nature, chaps. IX and X.

[43] E.g. E.A. Burtt, "Some Questions About Niebuhr's Theology," Reinhold Niebuhr: His Religious, Social, and Political Thought, p. 357ff; Edward John Carnell, The Theology of Reinhold Niebuhr (Grand Rapids, Michigan: Wm. B. Eerdmans Publishing Company, 1960), passim; Rachel Hadley King, The Omission of the Holy Spirit From Reinhold Niebuhr's Theology (New York: Philosophical Library, 1964), passim.

[44] Niebuhr, Human Nature, p. 16.

[45] It may well be that sensuality is not the best world for this phenomenon. Since Niebuhr uses the term in this way at least once, however, we will continue to use it as well.

[46] Niebuhr himself echoes this viewpoint when he says, "The natural fact that the woman bears the child binds her to the child and partially limits the freedom of her choice in the development of various potentialities of character not related to the vocation of motherhood." Human Nature, p. 282.

[47] De Beauvoir, The Second Sex, p. xxi.

[48] Ibid., p. xxviii.

[49] Ibid. Niebuhr points out that sensuality is never "the mere expression of natural impulse," but always

partly a spiritual flaw. (<u>Human Nature</u>, p. 179.)
It cannot be said, however, that he adequately ex-
plores the complex dialectical relationship between
freedom and destiny in (women's) experience.

[50] De Beauvoir, <u>The Second Sex</u>, p. xxi.

[51] Lessing, <u>A Proper Marriage</u>, pp. 10, 32, 69, 296.

[52] Lessing, <u>Landlocked</u>, p. 115.

[53] De Beauvoir, <u>The Second Sex</u>, p. 511.

[54] McGinley, <u>Sixpence in Her Shoe</u>, p. 14. Quoted in
Janeway, p. 55.

[55] Niebuhr, <u>Human Destiny</u>, p. 124.

[56] Goldstein, p. 109f.

[57] Raines, pp. 4-8. Cf. Wolf, p. 241.

[58] Raines, ibid., p. 8. The original quotation from
Raines is written in the masculine singular. I
have not used brackets to indicate my changes because they would be so numerous as to interrupt the
flow of the passage.

[59] Daly, p. 8.

[60] Carol Christ helped me organize and clarify my ideas
as I prepared to write this section.

[61] Niebuhr, <u>Human Nature</u>, p. 27; <u>Faith and History</u>,
p. 174.

[62] Niebuhr, <u>Human Nature</u>, p. 190.

[63] Ibid., p. 191.

[64] Above, pp. 12-14, 24-28.

[65] See my article "On Carol Christ on Margaret Atwood:
Some Theological Reflections," <u>Signs</u> 2 (Winter, 1976):

331-339 for a discussion of the ambiguities of the woman/nature association.

[66]De Beauvoir, *The Second Sex*, pp. 446, 467.

[67]Drabble, *The Millstone*, p. 58.

[68]Sherry Ortner reminds us that the socialization of children is an important cultural task. ("Is Female to Male as Nature is to Culture?" p. 19.)

[69]De Beauvoir, *The Second Sex*, p. 341. It should be pointed out that de Beauvoir does not see women's naturalness as at all positive. Her thoroughgoing (Sartrian) existentialist perspective leads her to speak of human creatureliness (immanence) in terms even more negative than Niebuhr's. I have for the most part simply ignored this aspect of her thought and adopted those aspects of her categories useful to my purpose.

[70]Neumann, "The Moon and Matriarchal Consciousness," p. 68.

[71]It must be stressed once again that pregnancy is the only one of women's experiences which "naturally" illustrates the link between nature and spirit. Motherhood as a role, relatedness to nature, and "feminine consciousness" may all be seen as products of culture.

[72]Niebuhr, *Human Nature*, p. 272.

[73]Ibid., p. 278f. Emphasis omitted.

[74]Ibid., pp. 270, 272, 288f.

[75]Ibid., p. 286. The above discussion of essential human nature is based on ibid., chap. X.

[76]Niebuhr, *Human Destiny*, p. 68.

[77]Niebuhr, *Faith and History*, p. 171.

[78]Niebuhr, *Human Destiny*, p. 74.

[79]Niebuhr, Human Nature, p. 296.

[80]Niebuhr, Human Destiny, p. 82.

[81]Ibid., p. 84. I have slightly altered the context of this quotation.

[82]Ibid., p. 86.

[83]Ibid., p. 247.

[84]Ibid., p. 87.

[85]The above discussion of sacrificial love is based on ibid., chap. III.

[86]Ibid., p. 98. The following discussion of grace is based on ibid., p. 54ff and chap. IV.

[87]Ibid., p. 99.

[88]Ibid., p. 100.

[89]Ibid., p. 108.

[90]Ibid., p. 109.

[91]Ibid., p. 110.

[92]Ibid., p. 114.

[93]Ibid., pp. 135, 148, 185ff.

[94]Ibid., pp. 134-148.

[95]Ibid., p. 188.

[96]Ibid., p. 204.

[97]Paul Lehmann, "The Christology of Reinhold Niebuhr," Reinhold Niebuhr: His Religious, Social, and Political Thought, p. 277.

[98]Wolf, p. 248.

[99]Niebuhr, _An Interpretation of Christian Ethics_, p. 217; _Human Destiny_, p. 123.

[100]This is true of Tillich, for example, as we shall see below.

[101]The fact that Niebuhr's discussion of general revelation is based on and intermingled with discussion of "the Christian view of man," mitigates the harshness of this criticism.

[102]Niebuhr, _Human Destiny_, chaps. VIII and IX.

[103]Ibid., p. 217.

[104]Ibid., p. 246.

[105]Niebuhr, _Human Nature_, p. 282. See also _An Interpretation of Christian Ethics_, p. 148; _Christianity and Power Politics_ (n.p.: Archon Books, 1969), p. 27; _Moral Man and Immoral Society_ (New York: Charles Scribner's Sons, 1932), p. 46f; _The Self and the Dramas of History_ (New York: Charles Scribner's Sons, 1955), p. 191.

[106]Goldstein, p. 101.

[107]Niebuhr, _Human Destiny_, p. 108.

[108]Ibid., p. 108; also chap. IV passim.

[109]Ibid., pp. 113, 109.

[110]See, for example, pp. 58, 110.

[111]Ibid., p. 110.

[112]Emma Trout argues thus for Barth and Tillich in an unpublished paper, "The Doctrine of Justification in the Light of Sexual Differences," 1970.

[113]Niebuhr, _Human Destiny_, p. 69. I have slightly altered Niebuhr's punctuation.

[114]Lessing, _A Ripple From the Storm_, p. 189.

[115]De Beauvoir, The Second Sex, p. 451.

[116]Goldstein, pp. 108, 110.

[117]Doris Lessing, The Summer Before the Dark (New York: Alfred A. Knopf, 1973), p. 20.

[118]Ibid., p. 104.

[119]Ibid., pp. 102f, 104.

[120]Niebuhr, Faith and History, p. 177.

[121]Niebuhr, "Grace and Self-Acceptance," The Messenger (April 25, 1950), p. 6. See also his review of Erich Fromm's Man for Himself in Christianity and Society (Spring, 1948), p. 27f.

[122]Niebuhr, Man's Nature and His Communities, pp. 106, 112f, 116.

[123]Lessing, The Summer Before the Dark, pp. 104, 105.

[124]Paul Ramsey, "Love and Law," Reinhold Niebuhr: His Religious, Social, and Political Thought, p. 109.

[125]Daniel Day Williams, The Spirit and the Forms of Love (New York: Harper and Row, 1968), p. 195; "Niebuhr and Liberalism," Reinhold Niebuhr: His Religious, Social and Political Thought, p. 210.

[126]James Gustafson, "Christian Ethics and Social Policy," Faith and Ethics (New York: Harper Torchbooks, 1965), p. 130ff.

[127]See Niebuhr's autobiographical introduction to Reinhold Niebuhr: His Religious, Social, and Political Thought, esp. p. 5.

[128]Niebuhr, "The Church and Equal Rights for Women," Essays in Applied Christianity, p. 93ff; "An Answer to Karl Barth," ibid., p. 179f; An Interpretation of Christian Ethics, pp. 148, 153; Christianity and Power Politics, p. 27; Moral Man and Immoral Society, p. 46f; The Self and the Dramas of History, p. 191;

Human Nature, p. 282; Human Destiny, pp. 85, 197.

[129]Niebuhr, Human Nature, p. 282.


CHAPTER THREE - Paul Tillich

[1]See, for example, Daly, Beyond God the Father, pp. 6, 20,27,32,35,70,103,127; Joan Arnold Romero, "The Protestant Principle: A Woman's-Eye View of Barth and Tillich," Religion and Sexism, pp. 329-337.

[2]Paul Tillich, Systematic Theology, 3 vols, (Chicago: The University of Chicago Press, 1951-63), 1(1951): 59,60. Vol. I is hereafter referred to as ST, I.

[3]Ibid., pp. 30, 65.

[4]Ibid., p. 62.

[5]Ibid., p. 4.

[6]Ibid., pp. 18ff, 62.

[7]Ibid., p. 64. The following discussion is based on ibid., pp. 34-52.

[8]Ibid., pp. 64, 63.

[9]Paul Tillich, The Shaking of the Foundations (New York: Charles Scribner's Sons, 1948), p. 154; Systematic Theology, 2(1957): 46. Vol. II is hereafter referred to as ST,II.

[10]Tillich, ST,II, p. 45.

[11]Paul Tillich, "The Two Types of Philosophy of Religion," Theology of Culture (New York: Oxford University Press, 1959), p. 10.

[12]Paul Tillich, "Estrangement and Reconciliation in Modern Thought," Review of Religion 9 (November, 1944), p. 6f.

[13]Tillich, ST,II, p. 29. Tillich's discussion of the

fall is found in <u>ST</u>,I, p. 254ff and <u>ST</u>,II, pp. 29-44.

[14]Tillich, <u>ST</u>,II, p. 33f.  See also <u>ST</u>,I, p. 254f.

[15]Tillich, <u>ST</u>,II, p. 34.  Cf. Niebuhr, Above, p. 56f.

[16]Tillich, <u>ST</u>,I, p. 255; <u>ST</u>,II, p. 34ff.

[17]Tillich, <u>ST</u>,I, p. 255.

[18]Tillich, <u>ST</u>,II, p. 44.

[19]Guyton B. Hammond, <u>Man in Estrangement</u> (Nashville, Tennessee: Vanderbilt University Press, 1965), p. 158.

[20]Ray L. Hart, "Recent Tillichiana--A Review Article," <u>The Drew Gateway</u> (Winter, 1961), p. 104.

[21]Tillich, <u>ST</u>,I, p. 182; <u>ST</u>,II, pp. 32, 38; <u>The Shaking of the Foundations</u>, p. 155.

[22]Tillich, <u>ST</u>,II, p. 44.

[23]Ibid., pp. 46, 56.

[24]Ibid., p. 47.  Tillich's discussion of sin is found in ibid., pp. 44-59.

[25]For a discussion of Tillich's doctrine of sin which focuses on its cognitive aspects, see David Kelsey, <u>The Fabric of Paul Tillich's Theology</u> (New Haven: Yale University Press, 1967), chap. 3.

[26]Tillich, <u>ST</u>,II, p. 48.  Tillich of course uses self-love in an ontological sense, Niebuhr in a moral sense.  The difference will be discussed further below.

[27]Ibid., pp. 48, 47.

[28]Ibid., p. 50.

[29]Ibid., p. 51.

[30]Paul Tillich, <u>The Interpretation of History</u> (New York: Charles Scribner's Sons, 1936), p. 93.  The essay in

question, "Das Damonische," was originally published in 1926.

[31]Tillich, _ST_,II, p. 60. The following discussion of evil is based on ibid., pp. 59-78 and _ST_,I, pp. 168-204.

[32]Tillich, _ST_,II, pp. 62, 61.

[33]For a full analysis of anxiety and courage see Paul Tillich, _The Courage to Be_ (London and Glasgow: Collins, the Fontana Library, 1952). Tillich does not distinguish between essential and existential anxiety in this book, and it is often difficult to tell whether he is dealing with essential anxiety or the mixture of the two in life. Sometimes it seems as if these categories simply cannot be applied.

[34]Tillich, _ST_,II, pp. 67-69.

[35]Ibid., p. 75.

[36]Ibid., p. 78f.

[37]Ibid., p. 86.

[38]Tillich's discussion of life processes is found in _Systematic Theology_ 3(1963):30-106. Vol. III is hereafter referred to as _ST_,III.

[39]Ibid., p. 32.

[40]Ibid., pp. 40f, 45.

[41]Ibid., p. 69.

[42]Ibid., p. 75.

[43]See, for example, _ST_,I, pp. 110,113,119,156.

[44]Tillich, _The Interpretation of History_, pp. 84, 94.

[45]Tillich, _ST_,III, p. 102.

[46]Tillich, _The Interpretation of History_, p. 94.

[47]Tillich, _ST_,II, p. 44.

[48]Kenneth Hamilton, _The System and the Gospel_ (Grand Rapids, Michigan: William B. Eerdmans Publishing Company, 1963); George Tavard, _Paul Tillich and the Christian Message_ (New York: Charles Scribner's Sons, 1962).

[49]See above, p. 102f.

[50]The terms "exist" and, in the next sentence, "existential" are used in a nontechnical sense.

[51]Tillich, _ST_,I, p. 169.

[52]Tillich, _The Courage to Be_, p. 90. I assume he is discussing essential being here.

[53]Hammond, p. 174. Also above, p. 98f.

[54]Tillich, _ST_,II, p. 61.

[55]Tillich, _The Shaking of the Foundations_, p. 158.

[56]Ibid.

[57]See above, pp. 106-108.

[58]Tillich, _ST_,III, p. 44.

[59]Tillich, _Love, Power, and Justice_ (London, Oxford, New York: Oxford University Press, 1954), p. 69f.

[60]Tillich, _ST_,III, p. 75.

[61]Lessing, _Martha Quest_, pp. 36, 41f, 45.

[62]See above, pp. 87, 88, 90.

[63]Tillich, _The Shaking of the Foundations_, p. 159.

[64]Tillich, _The Interpretation of History_, p. 93f; _ST_,III, p. 93.

[65]Tillich, ST,II, p. 50.

[66]Tillich, ST,III, p. 39ff.

[67]Biographically, this fascination with the demonic may be explained by Tillich's experiences in Weimar, Germany. (See Hannah Tillich, From Time to Time.)

[68]See above, p. 100.

[69]Tillich, ST,I, p. 255; ST,II, p. 44.

[70]Tillich, ST,II, p. 36.

[71]Ibid., p. 38; Tillich, ST,I, p. 256.

[72]Tillich, The Interpretation of History, p. 93.

[73]Proudfoot, pp. 81, 83. Proudfoot focuses on the monistic strand in Tillich's thought to the neglect of those elements which conflict with it, but he is very helpful in documenting Tillich's monism.

[74]See above, p. 15. Also Barbara Welter, "The Cult of True Womanhood," American Quarterly 18 (Summer, 1966), p. 152ff; Friedrich Schleiermacher, Christmas Eve (Richmond, Virginia: John Knox Press, 1967), esp. pp. 54f, 83.

[75]Tillich, The Shaking of the Foundations, p. 83. This theological difference is also an expression of a personal difference between the two men. Tillich relates that when they took walks together in Riverside Park, his own attention would often wander from their conversation as he looked at the trees around them. Niebuhr would become impatient and call him a "German Romantic." ("Sin and Grace in the Theology of Reinhold Niebuhr," Reinhold Niebuhr: A Prophetic Voice in Our Time, Greenwich, Connecticut: Seabury Press, 1962, p. 39.)

[76]Tillich, ST,II, p. 43; ST,III, p. 107.

[77]Tillich, ST,III, p. 15.

[78]Tillich, ST,I, p. 49.

[79] See James Luther Adams, _Paul Tillich's Philosophy of Culture, Science, and Religion_ (New York: Harper and Row Publishers, 1965), p. 233.

[80] Tillich, _ST_,II, p. 119.

[81] Tillich, _ST_,III, pp. 107, 111.

[82] Kelsey, p. 16.

[83] Tillich, _ST_,III, p. 138f.

[84] Tillich, _ST_,I, pp. 108-115; _ST_,III, p. 111ff.

[85] There are a number of confusions in Tillich's concept of ecstasy, which broadens from the first to the third volumes of the _ST_. In volume I, ecstasy is the cognitive side of faith which is the "state of being grasped by the ground and abyss of being and meaning." ("Reply to Interpretation and Criticism," _The Theology of Paul Tillich_, C.W. Kegley and R.W. Bretall, eds., New York: Macmillan Company, 1964, p. 338.) In volume III, ecstasy is the "state of being grasped by the Spiritual Presence" (p. 112). This would seem to make it identical to faith. But at other points, Tillich speaks of faith as an aspect of ecstasy (pp. 129, 135), while at still others, he seems to imply that ecstasy is a characteristic of faith which does not include courage (p. 242). In any event, ecstasy becomes the broadest term for describing the response of the human spirit to the transcendental unity of unambiguous life. The term will be used here in its broadest sense.

[86] Tillich, _ST_,I, pp. 115-118.

[87] Ibid., p. 117.

[88] Ibid., p. 118ff; Tillich, _ST_,III, pp. 120ff, 139f.

[89] Tillich, _ST_,I, p. 133f.

[90] Tillich, _ST_,III, p. 144; _ST_,I, p. 136.

[91] Tillich, _ST_,II, p. 133f.

[92]Tillich, _ST_,II, pp. 121-125.  I occasionally use "Jesus" as shorthand for "Jesus as the Christ."  The usage is not meant to imply that Tillich is concerned with the historical Jesus.

[93]Ibid., pp. 121, 125.

[94]Ibid., p. 125.

[95]Ibid., p. 126.

[96]Ibid.

[97]Ibid., p. 129.  The discussion of temptation is based on ibid., pp. 127-131.

[98]Ibid., p. 170.

[99]Ibid., pp. 170-176.

[100]Ibid., pp. 174, 176.

[101]Ibid., pp. 176-180.

[102]See above, p. 120.

[103]Tillich, _ST_,II, p. 177.  See also Tillich's "Redemption in Cosmic and Social History," _The Journal of Religious Thought_ 3 (Autumn-Winter, 1946), pp. 17,21f.

[104]Tillich, _ST_,II, p. 179.

[105]Tillich, _ST_,III, p. 229.

[106]Ibid., p. 129.  The following discussion of faith and love is based on ibid., pp. 129-138.

[107]Ibid., pp. 130, 131, 133.

[108]See Tillich's _Dynamics of Faith_ (New York: Harper and Row, Publishers, 1957), esp. chaps. 1 and 2.

[109]Tillich, _ST_,III, p. 134.

[110]Tillich would probably argue that Niebuhr, in equating agape and self-sacrifice, again confuses a religious term with a moral one. (Ibid., p. 137.) This makes sense because Tillich argues that pride, to which self-sacrifice is a response, is a moral and not a religious flaw.

[111]Paul Tillich, "Being and Love," Moral Principles in Action, Ruth Ashen, ed. (New York: Harper, 1952), pp. 664f, 668. See also, Tillich, ST,III, p. 169; ST,I, p. 280.

[112]Tillich, ST,I, p. 280. Also Love, Power and Justice, pp. 28-33; ST,III, p. 137.

[113]Tillich, Love, Power, and Justice, p. 33 (quotation); ST,I, p. 280.

[114]Tillich's discussion of regeneration, justification, and sanctification is found in ST,III, pp. 221-243.

[115]Ibid., p. 222.

[116]See Tillich, "Redemption in Cosmic and Social History," p. 27.

[117]Tillich, ST,III, p. 225.

[118]Ibid., p. 226. See also, Tillich, The Shaking of the Foundations, p. 156; Hart, p. 99; Daniel Day Williams, "Paul Tillich's Doctrine of Forgiveness," Pastoral Psychology 19 (February, 1968), pp. 17-23.

[119]See Tillich, The Courage to Be, chap. 2.

[120]Hart, p. 99.

[121]Tillich, The Courage to Be, pp. 53-58, 169ff; ST,III, p. 227f.

[122]Tillich, ST,III, pp. 228, 231, 237.

[123]Ibid., pp. 233, 234.

[124]Ibid., p. 235.

[125]Ibid., p. 139.

[126]Ibid., p. 149ff.

[127]Tillich's discussion of the Spiritual Presence and the ambiguities of life is found in ibid., pp. 162-275.

[128]Ibid., p. 158.

[129]Ibid., p. 273.

[130]"Existential" is used here in a nontechnical sense.

[131]Hammond, p. 169.

[132]Tillich, <u>ST</u>,III, p. 144.

[133]Tillich, <u>Love, Power, and Justice</u>, pp. 25-27, 68; "Being and Love," p. 663. Hammond feels that one cannot argue that Tillich affirms finite individualization on the basis of his treatment of love alone, because Tillich does not indicate <u>how</u> separation is both preserved and overcome in love between human beings and God (p. 168). It seems to me, however, that Tillich's treatment of love (which is, after all, one side of ecstasy) is no less (or more) clear than his treatment of ecstasy in this regard. (See below, pp. 142-145.)

[134]Tillich, <u>Love, Power, and Justice</u>, p. 121.

[135]Tillich, <u>ST</u>,III, pp. 232-235. See also <u>The New Being</u> (New York: Charles Scribner's Sons, 1955), p. 21.

[136]Tillich, <u>ST</u>,III, pp. 232, 235.

[137]See above, p. 114-116.

[138]Tillich, <u>The Shaking of the Foundations</u>, p. 162; <u>ST</u>,III, p. 228.

[139]Tillich, <u>ST</u>,III, p. 232f.

[140] Ibid., p. 262. Tillich, _Love, Power, and Justice_, p. 58 is equally unhelpful.

[141] See above, p. 100; Tillich, _ST_,II, pp. 35-44.

[142] See above, pp. 124-126 ; Tillich, _ST_,II, pp. 119, 127-130; _ST_,III, p. 269.

[143] Above, p. 100.

[144] For example, Tillich, _ST_,II, p. 44; _The Shaking of the Foundations_, p. 155; _Love, Power, and Justice_, p. 112.

[145] Hammond, p. 156ff.

[146] Tillich, _ST_,II, p. 91.

[147] Ibid., pp. 34-36. Tillich never suggests that it would be better to preserve dreaming innocence than to actualize oneself, but neither does he take the step of describing the fall as "happy."

[148] Tillich, _ST_,III, p. 242. Cf. _ST_,I, p. 9, where Tillich says that all theology is rooted in the experience of a "mystical a priori."

[149] See footnote 85 above.

[150] Tillich, _The Courage to Be_, pp. 153-158.

[151] Ibid., pp. 171-175.

[152] Ibid., p. 174.

[153] Ibid., p. 172.

[154] Tillich, _ST_,II, p. 12.

[155] The index to the _Systematic Theology_, which is fairly thorough, lists numerous references to participation (sometimes the word appears several times on a page) for part 3, section 2, and part 4,

sections 2 and 3 (<u>ST</u>,III, p. 437) but none to individualization (ibid., p. 433).

[156]See Proudfoot.

[157]Hart, p. 104.


CHAPTER FOUR - <u>Theology and Women's Experience</u>

[1]Above, p. 3.

[2]Niebuhr, <u>Human Nature</u>, p. 179.  See above, p. 57.

[3]Niebuhr seems to have recognized this later in his
life and decided that pride was too narrow a term
for the universal character of sin he had in mind.
(Tillich, "Sin and Grace in the Theology of Reinhold
Niebuhr," p. 38.)

[4]Tillich, <u>ST</u>,II, p. 46.

[5]See above, pp. 116-119.

[6]Reinhold Niebuhr, "Biblical Thought and Ontological
Speculation in Tillich's Theology," <u>The Theology
of Paul Tillich</u>, p. 219.

[7]Niebuhr, <u>Human Nature</u>, p. 179.

[8]Niebuhr, <u>Human Destiny</u>, p. 123f.

[9]Niebuhr, <u>Human Nature</u>, p. 228.

[10]Ibid., p. 184.  See above, pp. 60, 63.

[11]Niebuhr, <u>Human Destiny</u>, p. 68.

[12]Niebuhr, <u>Faith and History</u>, p. 177; "Grace and Self-
Acceptance," p. 6.

[13]This means that Niebuhr's concern for justice cited
at the end of chapter two (p. 93), could not be met
simply by expanding the category of sensuality.

[14]It is solved only on a very high level of abstraction, however.

[15]See above, pp. 114-116.

[16]See, for example, Tillich, The Shaking of the Foundations, p. 158; The New Being, p. 20f.

[17]See above, pp. 117, 118.

[18]Niebuhr, Human Nature, p. 282; An Interpretation of Christian Ethics, p. 148.

[19]Tillich undoubtedly emphasizes the unity of all life partly because he is a monist--and his monism has been found problematic from the perspective of women's experience. It is not clear, however, that this throws into question his view of the relation between humanity and nature, for it is not clear that one would have to be a monist to take his position on this issue. The question requires further exploration.

[20]Tillich, ST,II, pp. 39-44; ST,III, pp. 15ff; The Shaking of the Foundations, pp. 76-86.

[21]This prediction is not meant to suggest that the doctrine of grace is derived from the analysis of sin. Even if one were to begin with grace, inadequacies in one doctrine would probably entail inadequacies in the other. Of course, a theologian may develop one doctrine more fully than the other, as many critics claim Niebuhr does.

[22]Niebuhr, Human Destiny, p. 108f.

[23]Ibid., p. 105.

[24]Ibid., p. 120.

[25]See above, p. 139.

[26]See Trout.

[27]Niebuhr, Human Destiny, p. 100ff and passim.

[28]Ibid., pp. 100, 110, 114, 119f.   Quotation, p. 110.

[29]Lehmann, p. 277.   See Human Destiny, p. 98; above, pp. 81-83.

[30]Tillich, ST,III, p. 229.

[31]Ibid., pp. 112, 129.

[32]Ibid., p. 233.

[33]See above, pp. 139, 140.

[34]Niebuhr, Human Destiny, p. 68ff.

[35]See above, p. 81.   See also Niebuhr, Human Destiny, pp. 70-95.

[36]See above, p. 91.   For an alternative interpretation of the significance of Jesus, one explicitly linked to women's experience, see Dorothee Soelle, Beyond Mere Obedience (Minneapolis: Augsburg Publishing House, 1970).

[37]Tillich, ST,I, p. 133f; ST,III, p. 122.

[38]See above, p. 141f.

[39]This is not the same thing as saying that the picture itself is not concrete.   See Tillich, ST,II, p. 114f.

[40]See above, pp. 142-144.

[41]Tillich, ST,I, p. 133.

[42]E.g., above, pp. 129, 130, 137, 155.

[43]Erich Neumann, The Great Mother: An Analysis of the Archetype, Bollingen Series, XLVII (Princeton: The Princeton University Press, 1972), p. 25.

[44]Tillich, ST,III, p. 293f.

[45]Tillich, Love, Power, and Justice, p. 112.

[46]Tillich, The Shaking of the Foundations, p. 155.

[47]Niebuhr, Human Nature, p. 137f.

[48]Although it was not his thesis which brought the differences between Niebuhr's and Tillich's doctrines
of God to my attention, the patterns sketched here
correspond to Proudfoot's monistic and individualis-
tic types.

[49]Niebuhr, Human Nature, pp. 28, 58. Cf. Human Destiny,
p. 246 and passim.

[50]As Mary Daly says, "If God is male, then the male is
God." (Beyond God the Father, p. 19.)

[51]Report of the Special Committee of the House of
Bishops on the Ordination of Women" (October, 1972)
p. 7, cited by Elizabeth Farians, "Phallic Worship:
The Ultimate Idolatry," Women and Religion, p. 84.
Andrea Dworkin has pointed out that the American
ultra-right is drawing on images of the maleness of
God to reinforce female submission to husbands and
male authority structures generally. ("Safety,
Shelter, Rules, Form, Love--The Promise of the
Ultra-Right," Ms, June, 1979, pp. 62ff.)

[52]See above, pp. 86-90.

[53]See Soelle, and Tillich, Love, Power, and Justice,
p. 69.

[54]See Rita Gross, "Female God Language in a Jewish Context," Womanspirit Rising, pp. 167-173.

[55]A number of recent feminist thinkers have begun to
explore Goddess imagery as a resource for feminist
theology and have at the same time insisted on the
importance of female will in Goddess religion.
(See, e.g., Starhawk, "Witchcraft and Women's Culture," pp. 259-268; Budapest, "Self-Blessing Ritual,"
pp. 269-272; and Carol Christ, "Why Women Need the
Goddess," pp. 273-287, in Womanspirit Rising.) Up
to this point, writing on the Goddess has been experiential and impressionistic. It would be interesting
to see a coherent philosophical account of how the

207

Goddess as life force allows for finite self-actualization.

[56]See Dorothee Soelle, _Political Theology_ (Philadelphia: Fortress Press, 1974), chap. 8.

[57]Niebuhr, _Human Nature_, pp. 208-219.

[58]Ibid., chaps. 7,8. Describing the social dimension of original sin would not dissolve its mystery, but it would make the dimensions of the mystery clearer.

[59]Where Niebuhr deals with the attitude of submissiveness with which oppressed groups have accepted their oppression, he does not seem to view this submissiveness as problematic. See _Moral Man and Immoral Society_, pp. 142f, 268.

[60]See Niebuhr, _Moral Man and Immoral Society_ vs. _Man's Nature and His Communities_.

[61]Niebuhr, _Faith and History_, p. 177; "Grace and Self-Acceptance," p. 6.

[62]Tillich, _ST_,III, p. 234. Emphasis mine.

[63]Nelle Morton, "The Rising Woman Consciousness in a Male Language Structure," _Andover Newton Quarterly_ 12 (March, 1972), p. 178ff; Judith Plaskow, "The Coming of Lilith: Toward a Feminist Theology," _Womanspirit Rising_, pp. 198-209.

[64]For descriptions of this experience see Morton, p. 179f; Daly, _Beyond God the Father_, pp. 23f,32,139, 171; Carol Christ, "Spiritual Quest and Women's Experience," _Womanspirit Rising_, p. 232f.

[65]Soelle, _Political Theology_, pp. 86-89.

[66]See the Third Passage of Daly's _Gyn/Ecology_ for a description of the way in which patriarchy continues to "spook" feminists.

[67]Morton, p. 180. Morton continually stresses the importance of "hearing."

[68] Richard R. Niebuhr, _Experiential Religion_ (New York: Harper and Row, 1972), p. 103.

[69] These words were suggested by a group of women (at the 1972 Grailville Conference of Women Exploring Theology) who tried to name God out of their own experience. ("Singleness/Community Group," _Women Exploring Theology at Grailville_, Church Women United, 1972, p. 4).

[70] See Tillich, _ST_,III, p. 226. Tillich is confusing on whether the self does or does not receive itself back again.

[71] See Daly, _Beyond God the Father_, chap. 6 and H. Richard Niebuhr, _The Responsible Self_ (New York: Harper and Row, Pub., 1963).

[72] Juan Luis Segundo, "Seminar--Introduction," paper circulated to the theology colloquium at Harvard Divinity School, May, 1974. (Mimeographed.)

[73] It is also an important characteristic of fiction or stories. Perhaps not surprisingly, the relationship between theology and story has become a significant issue for contemporary theology and feminist theology in particular. See, e.g. Christ's, "Spiritual Quest and Women's Experience," pp. 228-232 and Sheila Collins, _A Different Heaven and Earth_ (Valley Forge: Judson Press, 1974), p. 44.

[74] Daly, _Beyond God the Father_, p. 8.

[75] Ibid.

# INDEX

Absolutize: 5,58

Acceptance: 127,128,129.
130,132,137,138,139,
145,147,156,157,159

Adolescence: 32,33,34,
35,39,40,46,49,114

Agape: 76,91,92,107,129,
130,134,159,160,201
(n. 110)

Anthropology: 30,31,48;
theological, 4,6,50,
154,173

Anxiety: 56,58,61,100,
105,131,141

Atwood, Margaret: 38,39

Barth, Karl: 4

deBeauvoir, Simone: 12,
31,32,34,35,36,39,43,
44,47,48,49,64,66,71,
72,87,180 (n. 29), 190
(n. 69)

Biology: 13,14,17,18,28,
29,64,83

Body: 14,23,24,25,26,27,
29,31,55,72

Bronte, Charlotte: 10

Childbearing: 14,17,22,
23,26,27,66

Children: 13,16,24,27,
32,39,41,45,46,67,72,
88,90,171

Children of Violence
(Lessing): 34,35,40,
44,50,65,114

Choices (women's): 32,41,
65,67,116,152,167,171,188
(n. 46)

Christ: 53,73,76,77,78,79,
82,152,155,160

Christianity and Crisis: 68

Christology: 155,160-161

Church: 5,81,82,96,97,133,
158

Civilization and its Discontents (Freud): 20

Communism: 42,49

Community: 133,134,167,170,
171,172

Concrete: 13,14,29,72

Concupiscence: 101,103,104,
108,110,111,125,141,146,
169; vs desire, 126

Constructive: 3,4,5,149,166,
175,177 (n. 4)

The Courage to Be (Tillich):
143,144

Creativity: 16,17,46; in
Niebuhr, 56,69,70,73,89

Creatureliness: 51,54,55,
56,57,66,69,70,71,72,73,
74,92,120,154,190 (n. 69)

Creaturely freedom. See
finite freedom

Cross: 76,77,81,90,91,92,
125,127,158,160,161

Daly, Mary: 174,175

211